THE PERFECTION OF ENGLAND
Artist Visitors to Devon c.1750-1870

Sam Smiles & Michael Pidgley

THE PERFECTION OF ENGLAND
Artist Visitors to Devon c.1750-1870

Sam Smiles & Michael Pidgley

Royal Albert Memorial Museum, Exeter
Djanogly Art Gallery, University of Nottingham 1995

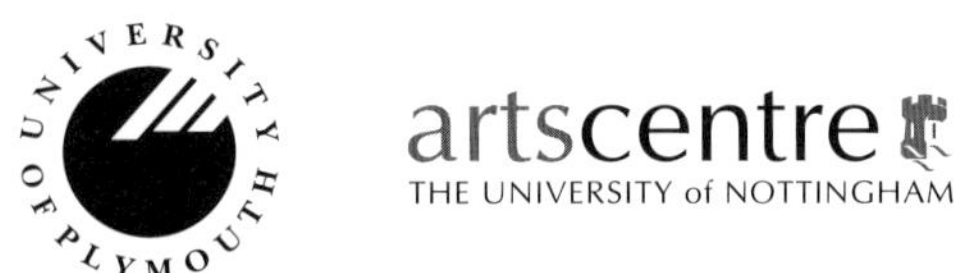

First published in Great Britain in 1995 for the exhibition
The Perfection of England: Artist Visitors to Devon c.1750-1870 by the University of Plymouth.

© University of Plymouth

© Copyright on essays retained by Sam Smiles and Michael Pidgley

British Library cataloguing in Publication Data.
A Catalogue record for this book is available from the British Library.

Designed, typeset and printed by Chas. Goater & Son Ltd., Nottingham.

ISBN: 0 905227 41 7

Front cover illustration: JOHN EAGLES, *A View of the River above Lynmouth* (1832)
Watercolour and bodycolour on paper, 36.0 x 53.2 cm
Bristol Museums and Arts Gallery
(Cat.no.18)

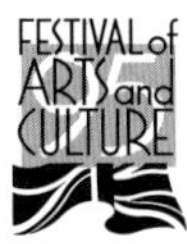 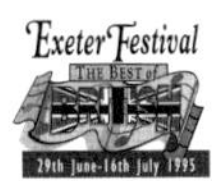

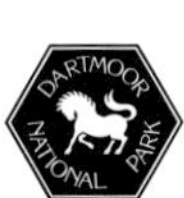 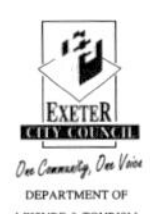

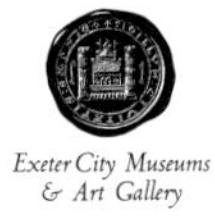 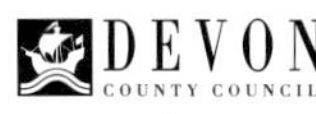

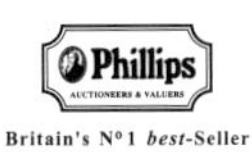 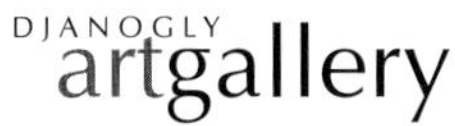

CONTENTS

ACKNOWLEDGEMENTS

The preparation of this exhibition has involved many people's efforts and we would like to record our thanks. David Jeremiah provided the initial institutional backing for the project which got it off the ground. Naomi Fabian-Miller was an invaluable research assistant in the early stages of contacting potential lenders and establishing what potential material was out there. At the Royal Albert Memorial Museum David Scruton, Exhibitions Officer, and Kevin Jones managed the in-house arrangements and administered the formal negotiations between Exeter and other collections. C. Jane Baker, Curator of Fine Art, was unfailingly helpful in assisting us with loans from the museum's collection and in supervising the exhibition's installation. David Griffiths, of Plymouth University Media Services, provided help in photography. Charlotte and Stephanie Pratt kindly agreed to proof-read the manuscript. Brian Rogers, Plymouth University Geographical Studies, prepared the map.

In Nottingham Joanne Wright has been consistently enthusiastic and her unflagging support for this exhibition has been a key factor in ensuring its success. The catalogue was designed in Nottingham by Jacqui Grafton and Albert Haynes of the printing company of Chas Goater and Son. David Bickerstaff advised on the design. Colour separation for publicity was generously provided by John Mullis of Mullis Morgan. We have secured loans from a number of private individuals, institutions and public collections and it is only space that stops us thanking them all individually for their co-operation. Financially, we are grateful to have received support from the Research Committee of the Faculty of Arts and Education, University of Plymouth.

We would also like to thank the following sponsors without whose help this exhibition would not have taken place: Phillips, Dartmoor National Park, Devon County Council, the Exeter Festival, Exeter City Council. The Paul Mellon Centre for Studies in British Art provided a generous grant towards photography.
We would like to thank the following for permission to reproduce the exhibits: Birmingham Museums and Art Gallery; Bristol Museums and Art Gallery; the Trustees of the British Museum; Ian Cook; Courtauld Institute Galleries, London; the Devon and Exeter Institution; Exeter City Museums and Art Gallery; the Fitzwilliam Museum, Cambridge; the Laing Art Gallery, Newcastle upon Tyne (Tyne and Wear Museums); Leeds Museums and Galleries, City Art Gallery; Lincolnshire County Council: Usher Gallery, Lincoln; Manchester City Art Galleries; the National Trust; the National Library of Wales; the National Museum of Wales, Cardiff; Norfolk Museums Service (Norwich Castle Museum); Plymouth City Art Gallery; Harris Museum and Art Gallery, Preston; Prudential Corporation plc; Sheffield City Art Galleries; Astley Cheetham Art Gallery - Tameside M.B.C. Leisure Services; the Tate Gallery; Borough of Torbay, Torre Abbey Collection; Royal Institution of Cornwall, Royal Cornwall Museum, Truro; the Board of Trustees of the Victoria and Albert Museum, London; Stephen Wildman.

FOREWORD

It is perhaps surprising that the diverse and beautiful Devon landscape has never before been the subject of a major exhibition. Often regarded as quintessentially English, Devon has, over the last 200 years, provided artists with a rich source of inspiration. This exhibition has sought to bring together for the first time a wide range of work produced by artists in response to their experience of Devon.

The project has been a collaboration between Exeter City Museums and Art Gallery, the University of Plymouth and the Djanogly Art Gallery at the University of Nottingham. We are very grateful to Dr Sam Smiles and Dr Michael Pidgley of the University of Plymouth whose original idea the exhibition was, and whose expertise has informed every aspect of its realisation.

It is particularly appropriate that the Royal Albert Memorial Museum, Exeter should stage an exhibition which celebrates the aesthetic riches of its local landscape as part of the 1995 Exeter Festival. In Nottingham, where it will be shown later in the year, it will reflect the Djanogly Art Gallery's commitment to mounting exhibitions which explore widely varied aspects of the landscape tradition in British Art. Many of the subjects will be as familiar to a Midlands audience as to those seeing the show in Devon, for eighteenth- and nineteenth-century artists often chose to represent views which are still admired by today's visitors for their great natural beauty.

Works of art depicting the glorious Devon landscape have, not surprisingly, found their way into public and private collections throughout Britain and the bringing together of the works for this exhibition has been a long and complicated task. We are extremely grateful to all those who have aided us in this as we are to those who have lent pictures to the show and those who have sponsored it. Without their cooperation and generosity the exhibition would not have been possible.

Katherine Chant
Head of Museums Service, Exeter City Council

Joanne Wright
Director, Djanogly Art Gallery, University of Nottingham

Map produced by Brian Rogers, Geographical Sciences, University of Plymouth.

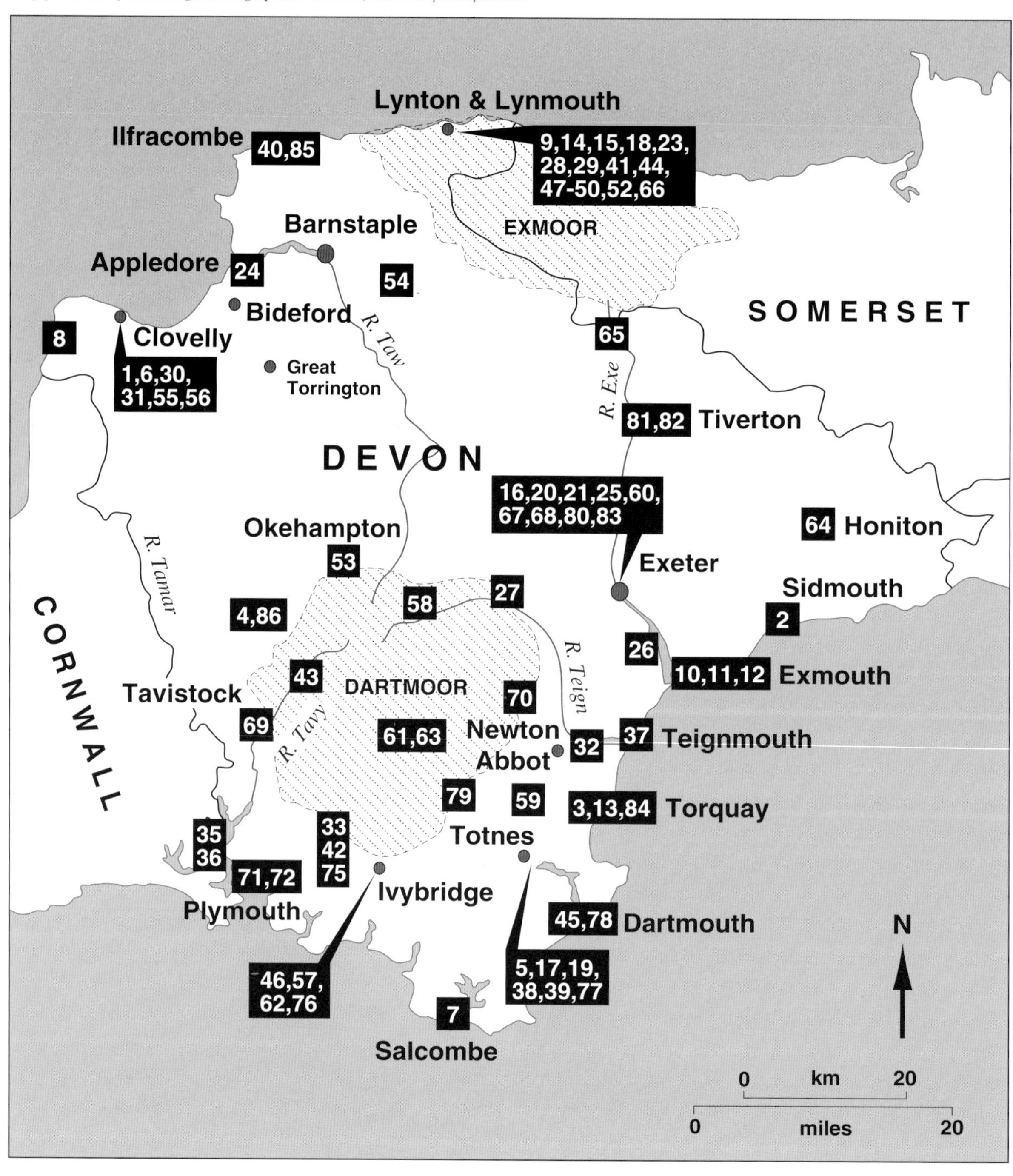

ARTISTS, TOURISM AND THE DISCOVERY OF DEVON

Sam Smiles

INTRODUCTION - DREAMING OF DEVON

> For those fanciful observers to whom broad England means chiefly the perfection of the
> rural picturesque, Devonshire means the perfection of England. I, at least, had so
> complacently taken for granted here all the characteristic graces of English scenery, had
> built so boldly on their rank orthodoxy, that before we fairly crossed the border I had
> begun to look impatiently from the carriage window for the veritable landscape in
> watercolours.[1]

The title for this exhibition comes from an essay by the novelist Henry James, one of a series of travel sketches he wrote for the American weekly, the *Nation*, in 1872. That an American visitor should already know what to expect of the Devon landscape is testament to its late nineteenth-century fame. James's account of what he found here can be seen as the product of a slowly developing process which established the Devon landscape as somehow representative of England at its best. It is that process which this exhibition sets out to illustrate, starting with artists working in the second half of the eighteenth century, when the artistic potential of the county was unexplored, and then witnessing a growing interest in the landscapes to be found here and how they might be painted. From the 1750s to the 1870s Devon was thoroughly investigated by artists whose experience of sketching grounds, in Britain and abroad, often prompted a keen appreciation of its potential. The dramatic appeal of the north Devon coast and the serenity of the south, the pastoral inland landscapes, fashionable resorts, urban scenes, and more abstract qualities of light, colour and atmosphere were all scrutinised for their artistic possibilities.[2]

If this artists' landscape naturally privileged an aesthetic understanding of the county it nevertheless needs to be distinguished from that image of Devon which sustains the tourist industry and, less tangibly perhaps, has created an imaginary concept of Devon which is shared even by those who have never visited the south west. Thus, while the majority of artist visitors interpreted the county in picturesque terms, few of the pictures in this exhibition could be confused with the idylls of imaginary Devon which are largely the product of the last 100 years. This imaginary Devon means yellow sands and blue seas, warm sun, hedgerows, winding lanes, thatched roofs on whitewashed cob-walled cottages, cider orchards and crystal streams. It means rolling hills, pastoral agriculture, small farms, fishermen, close-knit village communities, small market towns, an older and simpler way of life, a place where countless generations have conspired together to produce an English idyll of coastal beauty and rural charm. As such it registers a nostalgic dream of England, a place of recuperation from the stresses of modern life.[3] In this imaginary Devon quite ordinary things take on a symbolic resonance:

> a deep-sunken earth lane, just wide enough for the passage of a cart... might have been a little artery wandering into the very heart of Arcadian England.[4]

The pictures assembled here are not invested with those sentiments to anything like the same extent; indeed, one of the intentions of this exhibition is to demonstrate how diverse were these earlier responses to Devon. Yet, as the nineteenth century wears on it is evident that artists and writers alike were beginning to converge around the idea of Devon as an especially beautiful part of England. James's talk of perfection is very much the consensus view in the later nineteenth century and within a generation Devon's real qualities were being transformed into a pastiche of themselves. What had started as discovery often ended as formula and cliché.

THE GROWTH OF TOURISM

Devon's watering places, at first catering chiefly to local visitors, were established relatively early with Exmouth and Teignmouth developing from the 1750s, and Sidmouth, Dawlish and Ilfracombe from the 1770s. In truth, their facilities were rudimentary as yet, but sea-water cures for a variety of ailments were enthusiastically promoted and Exmouth and Teignmouth boasted of the introduction of bathing machines in 1759 and 1762 respectively.[5] France's declaration of war and the subsequent restriction of continental travel changed this situation radically. The climate of South Devon was compared to that of the Mediterranean and those who had been accustomed to winter in Montpellier or Nice turned now to the south Devon resorts.[6] With increased visitors came more cash, allowing local entrepreneurs to develop better facilities for the *bon ton* they wished to attract. The Devon resorts were transformed from fishing villages into sophisticated spas, with assembly rooms, libraries, theatres, promenades and purpose-built accommodation to which were attracted not just the sick, but the fashionable as well (fig.1). The temperate winter climate meant that the south Devon resorts in particular could enjoy two seasons in the year.[7] Torbay's safe anchorage and sheltered situation encouraged the families of navy officers and, alongside them, the gentility to build villas in and around Torquay. Within thirty years it had become the pre-eminent watering place on the south coast after Brighton, with a particular reputation for its mild winters and its suitability for invalids.

For Devon the threat of war had another immediate economic impact. Devonport (originally known as Dock) had been established by William III in 1692 as an important naval base, and was progressively transformed from the 1760s into a huge naval arsenal, the key port guarding the western approaches and a major centre for ship-building, munitions and repairs. The naval facilities built in these years and the later construction of the breakwater became an object of tourist interest, mixing patriotic pride with appreciation of industrial expertise, to add to the pleasures of Plymouth, Mount Edgcumbe and the surrounding countryside.[8]

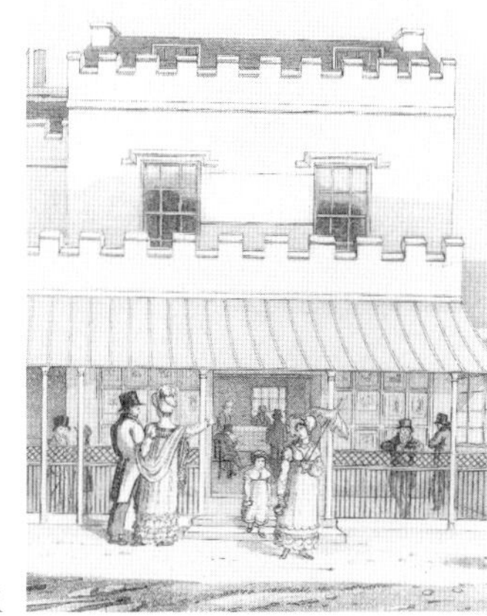

1

For the intending tourist the good news was that transport was improving. As late as the 1750s Devon had no turnpike trusts and in 1760 it still took four days to travel the 170 miles from London to Exeter. By 1764 this had been cut to 48 hours, by 1783 to 32 hours and by 1785 to 24 hours.[9] Thereafter, improvements in journey times were less spectacular but they were continual none the less. At the end of the coaching era the Exeter Telegraph had the journey down to 17 hours, while the Quicksilver (Devonport) Mail was half an hour faster still.[10] Of course, once arrived at the major towns, travelling elsewhere in the county could still be very slow. Travel to north Devon in particular was notoriously difficult with coaches taking almost a whole day to cover the 39 miles from Exeter to Barnstaple and worse horrors awaited the traveller trying to reach Ilfracombe, let alone Lynton and Lynmouth. Charles Dibdin's account of the roads near Torrington sums up what some travellers had to endure.

> The roads became worse and worse…the large hard and flat stones yielded to the
> slightest pressure and no dependence was to be placed on a single inch of the ground.
> All this uncomfortableness induced us to quit the carriage and clamber those
> declivities from whence the laughing hills and vallies presented a most romantic and
> luxuriant effect. It was a mischevious kind of laugh to say the truth for it seemed to be
> at people's misfortunes.[11]

It was not until the 1830s that Ilfracombe and other north Devon resorts were accessible on good roads and many came by sea instead, on steam packets from Swansea and Bristol.[12]

The pace of change was quickening. The arrival of the railways brought a wider cross-section of society to Devon in the summer months and the development of less exclusive resorts to cater for them (fig.2). From Exeter the South Devon Railway had opened stations to Torquay and Plymouth by the end of 1848, the North Devon Railway carried the line to Barnstaple in 1854 and by the 1870s a network

Fig.1. 'The Marine Library', detail from Hubert Cornish, *Sidmouth, Devon*, engraved in aquatint by (?D.) Havell, published Sidmouth, November 10, 1840, by J. and S. Harvey and in London by J. and E. Wallis and R. Ackermann. Dedication: 'To Emanuel Lousada Esqr. to whose active exertions and liberality of spirit the Environs of Sidmouth are indebted for their principal charms, this Panoramic View of that celebrated Watering Place taken from the Beach immediately opposite the Marine Library, and including an extent of Country from Torbay to Bridford is most respectfully inscribed by his much obliged and Obedient humble Servants, J & S Harvey.'

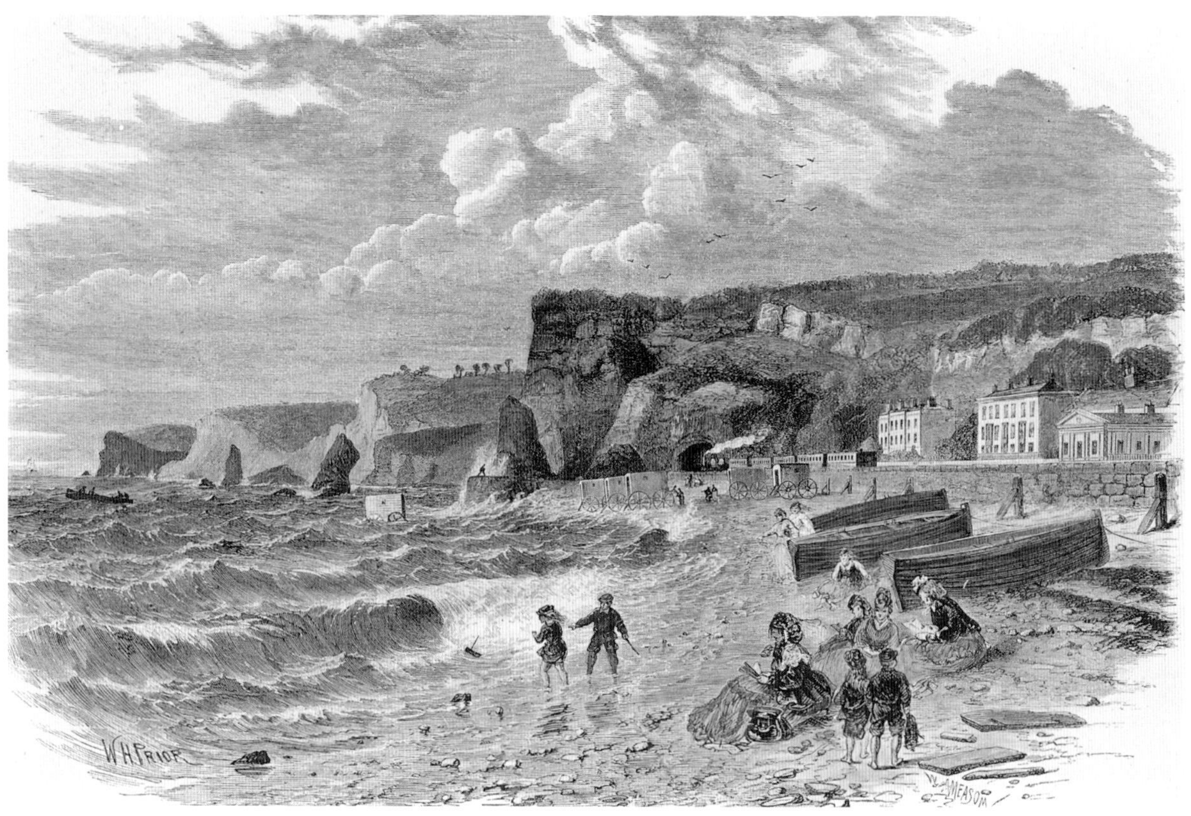

2

of branch-lines connected smaller towns like Dartmouth, Exmouth, Seaton, Sidmouth, Ilfracombe and Bideford to the main lines. This influx of tourists to all parts of the county was enough to inspire local entrepreneurs to create the holiday resort of Westward Ho! in the 1860s to capitalise on the popularity of Kingsley's novel.

This mid-century tourism was enhanced by the new pre-occupations of amateur naturalism which in Devon meant collecting marine organisms from rock pools and stripping ferns from inland. It was Philip Henry Gosse who was largely responsible for the former craze. In January 1852 he began to visit St. Marychurch, Torquay, collecting marine specimens and experimenting with the development of an aquarium to keep them alive. The first fruits of these investigations were published in 1853 as *A Naturalist's Rambles on the Devonshire Coast* and it helped to stimulate a mania for the aquarium among the middle-classes.[13] Gosse followed it with *Seaside Pleasures: Sketches in the Neighbourhood of Ilfracombe* (1853) and *Land and Sea* (1865) which between them championed Devon's shoreline as a centre of marine discovery and led inevitably to its subsequent despoliation by over-eager collectors. Fern collecting was launched by Kingsley's sister Charlotte Chanter who published *Ferny Combes. A Ramble after Ferns in the Glens and Valleys of Devonshire* (1856), concentrating mainly on north Devon. Other studies appeared in the early 1860s on the ferns of south Devon but it was Francis Heath's *The Fern Paradise* (1875) which set the seal on the identification of Devon with a natural wonderland.[14]

Fig.2. *Dawlish*, drawn by W.H. Prior, engraved by W. Measom, wood engraving. No. IX of 'Pictures on the Great Western Railway',
published in *The Illustrated Newspaper*, 1871.

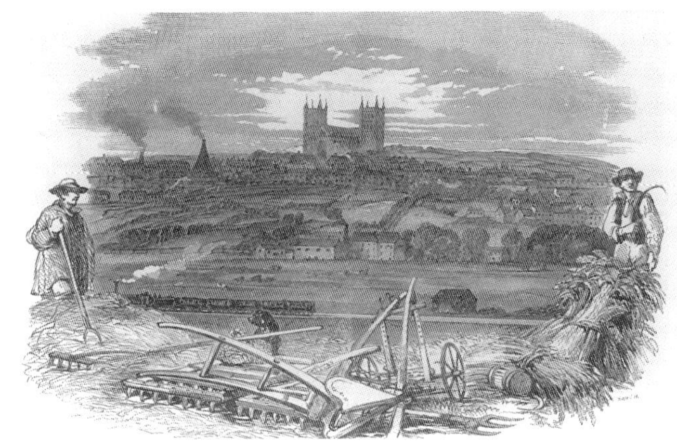

Reading his prose poems of admiration for the richness and diversity of the natural scene in Devon it is easy to understand how this landscape might become identified as an English arcadia.

The descriptions of Devon scenery contained in these and similar natural history books were matched by the more lyrical passages inserted into topographical guides to the region, a burgeoning travel literature[15] and by the literary representation of Devon. Charles Kingsley, who was born in Holne, wrote *Westward Ho!* (1855) and *Glaucus: or the Wonders of the Shore* (1855), both of which contain romantic evocations of Devon scenery. R.D. Blackmore's *Lorna Doone* (1869) associated north Devon in particular with a romance borrowed from legend and a glamorous retelling of history.[16] There is no doubt that tourists were eager to see the county through the imagination of writers and in 1884 William Everitt, an Exeter clergyman, capitalised on the fact by publishing *Devonshire scenery - its inspiration in the prose and song of various authors*. The fame of the county's scenic richness was by now firmly established.

THE LAND AND ITS PEOPLE

This enthusiasm for the Devon landscape should be seen as a choice, a decision to represent Devon in particular ways, to exploit its picturesque appeal. Even when written descriptions and artistic representations are rooted in observation, not cliché, they are none the less selective about what they choose to examine. Needless to say, seen from a different vantage point the image of Devon is markedly different. Contemporary agricultural reports and sociological accounts (as we would term them) are often strikingly at variance with artists' or poets' understandings and to read these reports is to see immediately the limitations of an aesthetic interpretation of the countryside.[17] This is especially true in respect of those who worked in this landscape but who rarely figure in its artistic representation, the fishermen and rural labourers (fig.3). Most commentators were charmed by the locals' politeness and friendliness. For some, like Robert Fraser, these genial inhabitants were further testament to Devon's special status.

Fig.3. 'Royal Agricultural Society of England', Twelth Annual Meeting and Exhibition, Exeter, engraved by Smyth, wood engraving, *Illustrated London News*, July 20, 1850.

The mild dispositions, affability, and kindness of its inhabitants, conspire with the
temperature of the air, the fertility of the soil, and the great beauty and variety of
scenery, to render many districts of this county, particularly the southern, the most
interesting and pleasing of any in the kingdom.[18]

Charles Vancouver endorsed Fraser's remarks, commenting on the inhabitants' 'openness of heart
and mildness of character... a general urbanity of manners, and desire to please and meet the wishes
of the stranger' which could not be excelled anywhere in England.[19] But he also observed that labourers'
wages of 14d a day were insufficient to avoid poverty and wretchedness and worried that the
introduction of education would breed restlessness and dissatisfaction with their lot.[20] Fraser and
Vancouver were writing during the war years when farming was prosperous but with peace came
economic difficulties and a worsening situation. Devon's farming practices were slow to change and
by mid-century it was widely regarded as hopelessly behind the times in terms of agriculture. The
agricultural workers suffered accordingly and their plight was so desperate in the 1860s that the vicar
of Halberton, Edward Girdlestone, organised emigrations to the north of England and elsewhere
where a decent living might be had.[21]

Not a breath of this disturbs that placid image of Devon so often portrayed by artists. A picturesque
and time-worn scene of rural England masks agricultural inefficiency and low wages; winding, rutted
lanes may be the bane of travellers and restrict economic growth; the thatched cottage, as James
pointed out, often harbours disease and poverty.

Crushed beneath its burden of thatch, coated with a rough white stucco of a tone to
delight a painter, nestling in deep foliage and garnished at door-step and wayside with
various forms of chubby infancy, it seems to have been stationed there for no more
obvious purpose than to keep a promise to your fancy, though it covers,
I suppose, not a little of the sordid side of life which the fancy likes to slur over.[22]

Very few artists in the period covered by this exhibition were able to reconcile these two truths, the
documentary and the artistic. Attempts to do so occur sporadically elsewhere in Britain from about
the middle of the nineteenth century, but in the south west it was chiefly Cornish subjects which
inspired artists to paint the social as well as the natural scene, most notably those painters associated
with Newlyn in the 1880s and 1890s. In contrast, artists in Devon tended to develop a picturesque
approach to their subjects as a general rule, eschewing attributes of work and rarely addressing the
social scene.[23] Pictures of rural and sea-side Devon tend either to concentrate on natural features, the
coasts, moors, streams and rivers, or on picturesque villages but very rarely on scenes of agriculture
or fishing. Often the experience is very much one of a pristine environment, with little evidence of
man's intervention. And when pictorial investigations did include the inhabitants of the county the
sordid side of life was typically slurred over just as James suggested. For artists and tourists alike Devon
became a place chiefly identified with the beauty and variety of its landscape.[24]

We can catch a glimpse of these two interpretations of Devon colliding in T.H. Williams' *Picturesque
Excursions in Devonshire and Cornwall* (1804) (fig.4). He describes a summer evening near the river
Tavy and pauses in his description to consider the life of the cottagers whose chimney smoke is casting
such a pleasing indistinctness over the scene. To begin with he celebrates the virtues of a cottage life
and the importance of rural labour for the economy but then the mood darkens.

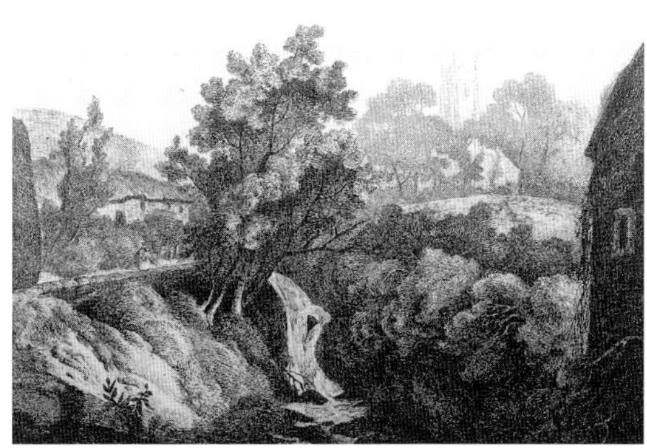

Can any mind receive delight from the richest assemblage of rural objects where there
is poverty among the inhabitants?... The common repast of the labouring families, in
this part of the country, is tea; it is their dinner, probably increased by a few potatoes,
and at the tea-hour of the evening it is alone their supper: on a Sunday the coarsest
part of animal food is their luxury... [knowledge of this poverty] embitters every rural
walk, renders as fabulous all the delightful visions of country life imbibed in youth, and
reduces to fictions, extravagant as Arabian tales, the descriptions of poets...[25]

Williams was a resident, keenly aware of the complexity of his social surroundings. Most visitors, it
would appear, chose not to let the fact of poverty spoil their enjoyment of Devon's idyllic scenery.

ARTISTS AND AMATEURS IN DEVON

The artistic discovery of Devon needs to be distinguished from artists' tours to Wales, the Lake
District and the Scottish Highlands in one important respect. Although some of the smaller villages
in Devon lacked amenities, visiting artists were not touring a remote region bereft of the comforts of
civilised living. Instead they were working in an area already established as a tourist destination,
fringed by coastal watering places, and even in the remotest parts of Dartmoor or Hartland they were
never more than fifteen miles from a resort or a market town.[26] Furthermore, both Plymouth and
Exeter contained small communities of artists, patrons and amateurs whose knowledge of the local
scene might be drawn on. In addition, there were a number of Devon-born artists working in London
who helped to forge links between the metropolis and the county which benefitted both communities.

The artistic scene in Plymouth and Exeter never developed that distinctive identity seen in Norwich,
Birmingham or Liverpool, for example, but exhibitions were a regular feature in Plymouth from 1815
and, more sporadically, in Exeter from 1821 and both towns boasted a population of resident artists.
In the 1820s each of them supported about half a dozen artists, in the 1830s this rises to a figure
averaging about 25 and while this number remains static for Exeter the artistic population at Plymouth
climbs to over 40 by the 1860s.[27] In Exeter and Plymouth the more successful artists earned good

livings through teaching, sales of work on the local market and business pursuits such as picture dealing. Some, like Exeter's John Gendall who had worked in London for Ackermann, would have maintained connections with the capital through their business interests.[28] Others, like Plymouth's A.B. Johns were involved in a complex network of artists and patrons in London and Devon.[29]

Visiting artists evidently made use of this sympathetic community when touring the region. Thomas Gainsborough, for example, was on intimate terms with the Exeter musician William Jackson and doubtless relied on Jackson's knowledge of the local scene when he visited Devon in the 1770s.[30] It is a reasonable assumption that visiting artists often made use of such local knowledge. For example, in the summer of 1819, two years after his arrival in Exeter, Francis Stevens accompanied a visiting artist by the name of Turner on a sketching trip to north Devon.[31] When Joseph Farington toured Devon in 1809 he called on the Rev. John Swete at Oxton House, Kenton, to get advice on picturesque touring; on his second visit in 1810 he was introuced to the Rev. Gayer Patch, a patron and collector, and met two local artists, James Leakey and William Traies.[32] In Plymouth Henry Woollcombe's circle of artists and amateurs extended hospitality to a number of artists as they passed through: John Downman and Samuel Prout in 1806, Benjamin Robert Haydon and David Wilkie in 1809, J.M.W. Turner and James De Maria in 1813, Henry Bone in 1814, William Collins and Francis Chantrey in 1821.[33] The Plymouth banker Sir William Elford played host to Joseph Farington in 1809 and was visited by Collins in 1819 and 1821.[34] The Bastard family at Kitley were probably involved with Thomas Girtin's visit of 1797 and with Collins in 1821.[35] John Hoppner and Turner were invited to spend some time at Saltram in 1803 and 1813 respectively.[36] The Champernownes at Dartington were connected with Farington, F.C. Lewis and Peter De Wint.[37] The Rev. and Mrs. Bray at Tavistock were hosts to James Duffield Harding in 1826 and F.C. and J.F. Lewis in 1829 and 1835, among others.[38] Of those who stayed on in Devon rather than merely visiting it on a sketching tour, William Tomkins worked for the Parkers at Saltram, Hendrik de Cort and after him John Varley were drawing masters for the Cliffords at Ugbrooke, William Marshall Craig did the same for the Courtenays at Powderham and Francis Nicholson worked for the Aclands at Killerton.[39]

Devon-born artists, temporarily revisiting their native county, could also help the visitor find his way. Haydon accompanied Wilkie to Plymouth in 1809, giving the latter access to that community. Collins was introduced by William Brockedon to his patrons Archdeacon Froude in Totnes and Governor Holdsworth at Dartmouth in 1819 'through whose knowledge of the scenery of this neighbourhood, I am enabled to see much more of the place than under other circumstances I could have expected.'[40] The evidence suggests that Collins' experience was not unusual and that artist visitors could choose to move around a network of artists and amateurs eager to facilitate their stay and to show them the best sketching grounds. And if Turner's experience of Plymouth hospitality in 1813 is a reliable guide sketching in south Devon, at least, could be a very comfortable and entertaining business for the visiting artist.

'ENCHANTED LAND'
~ THE DISCOVERY OF THE DEVON LANDSCAPE ~

As James points out, by the 1870s the artists had done their work: the image of Devon was already established in countless oils and watercolours by professionals and amateurs and the visitor arrived to confirm his or her already established expectations.[41] In fact, by the mid-nineteenth century Devon was second only to Kent as the most represented county in exhibitions held at the Royal Academy and it maintained this position until the end of the century.[42] Given that the Home Counties offered much easier access to artists, who could visit them regularly and cheaply from London, Devon's popularity is especially significant. It cannot simply be ascribed to the coming of the railways, important though that is, for that does not explain why Devon alone of the remoter regions profitted to this extent from better communications. Equally, the rise in Devon's popularity is detectable in the 1830s, the decade before the arrival of the Bristol and Exeter Railway at Exeter in 1844. Evidently, there was something intrinsic to the Devon landscape which suited particular aesthetic needs

We need to ask what this was. What prompted so many artists to choose Devon for a sketching tour and what factors led them to choose to paint the county in the ways that they did? A partial answer to the first question is relatively straightforward: what made Devon such a draw was its variety of terrains. It does indeed include 'all the characteristic graces of English scenery' and, as a result, could accommodate changes in artists' enthusiasms for different sorts of landscape. As a sketching ground, therefore, it maintained and developed its popularity while other regions, like the Lake District and the River Wye, lost theirs because they satisfied a narrower spectrum of aesthetic ideals. William Howitt's *Rural Life of England* makes this point emphatically, enthusing over the variety he encountered in 'the enchanted land of Devon'.

> If you want stern grandeur, follow its north-western coast; if peaceful beauty, look down into some one of its rich vales, green as an emerald, and pastured by its herds of red cattle; if all the summer loveliness of woods and rivers, you may ascend the Tamar or the Tavy, or many another stream; or you may stroll on through valleys that for glorious solitudes, or fair English homes, amid their woods and hills, shall leave you nothing to desire. If you want sternness you may pass into Dartmoor. There are wastes and wilds, crags of granite, views into far-off districts, and the sound of waters hurrying away over their rocky beds, enough to satisfy the largest hungering and thirsting after poetical delight.[43]

In this exhibition it is possible to witness the ways in which different types of Devon landscape come into focus to satisfy these different concerns, to observe how earlier tourists tended towards views of notable landscape features, how these views are supplemented by explorations of more intimate terrain in the first half of the nineteenth century and how, finally, Dartmoor itself is brought into artistic recognition of the sort Howitt promotes (fig.5). Yet it is important to remember that Howitt's appreciation of Devon is the culmination of a slow process of discovering the county. Eighteenth-century writers were much less enthusiastic about what they found here, as a general rule, and to compare Howitt with William Gilpin is to witness a real clash of aesthetic sensibilities.[44]

Those intrepid souls who ventured to the West Country before the 1750s were few and far between

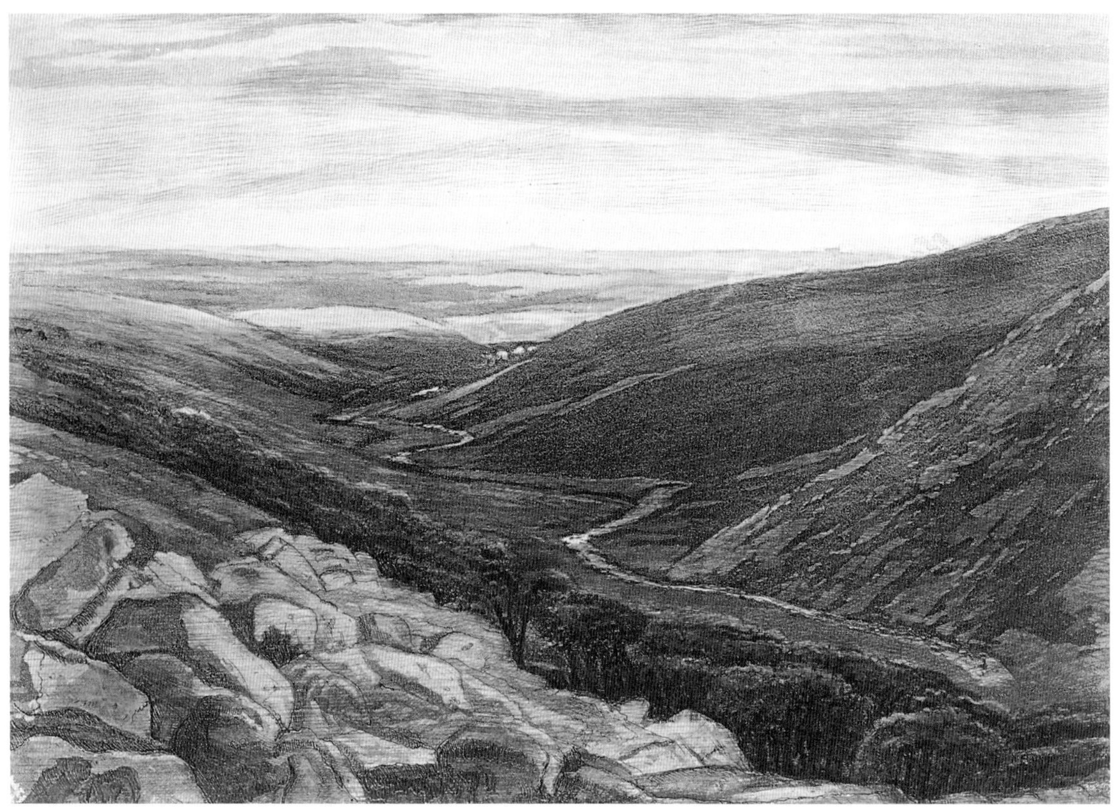

5

and practically all of them complained bitterly about the state of the roads. The most well known of these early visitors are Celia Fiennes who toured here in 1698 and Daniel Defoe who visited the region shortly afterwards. Although both of their accounts are interesting as historical records it is significant that at this early date neither of them felt impelled to spend any great amount of time describing what they saw in aesthetic terms. That intellectual fashion had yet to develop and only on a couple of occasions does Defoe offer an appreciation of Devon scenery. This is true for most early eighteenth-century descriptions of Devon which are routinely prosaic with only the occasional exception to mark a more poetic response, as for example the Bishop of Derry's enthusiasm for Exeter:

> ...the trees there shoot with a more luxuriant verdure; the flowers glow with warmer
> colours; and the fruits ripen to a richer flavour, than in any part of this island; and the
> fig and the grape scarce desire better skies.[45]

Although this sort of enthusiasm was scarce in the early years of the century, by its close the delights of the Devon landscape would be a constant stimulus for aesthetic response. This dramatic change in interest can be explained initially by the growth of domestic tourism in the later eighteenth century, a product of improved roads and faster travel on the one hand and a developing taste for tours in search of landscapes and antiquities on the other. This represented a cheaper and safer version of the

Fig.5. F.C. Lewis *On the River Dart from Wistmans Wood*, mixed method, from *Scenery on the Devonshire Rivers*, 1843.
'Original in the collection of Revd. Ewd. Bray.'

Grand Tour to continental Europe and it was encouraged and sustained by the appearance of topographical guides which explored the pleasures of domestic sites and scenery.[46] Robert Southey, writing in the guise of a Spanish visitor, captured the lure of picturesque tourism in his *Letters from England*, first describing the popularity of sea-cures and then moving on to picturesque tourism.

> Within the last thirty years a taste for the picturesque has sprung up; - and a course of summer travelling is now looked upon to be as essential as ever a course of spring physic was in old times. While one of the flocks of fashion migrates to the sea-coast, another flies off to the mountains of Wales, to the lakes in the northern provinces, or to Scotland; some to mineralogize, some to botanize, some to take views of the country, - all to study the picturesque, a new science for which a new language has been formed, and for which the English have discovered a new sense in themselves, which assuredly was not possessed by their fathers... I have myself caught something of this passion for the picturesque, from conversation, from books, and still more from the beautiful landscapes in water colours, in which the English excel all other nations.[47]

As Southey indicates, the rise of Picturesque theory, associated particularly with William Gilpin in the 1770s and afterwards,[48] did much to promote the aesthetic contemplation of British landscape scenery as a valid constituent and sometimes the chief motive of these tours. With the outbreak of war with France in 1793, what had started as an alternative to European travel became a virtual necessity for the less adventurous British tourists; apart from the brief Peace of Amiens in 1802 the continuing hostilities affected Continental travel until 1815. Gilpin toured Devon and Cornwall in 1775, publishing his *Observations on the Western Parts of England* in 1798. His account of what he found makes fascinating reading if only because the Devon landscape often resisted his insistence on discovering well-formed pictorial compositions in nature. Thus, while he admired Lydford gorge ('no part of this magnificent scenery would be a disgrace to the wildest and most picturesque country') and the view over Exeter from Haldon Hill, and endorsed at second hand the mouth of the Dart,[49] he was often disappointed with what he had been led to expect. On the road from Dulverton to Tiverton

> ...the country affords nothing that is striking. We had hills; but they were tame and uniform, following each other in such quick succession, that we rarely found either a foreground or a distance. As we mounted one, we had another immediately in view.[50]

The view from Mount Edgcumbe was too extensive from the heights, and although pleasing lower down it was not picturesque.[51] His trip up the river Tamar was equally disappointing, necessitating ten miles of navigation before finding any picturesque appeal, the Tamar being 'amusing, but not picturesque; it is not sufficiently divided into portions adapted to the pencil.'[52] Ivybridge looked promising but he had no time to examine it and the road from Ashburton to Chudleigh was as uninteresting as the road to Tiverton, rising and falling across the hills 'so that all distance was shut out, and all variety of country intercepted.'[53]

By the time Gilpin got round to publishing his *Observations*, however, other writers had begun to examine the landscape in less fastidious aesthetic terms. Devon had begun to attract a rich descriptive literature which characteristically stressed its fertility, its mild climate and its scenic variety. At its most banal this literature produced routine effusions like the following.

> This land I greet, Devonia, as the land
> Of lovely aspect, and of zephyrs bland:
> I like thy hills, for though aloft they soar,
> The hand of Cultivation cloathes them o'er,
> While down each slope their fertile sides unfold
> Gay robes of verdure, trick'd with waving gold.
>
> Thy clime I greet, Devonia, as the clime
> For Fancy's sons to "wile away the time:"
> I love thy woodland shades, thy pastures green,
> Where interspers'd the fleecy groups are seen;
> Thy winding vales, where tender warblers throng,
> And where the silver streams so sweetly glide along. [54]

A measure of the attention now being paid to the landscape characteristics of Devon can be found in Robert Fraser's *General View of the County of Devon* (1794). This book was intended for the Board of Agriculture and Internal Improvement as a survey of the agricultural practices in Devon with suggestions for their development, yet the following passage is marked by an appraisal of the south Devon landscape which is more than simply economic.

> The scenery of this district is most admirable; whether we view the Teign, the Dart, or
> the Tamar, and their beautiful banks, or take a general view of the country, charmingly
> diversified with hill and vale: the vales interspersed with villages in the midst of
> orchards, and the hills fringed with wood, and cultivated to their summits.
> In addition to this delightful scenery, you have in most parts a view of the ocean,
> presenting itself in some grand and beautiful bay, covered with fleets, the sources of our
> wealth and commerce, and the proud bulwarks of England. On the other hand the
> range of the Dartmore *(sic)* mountains form a background to the scene, that give an air
> of magnificent finishing to the whole; forming altogether the most beautiful and
> interesting picture that is anywhere to be found. [55]

Fraser's account has, in embryo, all the features which will be elaborated in the nineteenth century. Devon is, above all, a rich land, teeming with flocks and cultivated in every corner; it is also a varied landscape, encompassing many different sorts of scenery; its most charming features are its vales, closed in and intimate; and above all this looms the majesty of Dartmoor, a sublime backdrop to a beautiful foreground (fig.6). It is this litany of praise that will be repeated again and again over the next hundred years. It is a vision of peace and prosperity, an idyll of mildness and tranquillity, the closest approximation England has to a land of milk and honey.

Perhaps the most telling description of Devon landscape in this vein comes from the diary of the painter Benjamin Robert Haydon, whose own upbringing in Plymouth gives his account a particularly fervent quality.

> Sept. 25 1829. Never more impressed in my life with the beauty of Devon. I walked to a
> favourite haunt when a child... and found it as woody and sequestered and beautiful as
> ever - never was such a spot!... I can now account for all my early aspirations; no
> wonder Devonshire is so prolific in painters.

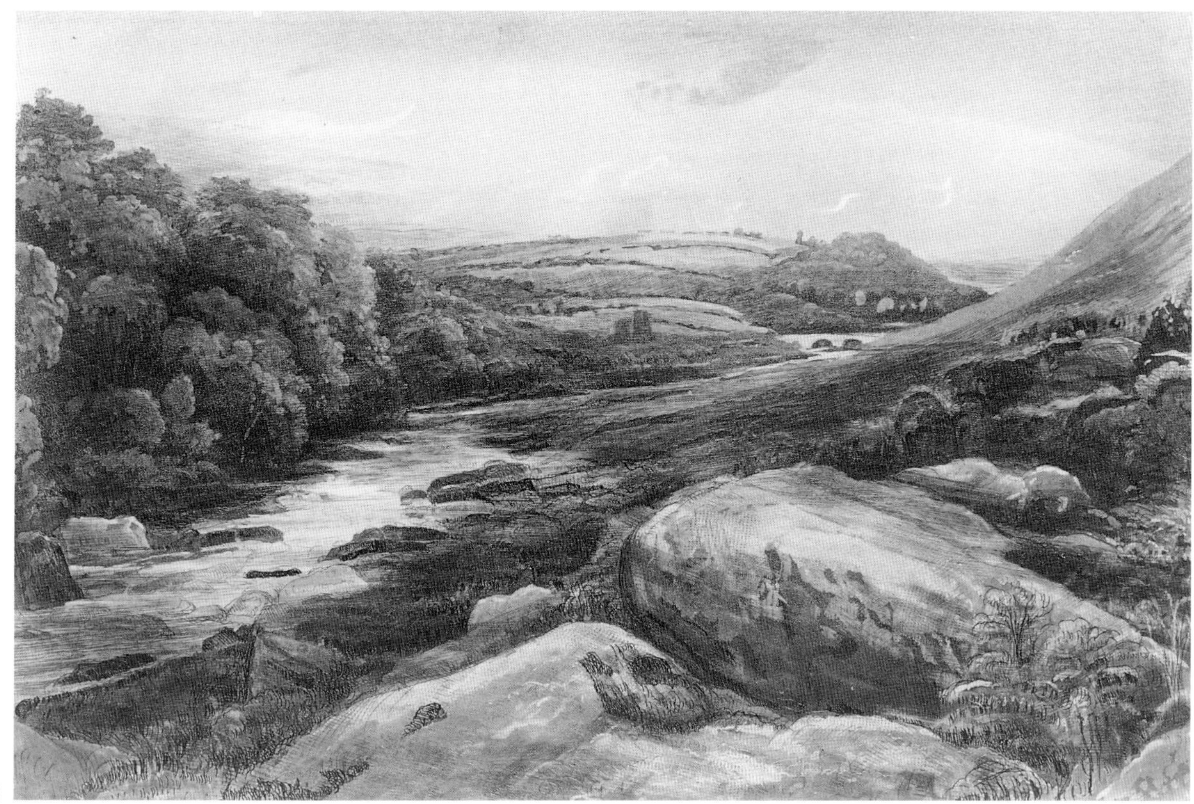

Devonshire is a gem. I remember when a child I used to loiter behind my nurse to look
and muse on the scenery of this enchanting place, and could not tell what was there to
make my heart beat so. The fact is, the Scenery is so poetic it was impossible not to
affect a Poetick mind. The deep shadows of umbrageous trees, the green emerald masses
of Foliage, the crystal ripple of the limpid springs, were fit to excite emotions
deep and passionate...[56]

What Haydon describes here is a sort of enchantment, an enchantment which obviously enthralled
many of his fellow painters who visited the county and which was the basis for Devon's attraction as
a tourist destination. A generation later, Gilpin's reservations had been entirely overcome by an
enthusiasm which brooked no criticism.

Fig.6. F. C. Lewis *Dartmeet Bridge (On the River Dart)*, mixed method, from *Scenery on the Devonshire Rivers*, 1843.
'The picture in his Possession.'

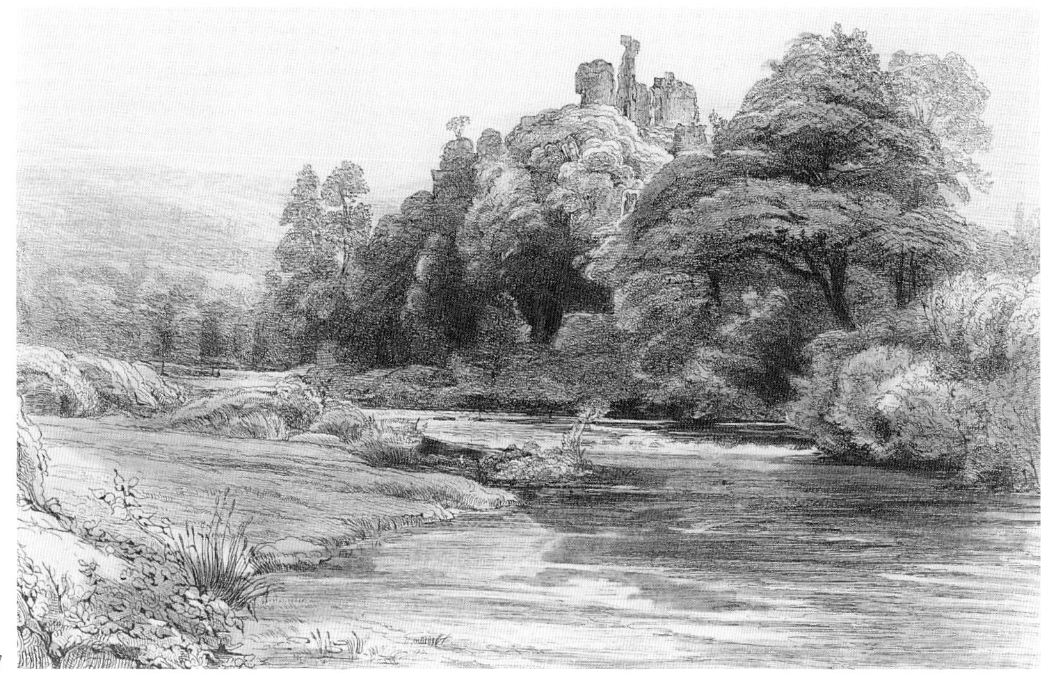

REPRESENTING THE LANDSCAPE
~ ARTIST VISITORS TO DEVON ~

A widespread popular appreciation of Devon should be seen as the appropriate context in which to examine the artistic representation of the county. The growth of landscape painting in Britain is inextricably bound up with tourism, for both activities find value in the natural scene, and artists only began to visit Devon in large numbers after tourism in the West Country was established in the 1790s. The growth of tourism in Devon not only included artists in its numbers, it also promoted an interest in the pictures they might produce. The paintings exhibited on the walls of the London exhibition rooms would quite likely be enjoyed and purchased by a class of people who had visited the county as tourists and wished to commemorate the fact. This is not to say, however, that all such paintings are topographical records alone. Ambitious painters owed their allegiance to art, to an understanding of the demands of picture making and to a tradition which required exacting standards of competence. The Devon landscape might inspire their imagination but it did not necessarily coerce it.

This exhibition sets out to examine the rise of Devon as an artist's landscape in the late eighteenth and early nineteenth centuries, but such visitors have left their impressions of the county from at least a century earlier. The journal written by the Dutch landscape painter William Schellinks is one of the earliest records of any of them, detailing his fact-finding tour made from July to September 1662. In Schellinks' journal Devon is described as a county of 'many woods and pleasant pastures

Fig.7. F.C. Lewis *Okehampton Castle (on the River Okement)*, mixed method, from *Scenery on the Devonshire Rivers*, 1843. 'Original picture collection of B.B. Cabell.'

and gardens, many villages and fine buildings'[57] but his written descriptions are disappointingly sparse and uninformative about the county's potential for landscape painting, concentrating instead on the agriculture, trades and occupations of the inhabitants. Another example of this fledgling interest in touring is found in the amateur artist and virtuoso Francis Place's visit of 1678.[58] Neither of these tours can be said to have helped promote the image of Devon, however; Schellinks took his drawings with him on his departure from England while Place's sketches would have been known only to a select group of his family and friends. The only seventeenth century artist to leave a public record was Wenceslaus Hollar who visited Plymouth in the 1670s and published three etchings of the harbour.[59] In any case, landscape painting itself was something of a novelty in this period as witnessed by Edward Norgate's mid-century declaration that it was 'an Art soe new in England, and soe lately come a shore, as all the Language within our fower Seas cannot find it a Name, but a borrowed one.'[60]

It is not until the mid eighteenth century that topographical images of Devon landscape and antiquities begin to appear with any frequency. Of these, the most important early collection was produced by Samuel and Nathaniel Buck for their *Antiquities, or Venerable Remains of Above Four Hundred Castles, Monasteries, Palaces etc. in England and Wales.* (London, 1726-52). The 1734 and 1736 volumes contain seventeen copper line engravings of castles, abbeys and priories in Devon as well as prospects of Exeter and Plymouth.[61] These prints were the staple fare of topography and the more picturesque buildings they recorded would remain popular well into the nineteenth century, as for example Berry Pomeroy Castle, Dartmouth Castle and Okehampton Castle (fig.7) (see cat.nos 19, 38, 39, 45, 53). Similarly, Mount Edgcumbe received early attention in a set of five line engravings published in London in 1755.[62] The subjects contained in these two sets of prints dominate the engraved image of Devon until the 1780s when one or two new subjects begin to appear, while the landscape itself starts to feature in prints from about the beginning of the 1790s.[63] It has to be said, however, that Devon topographical prints in the eighteenth century were not appearing in large numbers. Little more than 100 separate prints appear to have been produced in total, which represents a fairly meagre record. This situation is transformed in the first twenty five years of the nineteenth century when the production of Devon topographical images increases exponentially, about 500 prints being recorded. By 1870 over 3,500 prints of Devon had been produced, which indicates something of its extraordinary appeal.

The pictures in this exhibition demonstrate the same growth of interest. Eighteenth-century paintings and drawings like those of John Inigo Richards (1768), Richard Wilson (1771-2) and Anthony Devis (c.1780) are in the minority and are presented here as something of a prelude to the discovery of Devon. The next phase is represented by Thomas Girtin and J.M.W. Turner's work, in the 1790s and 1810s respectively, where a developing recognition of Devon's potential as a sketching ground for artists does not as yet elaborate a distinctive identity for the county. In the middle decades of the nineteenth century this identity begins to form; artists like J.D. Harding, William Collins, J.W. North and William Müller, notwithstanding their very individual styles, are consciously seeking out specific attributes of landscape, light and colour which have become identified as essentially Devonian. This is the image, often from lesser hands, which will eventually result in that clichéd representation James alluded to as 'the veritable landscape in watercolours.'

This exhibition closes just before the era of mass tourism in Devon, which had barely begun in the 1870s. As it developed, so too did a particular image of Devon, centred now much more on the needs

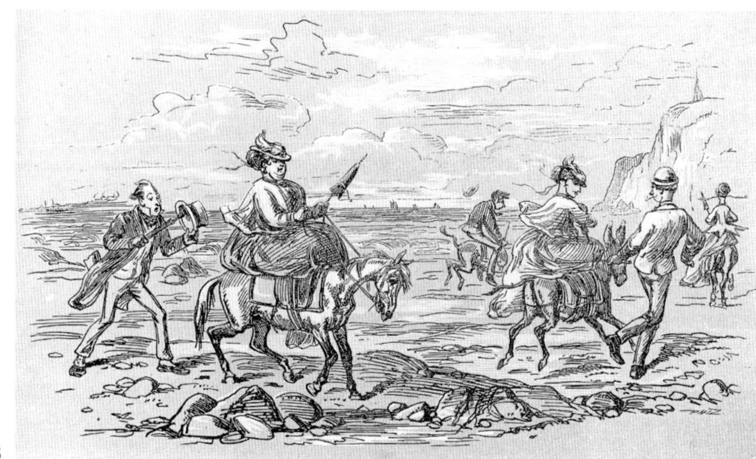

of the holiday-makers at the resorts (fig.8). This process was developed in G.W.R. posters and is still present in today's calendars and post-cards presenting a place perfectly suited to recreation and ease. In this manifestation Devon becomes that imaginary entity discussed earlier, a beautiful playground where dreams of an English arcadia can be entertained. The relationship between the pictures collected in this exhibition and that later image represents the same process as is indicated in Everitt's anthology of literary descriptions, the recycling of what had once been fresh experience to the point where its originality is dulled, its brightness tarnished and an ersatz experience is made to stand for the original.

Such a development, however, lies outside the scope of this exhibition. Even though the idea of Devon is taking shape in the mid-nineteenth century its emergence can only be discussed in the most general sense and it is important to pay equal attention to the individual artist's specific encounter with this landscape. The more abstract issues concerning the construction of an image of Devon are the necessary context for discussion of each of their endeavours but within that context there are as many differences as there are similarities. The motives behind these images, for example, could be very various. Girtin seems to have used the landscape to develop a much more abstract type of composition; Farington was looking for picturesque subjects suitable for engraving; John Varley came to Devon to work as a drawing master; Turner was originally on commission but was impressed enough to return twice for his own purposes, perhaps finding here a more luxurious colour than elsewhere in England; Müller, Collins (on his third visit) and De Wint were looking for rest and recuperation as well as landscape subjects; Danby had settled in Exmouth and was painting his new surroundings.

Whatever their motives, the pictures that resulted constitute a significant body of work not only for the image of Devon but more widely. With the signal exception of John Constable, virtually every major British landscape artist in this period visited the county and the work collected here can almost be regarded as a miniature history of British art. Devon was the last major sketching ground to be opened up; now that it has an exhibition devoted to it, it is possible at last to assess its place within the development of landscape painting in Britain.

Fig.8. Phiz (Halbot K. Browne) *Sketches of the Seaside and the Country*, the Graphotyping Company, London, (n.d. 1860s). 'Mrs. Bouncer - "Drat these seaside ponies, they're as weak as rats. I'm sure Jemima gets on a deal better with her donkey."'

SKETCHING FROM NATURE
Michael Pidgley

RESPONSES TO THE DEVON LANDSCAPE

If there is a county in England for which Nature, like a kind mother, has done much, it
is Devonshire: there she has lavished mountain and valley, ocean and river, rock and
forest, orchard and cornland, fruit and flower; and these gifts she has canopied over
with an azure curtain sometimes laced with golden sunshine, at others chequered with
fleecy clouds, such as our temperate zone only can present, and our Wilsons and Lees
alone can paint.

This glowing testimonial to the perfection of England was penned by Richard Ford.[1] Hyperbole was
common enough when dealing with Devon scenery. To the poet Carrington it was 'the land of the
matchless view' and to William Howitt it was an 'enchanted land.' Of the two artists singled out by Ford
only Richard Wilson, as an artist visitor, is represented in this exhibition (cat.no.86). Frederick Richard
Lee as a native of Devon, born in Barnstaple in 1798, is excluded. He came to represent the official
purveyor of Devon scenes through his many exhibits at the Royal Academy. At first, in the 1830s and
1840s, they were well received but what began as novelty soon degenerated into familiar formulae:

Whatever the cause may be, it seems to me that our landscape painters go on repeating
themselves, and not improving in the repetition. Else, why is it that ... Devonshire
moors, and Devonshire lanes, and Devonshire ferries, have become so stale, flat, and
unprofitable in the hands of Mr LEE? Is it that he paints them more feebly, or that we
are sick of the repetition?

So wrote Tom Taylor in a survey of landscapes at the Royal Academy in 1852.[2] Other reviewers noted
the Devon scenes without such condemnation of Lee:

The damp glades of Devonshire, glazed with green pea soup, those Naiad and Dryad
localities whose clear and tiny rills dance over shallow pebbly beds, now sparkling in a
sun-gleam, now sobered in the shadow of over-hanging copse-wood - are faithfully and
frequently presented in this Exhibition.[3]

The mere mention of Devon seemed to evoke this world of water sprites and wood nymphs, of dells and fairy glens. No wonder *Fun* magazine could imagine a mythic artist, Titian Tarbrush, working on 'his little thing called "Thirteen Fairies taking a Bath in the River Lynn, near Watersmeet, North Devon."'[4]

The mild, damp climate might be recommended for invalids but was less favourable for landscape sketchers and for tourists generally. Many had reason to lament the soggy nature of things. To Samuel Palmer it was 'dear spongy Devon' while to others, such as Joseph Farington it meant the postponement of their sketching activities outdoors. Richard Warner, on a walking tour of the West Country in 1800, put off his intended trek into Cornwall 'to longer days and clearer skies':

> I recollected with dread the appropriate name which had been imposed by a wicked
> French wit on the county of tin, (*Pot de Chambre d'Angleterre*) and concluded that if it
> only *drizzled* in Devonshire, it must *pour* in Cornwall.[5]

As a later guide book put it: 'The frequent showers which fall in Devon, have been objected to by some, as abridging the pleasures of the tourist.'[6] If the weather was an obstacle, so too were the roads which frequently prevented any of the fine scenery from being seen. The Devon volume of *Magna Britannia* (1822) described 'the general character of a great proportion of the county' as a succession of hills more or less of the same height.

> Views must of necessity be bounded in general by the top of the adjoining hill, perhaps
> a mile distant; and should any more interesting view occasionally occur, it is totally
> obstructed by the hedges.[7]

A 'true Devonshire road', wrote Warner, ran between high banks and was canopied over-head by trees. Views of lofty hills and rich valleys were occasionally afforded by 'a gateway, or accidental aperture in the hedges'.[8] Fortunately such natural hindrances proved to be challenges rather than obstacles to visiting artists.

SKETCHING FROM NATURE

Sketching outdoors became a significant artistic activity as more landscape painters devoted themselves to topography, to the accurate depiction of real places. Devon provided a rich harvest for the travelling artist as this exhibition proves. Sketching developed also among the educated classes who were the collectors of this new art, and who would frequently offer hospitality to the visiting professional artist and take lessons from him. The interaction is well expressed in a local guide-book:

> Seeking the picturesque the artist is often attracted by a spot, which an indifferent
> spectator might deem uninteresting. The lowly cottage, and serpentine sweep of a fine
> river, charm his eye, and he delights to imbody the scenery which has given him
> pleasure. Every lover of nature is irresistibly enamoured at seeing her happily imitated;
> but when taste and judgement are combined in a spectator, he feels a sublime pleasure
> in tracing the merits of the work.[9]

Francis Stevens, an artist who settled in Exeter (cat.no.70), wrote in 1815:

> At no period do we find the fine arts cultivated so generally as at the present epoch,
> and in our own favoured isle, wherein few families holding any rank have not some
> members who practise, among other elegant studies, the arts of drawing and painting:
> hence the enlightening radii of taste have spread to the extremity of our shores.[10]

Lessons would progress from simple line drawings, to pencil shading and then to the use of colour. 'Such as only make sketches in black lead pencil,' postulated Stevens, 'can never form pleasing pictures.'[11] This exhibition has some excellent examples of pencil sketches by Henry Edridge, Joseph Farington, Cornelius Varley, J.F. Lewis, William Pitt and others as well as examples of coloured studies from nature by the most assured sketchers of the mid-nineteenth century, William Müller and John Middleton. (cat.nos.19-21, 42-44, 46, 48-50, 55, 56, 82) Less appreciated artists, such as William Collins, are shown to have been exceptional sketchers (cat.nos.7, 8). In fact, his Devon sketches were singled out as 'among the most striking of the studies' in his posthumous sale of 1847.[12]

'In a climate like that of England', notes Stevens, 'there are few days that will admit of this useful and necessary mode of studying in the open air'.[13] Colouring on the spot required great dexterity and keen observational and practical skills. Farington in Exeter in 1809 made careful drawings with detailed colour notes. In 1810 he returned and coloured some of these drawings on the spot. He sketched in pencil and colour in his small sketchbook, with particular attention paid to light effects. (cat.nos.20, 21)

Manufacturers were keen to supply improved colours and materials. 'Cartridge paper may now be had,' wrote Stevens, 'of clear tint and excellent texture, on which coloured studies can be made, that rival the power obtained by using colours ground in oil.'[14] A 'greater rapidity of effect' with 'a superior boldness of style' could be achieved. Later, James Duffield Harding, represented here with two Devon works (cat.nos.28, 29) pioneered a machine-made paper with different surfaces which was marketed with his initials 'JDH' stamped on it. This is a good example of the influence of a prominent drawing master.[15]

Sketching in oils outdoors posed more considerable problems. J.M.W. Turner was tempted to work in this way in Devon and produced some of his finest and most satisfying oil sketches (cat.nos.72-75). It was Turner's friend, the Plymouth landscape painter A.B. Johns who had equipped himself with the necessary box and prepared paper to work outdoors using oil paints, and who encouraged Turner to sketch in oils, which was not his usual way of working. Such equipment was cumbersome. Most artists preferred to travel light. Charles Robert Leslie, best known today as Constable's biographer, was in Devon in 1818. As he set out for Plymouth from Newton Bushel (travelling via Berry Pomeroy, Totnes and Ivybridge) he had with him 'only a few shirts and cravats tied in a handerchief, and a sketchbook.' He had already sent his trunk back to London.[16] Samuel Palmer, too, preferred to keep things to a minimum. His son explained:

> Between 1848 and 1858 my father visited Devon and Cornwall four times, on each
> succeeding occasion becoming more enthusiastic in his admiration. His luggage and
> paraphernalia were simpler than ever, and after describing a beautiful South Devon
> route he says:- "This would be a thing to do very leisurely; no luggage, but one spare

shirt. Sketching portfolio with ... thin brown paper, which would weigh lightly. In
pocket, case of pencils and black and white chalk.[17]

Together with a few basic colours 'for slight indications of local colour', this provided him with all he needed for 'the most rapid method of sketching'. The exhibited sketch exemplifies his drawing skills and limited use of colour (cat.no.52). He eschewed, wrote his son 'costly umbrellas, elaborate boxes, or well-filled portmanteaus'. His portfolio was slung over his shoulder and his 'capacious pockets filled with sharp knives, chalks, charcoal, crayons, and sketchbooks'. He also 'carried a pair of ancient neutral-tint spectacles, with a little diminishing mirror, especially for sunsets'.[18]

The 'diminishing mirror' was a small convex mirror more commonly called a 'Claude glass' because it was intended to make the real landscape have the glow and tonality of paintings by Claude Lorrain, the great seventeenth-century painter of radiant, poetic Italian landscapes. ('Claudian' was a term often applied to the Devon landscape). The glasses were tinted to enhance the effect, reduce glare, and give a dark-toned quality. Picturesque tourists commonly carried them. Other instruments included the camera obscura (the forerunner of the small box photographic camera) which Farington used and which is listed among his sketching equipment in his notebooks. Samuel Prout also recommended it, as well as other drawing aids, such as the camera lucida (a small instrument with a combination of a prism and lenses). Stevens used a camera lucida to draw his simple but accurate views of Exeter (fig.28, p.97). Cornelius Varley used his own invention ('Varley's patent graphic telescope'), which combined a camera lucida with the added power of telescopic magnification. (cat.nos.81, 82). Such instruments were used by amateurs as well as professional artists.[19]

One writer, Isaac Taylor, extolling the joys of Devon scenery and particularly Dartmoor, advocated sketching out of doors as the best way of recollecting one's travels. Even if the results were 'far beneath the authentic artist-level', sketches would 'take a firmer grasp of the imagination' than 'even the most consummate of the lens-and-chemistry marvels of the photographic conjurer's box'.

> One for *one*, I would now gladly accept *another pencil sketch* in place of the same scene:
> especially if the instance were a Devonshire nook - a choice sample of the picturesque.[20]

(Francis Danby's opinion would have been much the same, as his 1857 Exmouth lecture on the 'Progress and Retardation of Art in England' demonstrates.[21]) Taylor also preferred earlier modes of transport:

> In what mode of locomotion is Devonshire to be seen to the best advantage? Certainly
> not from the prison-window of a carriage on the Great Western Railway![22]

Dartmoor was greatly to his taste. He contrasts the ever-changing agricultural scenes with never changing Dartmoor: '*here* it is not TIME that must be spoken of: it is DURATION'.[23] The temporal and the eternal were duly captured by Palmer who in 1859 exhibited a watercolour *The Comet of 1858, as seen from the Skirts of Dartmoor*.[24] When T.D. Acland and a companion were sketching on Dartmoor in 1867 their talk was of 'burning topics' including astronomy, ancient and modern. At their inn they met 'two professional artists, one from Plymouth, and the other from London', also on a sketching expedition.[25]

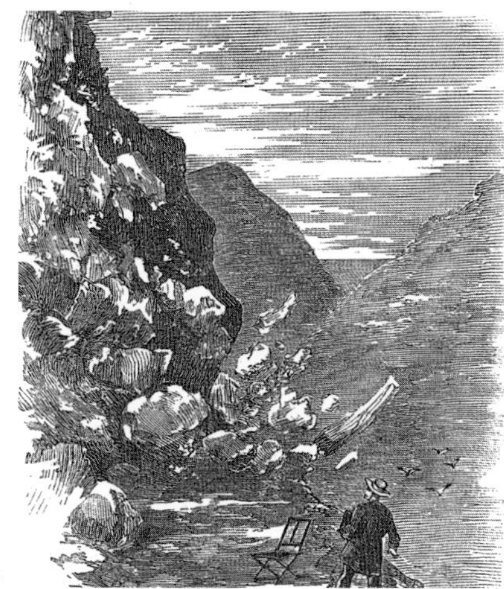

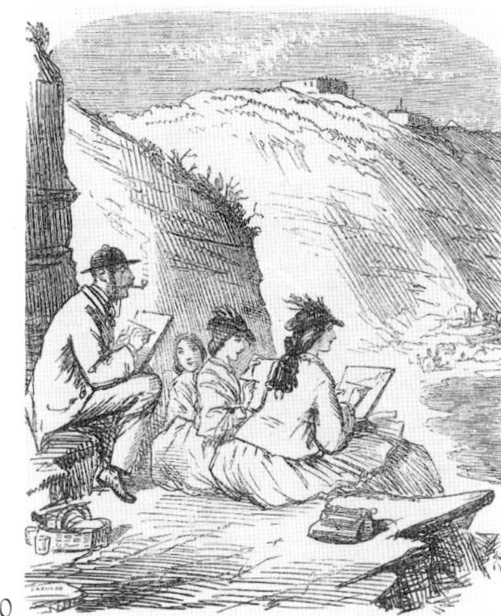

Other grand scenery is represented in this exhibition. The 'naked solitude, hopeless sterility, and wild desolation' of north Devon's Valley of the Rocks was sufficiently distinct to provoke very imaginative responses.[26] This sublime grandeur was not without its dangers. John Eagles nearly died when sketching on that coast in the 1830s.

> On the coast of Devonshire I had wandered on the ledge of a cliff, wide at first, but which narrowed and narrowed till it came to nothing. I had reached this extreme point, loaded with a heavy portfolio: some feet above me, the rock was perpendicular, and so beneath me, perhaps 200 feet. I could neither proceed nor recede. I had no space to turn in, for the wall of stone pressed upon me. What was to be done? About a yard before me I saw a mere bit of rock, just of a size to bear at least part of my foot, projecting from the otherwise smooth surface, and above that I perceived a tuft of earth and weedy grass growing from a crevice within arm's reach. If I could reach, and for a moment retain my foot upon this little projection, and at the same time take hold of the tuft - if that, peradventure, should be strong enough not to come away - I might scramble up to the top of the down, and be saved. I was able, in an instant, to see all, measure all with an accurate eye, and calculate my leap. There was not a moment's hesitation - the scheme of safety was concluded; I quietly let drop my portfolio, and the bit of rock and grass tuft were firm, and I escaped. But when I reached the top, there being no further need for action, I fell on my face, and trembled like a leaf. It was only then that the fear of danger came upon me.[27]

Similarly, the Plymouth artist Philip Mitchell was once nearly caught in a rock slide near Lynton, an event which became an illustrated newspaper story (fig.9).[28] The subject of the artist sketching thus becomes the image, rather than, or as well as, what he is actually depicting. Artists themselves (but more particularly caricaturists) occasionally took up this theme, sometimes with an element of self-parody. One such example, exhibited in 1858 was entitled *Painting from Nature out of Doors* and showed:

Fig.9. 'Landslip Near Linton, North Devon. Remarkable Escape,' wood engraving (probably from *Illustrated London News*).

Fig.10. John Leech, engraved Swain, 'Sketching the Castle', wood engraving from *Once a Week*, July 16, 1859, p. 50.

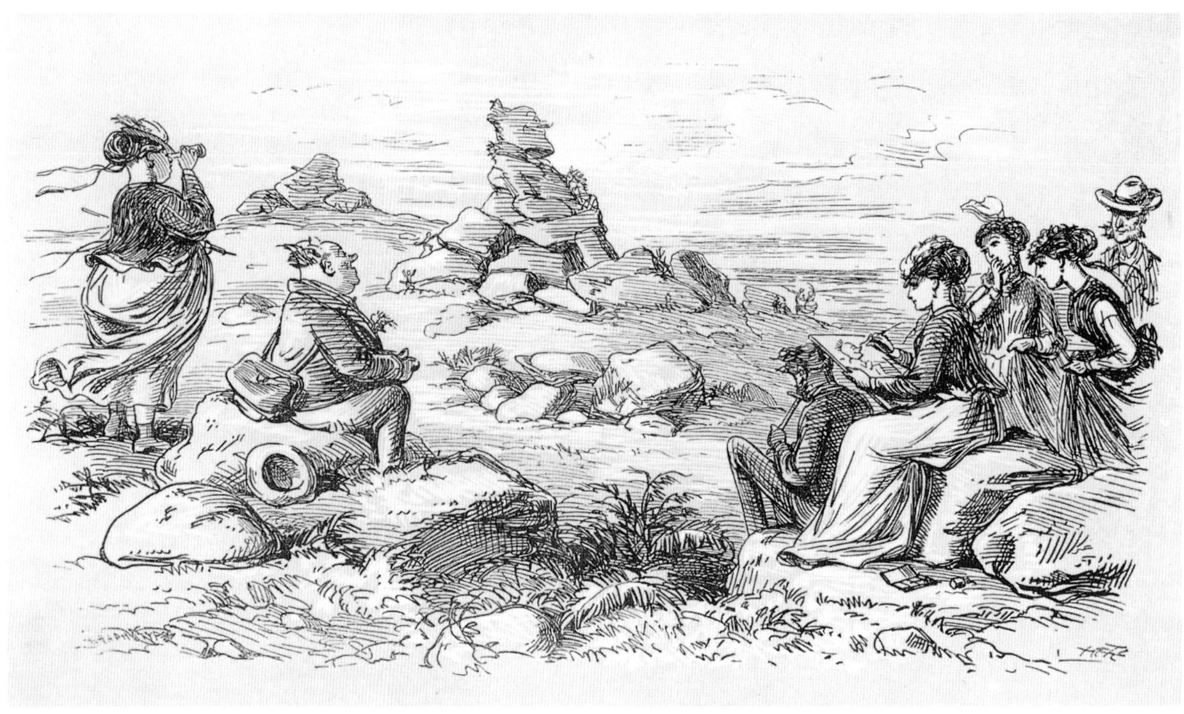

11

a tramping artist in the street of some Devonshire fishing village, say Clovelly, fixed on
his tripod of a camp-stool, his sketching canvas, white and tight as a drum-head, before
his ready hand, and steadily balanced on his permanent easel.[29]

The real subject turns out to be the artist molested by a variety of locals, young and old, as he attempts
his essay in the picturesque. Clovelly had already been 'discovered' by the artist James Clarke Hook
who was 'the acknowledged painter of Devonshire life.'[30]

In the summer of 1855 he went to Devonshire and first saw Clovelly. Primitive and
unsophisticated as the place then was, it was already well known to artists and some
authors. I think he must have been sent there by his friend Samuel Palmer, who knew
most parts of Devonshire and Cornwall very well. And it may have been also on Palmer's
advice that he went to Chagford, another haunt of the landscape painters of the day.[31]

Hook's first Clovelly paintings were exhibited at the Royal Academy in 1856 and immediately stamped
him as the 'authentic' painter of Devon's fisherfolk. In order to be as true to life as possible he invented
a special portable easel, weighted down to prevent it blowing away. It was afterwards taken up by
many other painters and it enabled Hook to paint his exhibition pictures entirely out of doors,
capturing with great effect the figures, the surroundings and the sea.

Another artist also tried, with less success, to paint a large work outdoors, this time at Torquay.
Fred Walker was aiming for a quite different poetry in his unfinished *The Unknown Land* painted on

Fig.11. Phiz (Halbot K. Browne) *Sketches of the Seaside and the Country*, the Graphotyping Company, London, (n.d. 1860s). 'Mr. Pipkins is so delighted with
that picturesque rock "Bobb's Nose," that he prevails upon Miss Fotoe to make a sketch of it for him (which is pronounced by all to be *very* like.)'

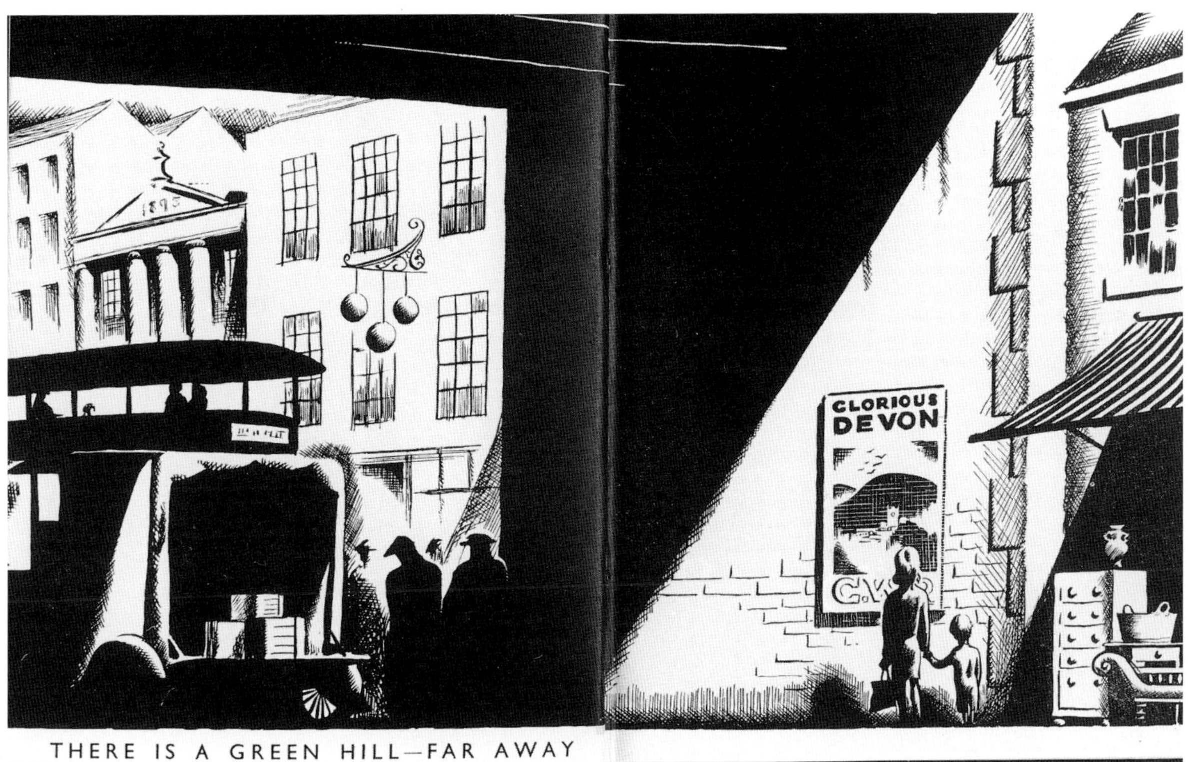

12 ___ THERE IS A GREEN HILL—FAR AWAY

the beach from a boat house between August 7 and September 7, 1873. He planned 'a glorious subject' based on the scenery near Anstey's Cove, 'the colour of the sea quite like the Mediterranean.' The picture is described as 'mariners, after a long voyage, arriving at an unknown shore, and beaching their boat with feverish eagerness.' Working from his boathouse he was able to cut himself off from 'the tourist beast', from 'bathers and other intruders'. Fortunately, as he told his sister, 'there aren't many people here, thank goodness, but what there are, you'd be disgusted with; vile excursionists and semi-plebians.' he worked for several weeks trying to hide himself from the view of the 'brutal people that infest the place.'[32]

Continental visitors sketched here too. In south Devon the cataclysmic landslide in 1839 at Dowlands, near Axminster,[33] a 'world in ruins', was marvelled at by the Dresden-based artist, Carl Gustav Carus for whom a landscape painting had to be an 'earth-life-picture'. He was particulalrly appreciative of Devon's coast and river scenery and made a number of coloured sketches.[34] The serious nature worship of Carus required an understanding which he felt was 'relatively speaking, the property only of the few', although, he conceded, many more now possessed a 'deeper insight into nature'. However, 'among the incapable many' this had 'degenerated into an actual caricature.'[35] Caricature was indeed much in evidence in the British response to Devon scenes as the examples here by Phiz (Hablot K. Browne) and John Leech (figs. 10 and 11) amply demonstrate.[36] Images of Devon, however, were enough to evoke 'the green hill far away' well into the twentieth century when the G.W.R. poster could offer escape from the socially deprived city into unspoilt nature (fig.12).[37]

Fig.12. Arthur Wragg, 'There is a Green Hill – Far Away,' from
Jesus Wept. A commentary in black and white on ourselves and the world today (n.d. 1930s, n.p.).

FREDERICK CHRISTIAN LEWIS AND THE RIVERS OF DEVON
Michael Pidgley

In his dual role as painter and printmaker F.C.Lewis was at one time highly regarded, locally and nationally, as an interpreter of Devon scenery. Today, sad to say, he is almost forgotten. Hopefully this exhibition will help to restore his neglected reputation.

Between 1820 and 1850 he regularly exhibited oil paintings and watercolours of Devon subjects at the London exhibitions.[1] He published three series of prints, all dealing with Devon rivers, with all but a few of them being etched and engraved by himself from his own sketches. These represented the Dart (1821), the Tamar and the Tavy (1823), and the Exe (1827).[2] Later he reworked a selection of the plates and re-issued them in much altered form, along with his own introductory text, as *Scenery on the Devonshire Rivers* (1843).[3] The plates in that volume constitute some of the most original contributions to landscape printmaking in this period.

One has only to look at the list of subscribers to the Exe etchings to see how important Lewis must have been in spreading an appreciation of the richness of Devon's river scenery. Among the artists whose Devon works are represented in this exhibition, and who were subscribers, are Turner, Danby, Collins, Chantrey, Eagles and Stevens. Other artist subscribers include Constable, Callcott, Lawrence and Wilkie. Non-artists were represented by royalty, peers of the realm, gentry, landowners, connoisseurs and cultured folk.

In Exeter Lewis established contacts with local artists and included in his Exe volume a few etchings after outlines by Francis Stevens (q.v.) and a facsimile of a wash drawing by John White Abbott. Also included is a view of Killerton from a sketch by Sir Thomas Dyke Acland, to whom the whole volume is dedicated. He received, as he acknowledges, 'very liberal and hospitable treatment' in Devon.

Among his hosts were the Reverend and Mrs. Bray at Tavistock. Anna Bray gives us her first hand account of introducing Lewis and his son, John Frederick Lewis (q.v.), to the local scenery:

> That most worthy man and meritorious artist, Mr. Lewis, has made some beautiful
> drawings in this neighbourhood from nature. And one of the finest landscapes of
> modern times, a view on the Tavy, was painted by him in oil, from his own sketch, and

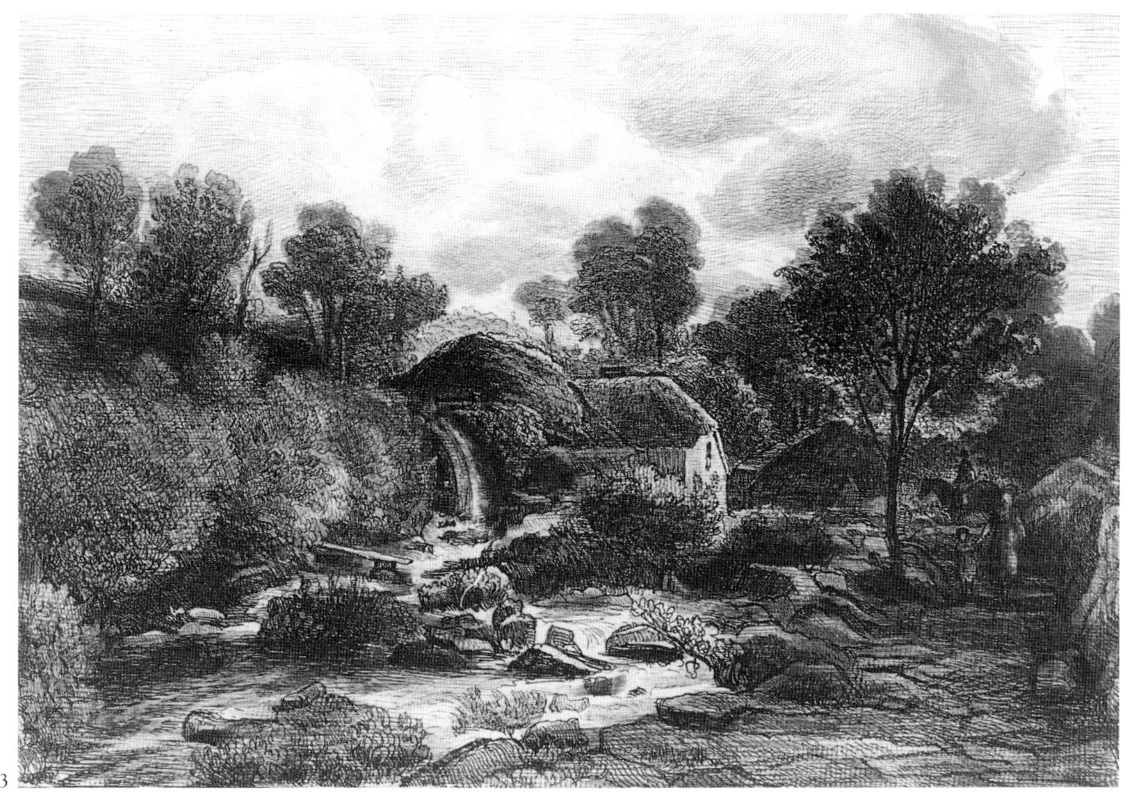

purchased by the Duke of Bedford, who gave it to Mr. Wilson, the gentleman who
manages his property at Tavistock.[4]

The Duke of Bedford acquired quite a few works by Lewis, who represented the Duke's Devon
properties among his subjects and to whom he dedicated his Tamar prints (1823). The extent to which
Lewis came to be associated particularly with Devon can be judged from the following review:

Mr. F.C.Lewis's *By the Rivers of Babylon* &c (114) is just one of those Devonshire scenes
on the estate of the Duke of Bedford, near Tavistock which the painter has contributed
for many years to succeeding exhibitions.[5]

There is a distinct sense of *déja vu* in these comments, more than a hint perhaps that Lewis had worn
out his formulae for wooded river scenes which were now automatically associated with Devon!
A kind of over-green, lushly foliaged, round-hilled landscape, preferably with a boulder-strewn, fast-
running river was almost synonymous with 'Devon'.

Lewis's etchings of the river Tavy were dedicated to the Marquis of Tavistock. Three are entitled
'Near Mary Tavy', an area Lewis declared 'to be unique in beauty and in subjects for an artist'.[6]
An example of how one particular subject could become a popular favourite is made clear by
Mrs. Bray:

Fig.13. F.C. Lewis *Mill at Peter Tavy. Property of the Revd. E. A. Bray*, mixed method, from *Scenery on the Devonshire
Rivers*, 1843. 'Picture in the collection of T. Webster.'

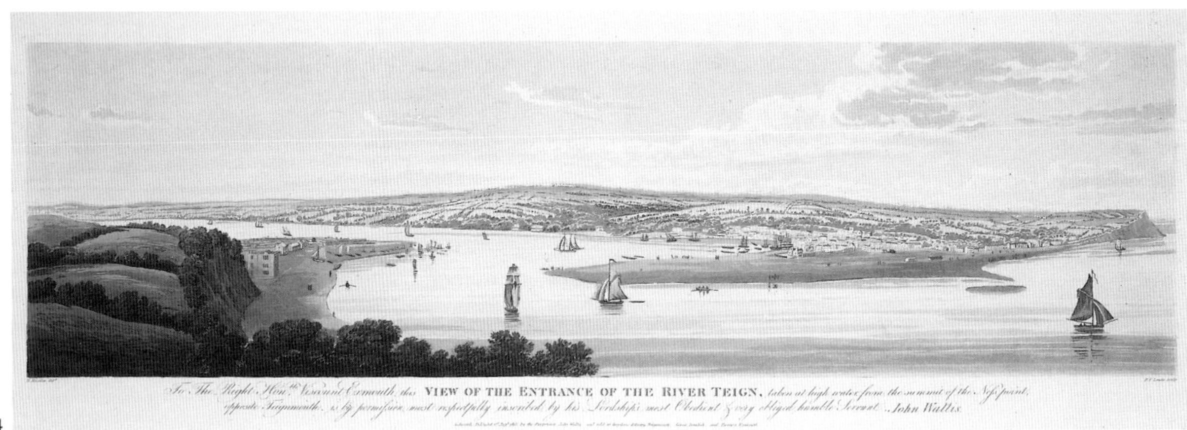

14

> All the artists who have hitherto visited Peter Tavy, and we have guided many thither,
> declare it to be an unrivalled village in the variety of beauties it affords as studies for
> the painter. A mill there, the property of Mr. Bray, has been drawn and painted over
> and over again, has been hung in Somerset House [the Royal Academy], and the
> Water-colour Exhibition, and was never yet returned unsold on the hands of an
> artist....The mill has been drawn by Mr. Lewis and his son more than once... the subject
> it affords is strikingly characteristic. - a rush of water turns the wheel, and forms a
> cascade that falls into a rapid mountain stream as clear as the brightest crystal; the
> thatched gable of the mill is covered with ivy; a little bridge crosses the stream opposite
> the cottage door, and as you stand on this you see the crystal waters come pouring down
> a shelving and rocky channel in a manner that the pencil alone could portray...[7]

No wonder that another pictorial cliché of Devon was the water mill! Lewis included it in his Tavy etchings and in the *Devonshire Rivers* set (fig.13).

Even before Lewis came to Devon to find his own subjects he had engraved some important local scenes by other artists including *Views of Sidmouth* after W.B.Noble (1816) and two large impressive panoramas of the Exe and the Teign by Henry Haseler (1818) (fig.14). He had also engraved some of the attractive plates in *Picturesque Views on the River Exe*, published in Tiverton in 1819. Working on such scenes may have quickened his interest in exploring the picturesque possibilities of Devon for himself. He saw his own work as complementing that of others. His Dart engravings could, he wrote, 'contribute to illustrate the History of Devon by the Revd. Danl. Lysons FRS FA & LS.' Lysons's volume on Devon (volume six of his *Magna Britannia*) was published after a long delay in 1822 as a weighty tome of 682 pages. It contained illustrations by, among others, Joseph Farington (q.v.) drawn on his trips to Devon in 1809 and 1810.

Lewis's first exhibited work depicting Devon was of Dartmoor which, in 1820, was still something of a novelty.[8] His Dart volume was published the following year with the title *Scenery of the River Dart*,

Fig.14. Henry Haseler, engraved F.C. Lewis, *View of the Entrance to the River Teign, taken at High water from the Summit of the Ness Point, opposite Teignmouth*, aquatint, published J. Wallis, Sidmouth, 1818. Dedicated to the Right Honble. Viscount Exmouth.

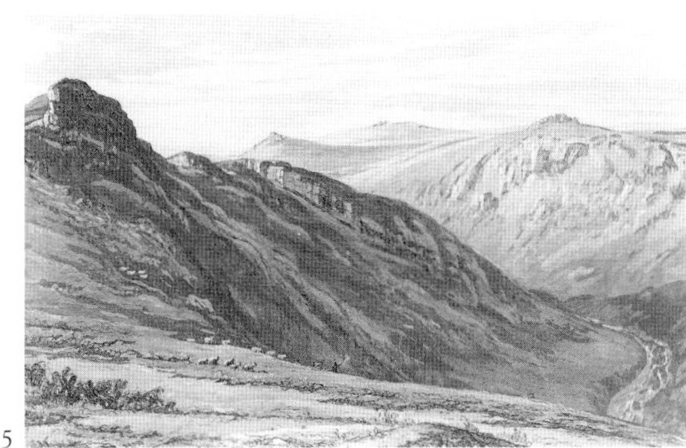

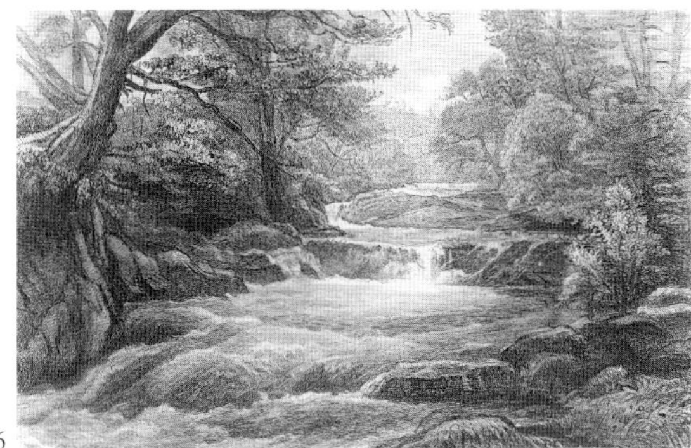

being a series of Thirty-Five Views, Representing the most interesting features in its Course, from its source in the wildest & most uncultivated parts of Dartmoor, to its Mouth in the English Channel. Lewis was, as Geoffrey Grigson remarked, 'an early reveller in the scenery of Dartmoor,' with 'an evident delight in granite, stream, and uncultivated width,' the beginnings of a concern which 'looked forward toward the Brontes and Thomas Hardy'[9] (fig.15).

Another avowed aim of the Dart series was expressed by Lewis. 'Executed to form as nearly as possible Facsimiles of the Drawings' he had calculated that his views would 'not only interest the admirers of Nature, and those unacquainted with the Country,' but would 'also form a set of studies for the Learner of Landscape drawing.'[10] This appears to have been exactly what John Sell Cotman, an original subscriber to these engravings, had in mind when he made his own lively interpretations of Lewis's prints in a series of drawings now in the British Museum. Far from being evidence of a personal trip to Devon, as Cotman's biographer S.D. Kitson not unreasonably imagined, Cotman's drawings were probably made from the prints at home in Yarmouth for the use of his pupils.[11] The Dart series was also subscribed to by other Norwich artists namely James Stark and George Vincent. Other artist subscribers included B.R. Haydon, John Martin, James Northcote, C.R. Leslie (who had visited Devon in 1818 [see *Sketching from Nature*]) and, from Boston, Leslie's fellow American, Washington Allston.

The local Devon newspapers took a keen interest in Lewis's publications. *Flindell's Western Luminary* in a review of the Tamar and Tavy volume (1823) pondered on the dilemma of topographical accuracy:

> The artist who delineates local scenery is involved in frequent difficulties. The finer his
> taste and science, the greater his temptation to swerve from fidelity. Turner will elevate
> his rock; his inferiors will represent its real altitude. However he may repine at the
> sacrifice, yet to illustrate topography the artist must faithfully represent his scene.

The significance of Lewis's work was put in a national context and expressed in a high moral tone:

> Should his efforts divert the torrents of idlers from their foreign destination, and thus
> check the present baleful traffic - the exportation of English riches, and the importation

Fig.15. F.C. Lewis *Benshe Tor*, 1820, etching and aquatint in sepia, from *Scenery of the River Dart*, 1821.

Fig.16. F.C. Lewis *On the River Okement*, mixed method, from *Scenery on the Devonshire Rivers*, 1843. 'Picture in the Collection of Rev. E. Coleridge.'

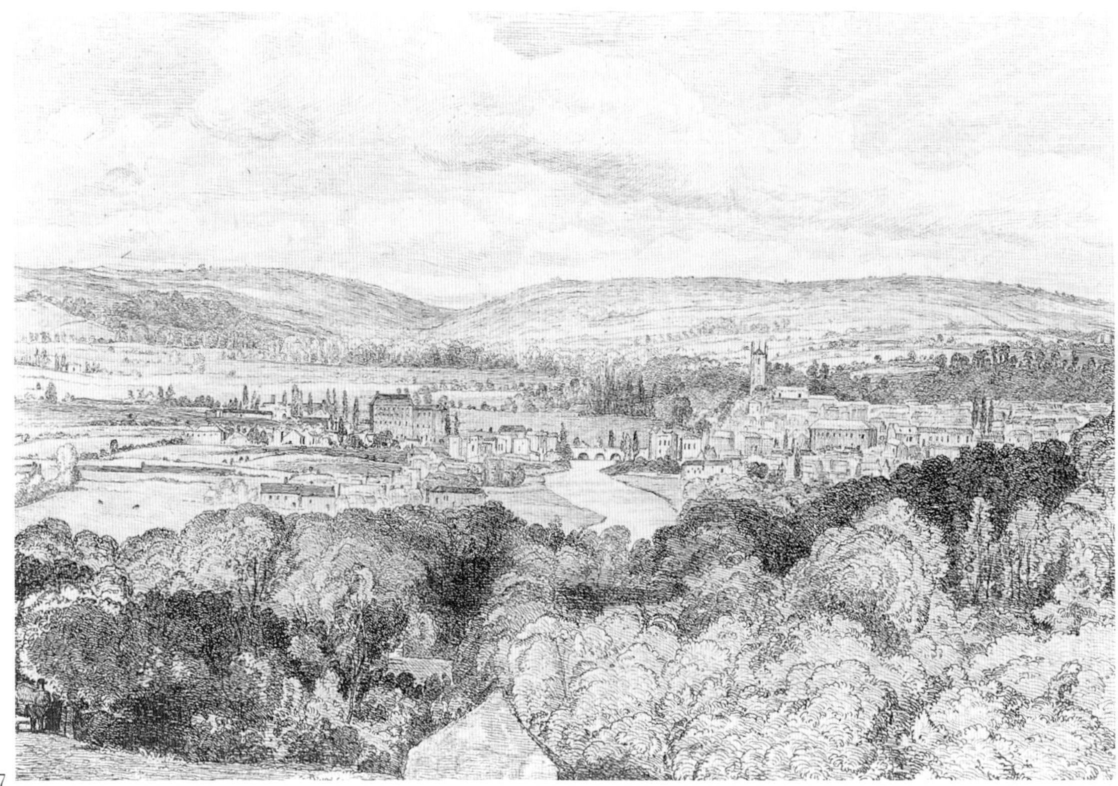

of continental immorality, the civic crown should be his reward and the verdict of
Britons, "this man has served his country."[12]

These delineations of Devon aroused patriotic feelings at a time when, according to the reviewer,
'fashion will allow no beauty on this side of the channel', when France and Italy were the destinations
of the higher classes, 'when nothing less than the Alps or Appennines are deemed capable of exciting
the admiration of accomplished young ladies.'

Lewis's third volume of Devon river scenery was devoted to the Exe (1827) and was equally well
received; it was 'consistent with his reputation, and with the patronage by which he is distinguished.'[13]
The Exe itself presented 'scenes of grace, variety, and tranquility, rivalling and frequently surpassing
the exquisite compositions of Claude Lorraine.' And Lewis had triumphed. His views were 'judiciously
selected, accurately drawn, and carefully engraved... None could imagine his representations deficient,
unless acquainted with the actual localities.'[14]

The help and hospitality that Lewis received on his trips to Devon he was able to reciprocate when
his Devon friends and acquaintances came to London. Lewis was very well connected in the art world
and took visitors to meetings of the Graphic Society, established in 1833, and whose president was
William Brockedon, himself a Devon-born artist (born Totnes, 1787). The society's meetings brought

Fig.17. F. C. Lewis *Tiverton. Looking over from Colypriest*, etching, from *The Scenery of the River Exe*, 1827.

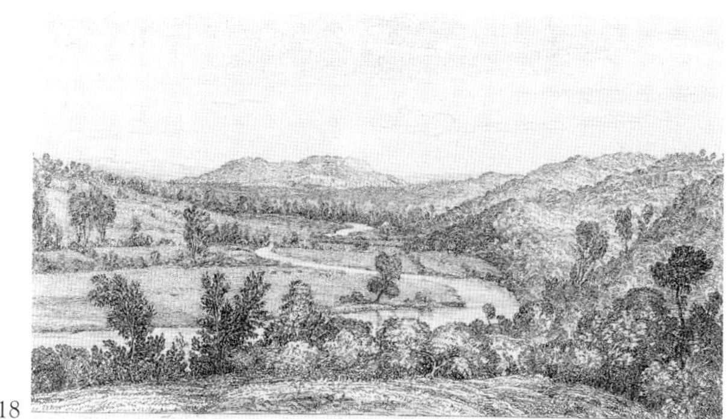

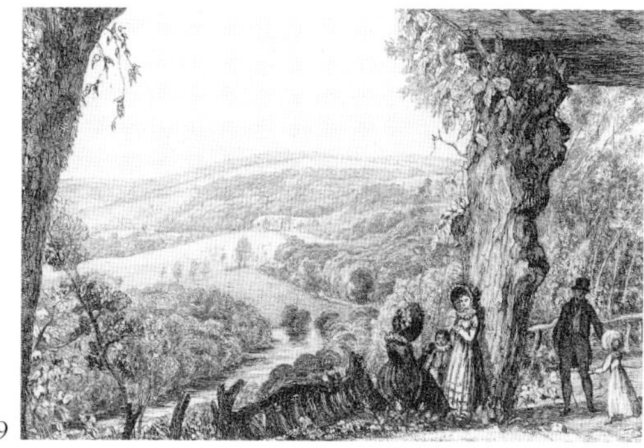

together artists, engravers, publishers and collectors. All kinds of art works were brought along by the members. At one meeting in 1836 the two Lewises, father and son, introduced Mr. Champernowne of Dartington Hall and the Rev. Edward Coleridge of Ottery St. Mary.[15] Also present was the Exeter-born engraver Samuel Cousins who was to have a long and illustrious career as a mezzotinter. Brockedon, Champernowne and Coleridge were all subscribers to Lewis's Devon prints. He was a guest at Dartington on a number of occasions.[16]

Lewis must have been gratified by the reception of his major and last collection of West Country scenes which he published in 1843 as *Scenery of the Devonshire Rivers*. His own introduction offered an explanation of his very painterly techniques:

> In every original picture there is much accident in touch, in chiaro oscuro, and in colour: the mind of the painter, ever vigilant, seizes on these accidents, and turns them to a new advantage. These can scarcely be copied, nor can they be transferred to the plates, by a too regular and precise method of engraving. The Author, by his mode of engraving, has endeavoured to give a freer scope for such accidents, of which he has taken advantage as they arose. The plates have, therefore, a greater air of originality than the more usual method of highly finished engraving supplies. It is for this original quality that painters' etchings are so much prized.

The *Athenaeum* commended his efforts for their distinctive qualities which would be recognised by the discriminating who wished for something beyond the standard product. Lewis, too, made this point:

> He does not pretend to offer a companion to an itinerary, nor to take the tourist from spot to spot. Numerous are the views, for such purpose, published every day, and in which considerable talent is often shown, though, perhaps they are generally too ambitious of effect, and are not always recognised upon a comparison with the real scenes.

Fig.18. Sir T.D. Acland, etched by F.C. Lewis *Killerton from the Exe, the Seat of Sir Thos. D. Acland Bt. MP*, from *The Scenery of the River Exe*, 1827.

Fig.19. F.C. Lewis *Endsleigh Cottage and Grounds from a Seat under the Rock. The Property of the Duke of Bedford*, etching, from *The Scenery of the Tamar and Tavy*, 1823.

He aimed more at the 'impression' of a scene, 'the large effect of simple truth,' in which the painter's personal expression took preference over 'dexterity of hand.' As the *Athenaeum* noted, Lewis had combined aquatint and mezzotint with his etchings 'to vary the quality of his chiaroscuro;' they were '"painters' etchings" in the true sense of the term... recalling to mind the etchings of Rembrandt, without suggesting the idea of imitation.'[17]

Lewis's introduction draws the reader's attention to a number of useful publications on the subject of landscape, including John Eagle's essays as "The Sketcher" written for *Blackwood's Magazine* in the 1830s. Eagles (q.v.) was a collector of Lewis's paintings and prints and an avid sketcher of Devon scenes.

It is the poetry of nature that comes through most strongly in this final volume of Devon scenes, a broadly treated and atmospheric landscape style, one that 'affects the mind and moves the feelings' and one separated from 'common obvious everyday nature,' as poetry is from conversation.

> Without mind there would be no music, no poetry, no beauty in external nature, for thus it shines, as it were, by that great reflected light that the creator has placed in the conception of man.[18]

CATALOGUE
~ OF EXHIBITS ~

1. SAMUEL HENRY BAKER, *At Clovelly* (c.1860)

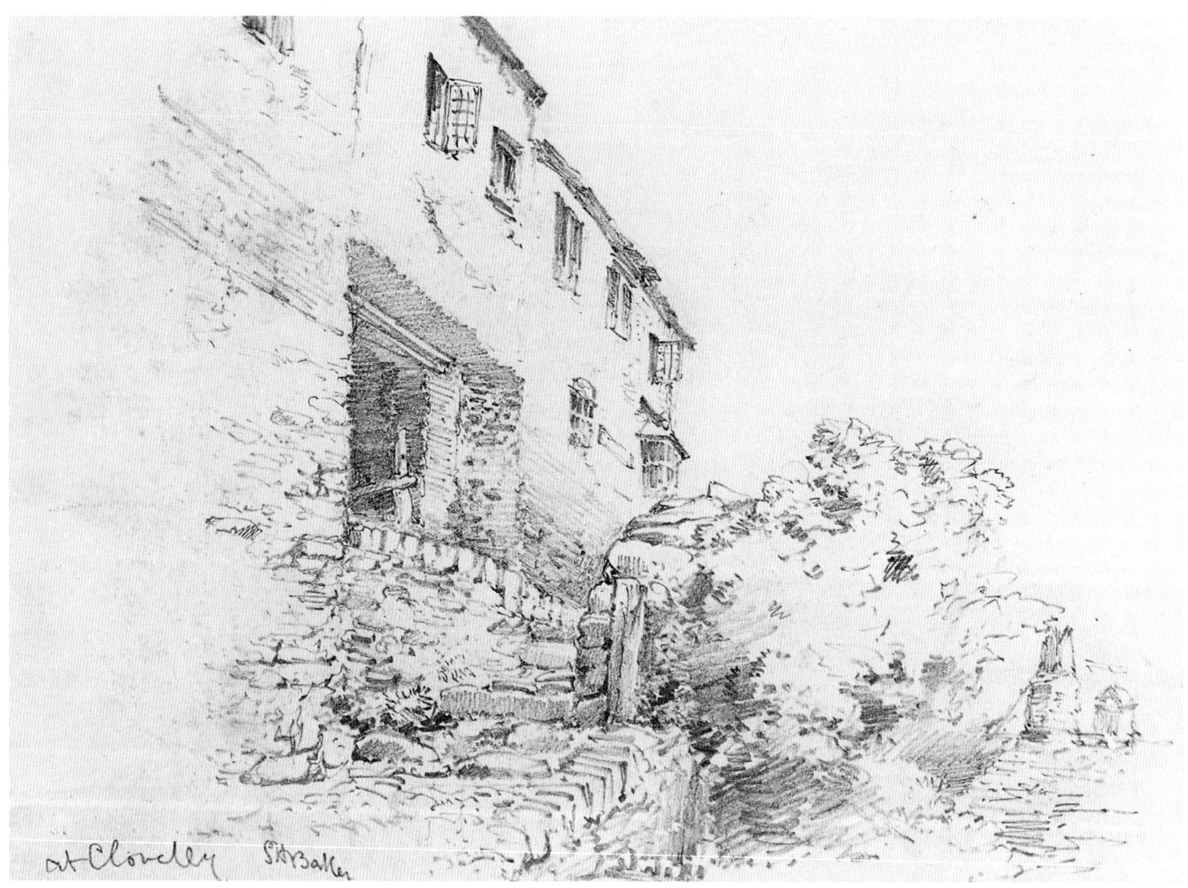

SAMUEL HENRY BAKER (1824-1909)

1. *At Clovelly* (c.1860)
Pencil on paper, 22.1 x 29.8 cm
Signed 'S H Baker' and inscribed
'At Clovelly' (lower left)
Stephen Wildman

Samuel Baker was originally apprenticed to a magic-lantern slide painter but soon enrolled at the Birmingham School of Design and then took lessons from the landscape painter Joseph Paul Petitt. He was a mainstay of the Birmingham Society of Arts, where he exhibited over 500 works, and his reputation today rests on the qualities of his draughtsmanship, of which this is a good example.[1]

The motif comprises a group of cottages, just up from the quayside at Clovelly, and Baker indicates the vertiginous nature of the spot by including the chimney pots of another house at our feet on the right. His technique is quite painterly here, using a soft pencil to emphasise tone, and should be compared to the more linear style used by his fellow townsman, William Pitt, to depict the same buildings (cat.no.55,56). Both motif and treatment owe a debt to that 'cottage picturesque' seen in Horsley's *Bishopsteignton* (cat.no.32) and ultimately associated with Samuel Prout (q.v.), whose soft-ground etchings of Devon cottages helped to establish the genre. (SS)

2. JAMES BOURNE, *View from near the Fort, Sidmouth* (1805)

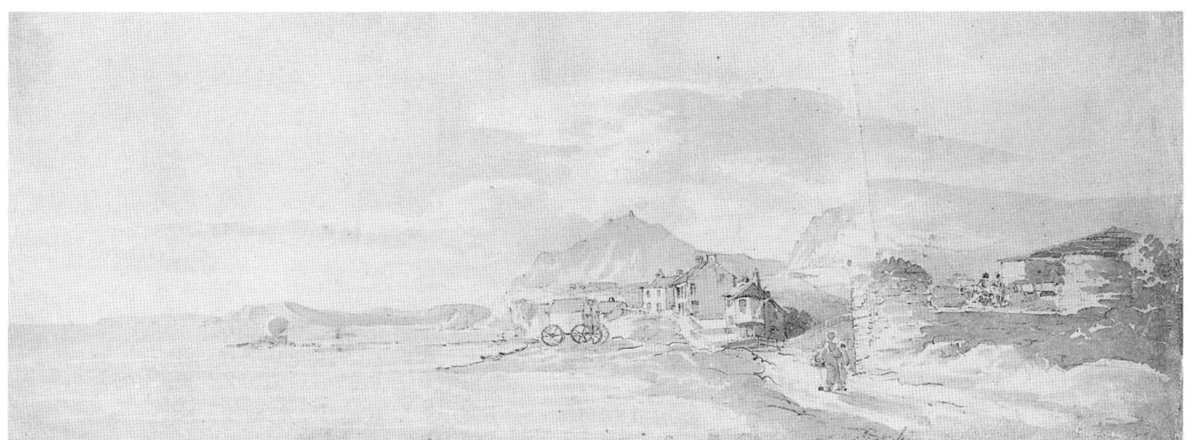

JAMES BOURNE (1773-1854)

2. *View from near the Fort, Sidmouth* (1805)
Pencil and wash, 20.2 x 53.5 cm
Birmingham Museums and Art Gallery

Bourne probably visited the West Country in 1799 but the date of this study and the fact that he exhibited a *View of Exeter* at the Royal Academy in 1809 show that he continued to work up his sketches many years later.[1] Little is known of his artistic training. He may have been self-taught although Bourne's monochrome style, as seen here, is vaguely reminiscent of the broad, sketchy approach outlined by Alexander Cozens in his various treatises on landscape composition.[2] Bourne may have been influenced in this by Sir George Beaumont, one of Cozens's pupils, with whom he was probably in contact at this period.[3]

This drawing is of interest insofar as it shows Sidmouth still relatively undeveloped; only the bathing machines hint at its fashionable reputation. Certainly, had Bourne returned to Sidmouth in 1805 he would have noticed the 'great number of new houses... erected... ranged upon the beach... numerous as the lodgings now are, there are frequently not enough to accommodate the company in the height of the season.'[4] (SS)

GEORGE PRICE BOYCE (1826-1897)

3. *Babbacombe Bay, Coast of Devonshire* (1853)
(Illustrated in colour on p.43)
Watercolour on paper, 32 x 53.5 cm
Signed and dated 'G.P. Boyce 1853' (lower right)
Astley Cheetham Art Gallery, Tameside Metropolitan
Borough Council Leisure Services

'Mr. Boyce's faculty of observing Nature is second only
to his power of reproducing her effects.'[1] Those
reviewer's words from 1862 are certainly applicable to
this view of Babbacombe, one of the most attractive
mid nineteenth-century depictions of the Devon
coast. It is rich in Pre-Raphaelite attention to detail,
particularly in the pebbly rock-strewn beach.[2] The
shimmering sea and the powder blue sky give an
overall sense of summer stillness and health-giving
atmosphere. This is a place to relax and enjoy the
pleasures of the seaside, an impression enhanced by
the discreet inclusion of the figures preparing for a
picnic, a note of eye-catching colour on the red cloth
drawing our attention to the wine and picnic basket.
An 1817 guide, intent on recommending 'the
wandering tourist to view the beauties of his own
native land,' suggested a water excursion to
Babbacombe where 'parties of pleasure' would find a
new inn. 'Visitors should stock themselves with wines,
&c, lobsters being the principal article to be procured'
on arrival.[3]
In William Daniell's *Voyage Round Great Britain*
Babbacombe is illustrated. (See Daniell's preparatory
sketch, cat.no.13). It is there described as a 'romantic
little watering-place deservedly a favourite with those
who prefer true seclusion to the questionable delights
of merely fashionable retirement.'[4] The number of
prints of it prove its growing popularity.[5]
Here we are in the presence of nature's wonders, the
rocks 'most various and gorgeous in colour' as Samuel
Palmer described them.[6] It is a sort of natural paradise
and it was at Babbacombe in 1852, the year before
Boyce painted his view, that the eminent Victorian
naturalist Philip Henry Gosse made many of his most
important discoveries in the marine life of the sea
shore. As soon as he had arrived in Devon from
London at the end of January 1852 Gosse 'went down
through the embowered hamlet of Babbicombe (*sic*)
"to see what promise the beach might afford."'[7]
It proved a veritable treasure trove of sea-weeds and
rare sea-anemones. He 'nourished a jealous and almost
whimsical affection' for one particular pool,
constantly fearing that its 'crystal beauty might be
profaned.' The pebbles on the beach were 'singularly
rich in those fantastic and gem-like creatures, the
rudibranch mollusca.'[8] His daily observations at
Babbacombe and elsewhere became *A Naturalist's*

Rambles on the Devonshire Coast, published in May
1853. This was an instant critical and popular success.
It is hard to imagine Boyce not having come across it
before he visited Devon in the summer of 1853. The
reviewers all commented on Gosse's singular ability to
describe scenery, and for his 'philosophically poetic
mind.' 'His description of scenic nature' was
'exceedingly rich.' 'His "pen pictures" of the scenery'
were charming, and he elucidated 'some of the most
wonderful mysteries of the creation.'[9] Gosse and others
popularized the collecting of marine life, of sea shells
and pebbles. 'Sea-Side Life' was written about widely.
The poor sea-anemones were under attack. 'How they
must hate the season and Mr. Gosse! Poor things!'[10]
Gosse himself hated it when 'idle men or lads
approached the scenes of his devotion.'[11]
An 1821 guide to the south Devon coast had a section
on Conchology, to draw attention to the 'amusement
and delight' to be gained from collecting shells, as well
as pointing to 'its more serious association with
geology.'[12] By the mid century it could be stated that
the study of shells had 'leaped at once out of the more
childish toy of conchology into the maturer science of
malacology'[13] Now it was the creature itself, its form
and habits that interested the newly informed seaside
visitor. Gosse himself gave up visiting Babbacombe
when his favourite pool was vandalised and Edmund
Gosse, his son, described the inevitable decline of its
secluded charms:
'The beach is now familiarized and vulgarized; carriage
roads wind down to it, where break neck paths used to
descend; it is all given up, with but a small trace of its
ancient wildness, to the comfort of nursemaids and
trippers. But in those days no bathing machines had
invaded its savage coves and creeks.'[14] (MP)

HENRY BRIGHT (1810-1873)

4. *On the Borders of Dartmoor* (c.1840)
(Illustrated in colour on p.44)
Pencil, watercolour and some scraping out on cream
paper, 45.6 x 75.9 cm
Norfolk Museums Service (Norwich Castle Museum)

On the Borders of Dartmoor was almost certainly
exhibited in 1844. It is a very self-conscious piece of
'picture-making' painted in what the *Art Union* called
'a manner the most masterly':
'The admirable scenery of the place reconciles us to
the word "Dartmoor" in some degree, which is surely
one of those standing in type from year to year, in
readiness for catalogues.'[1]
A hazy view of Dartmoor is seen in the background
beyond Lydford. The major pictorial component is the
stagey picturesque mill with the foreground figures
also striking a pose. Bright (who probably visited the

3. GEORGE PRICE BOYCE, *Babbacombe Bay, Coast of Devonshire* (1853)

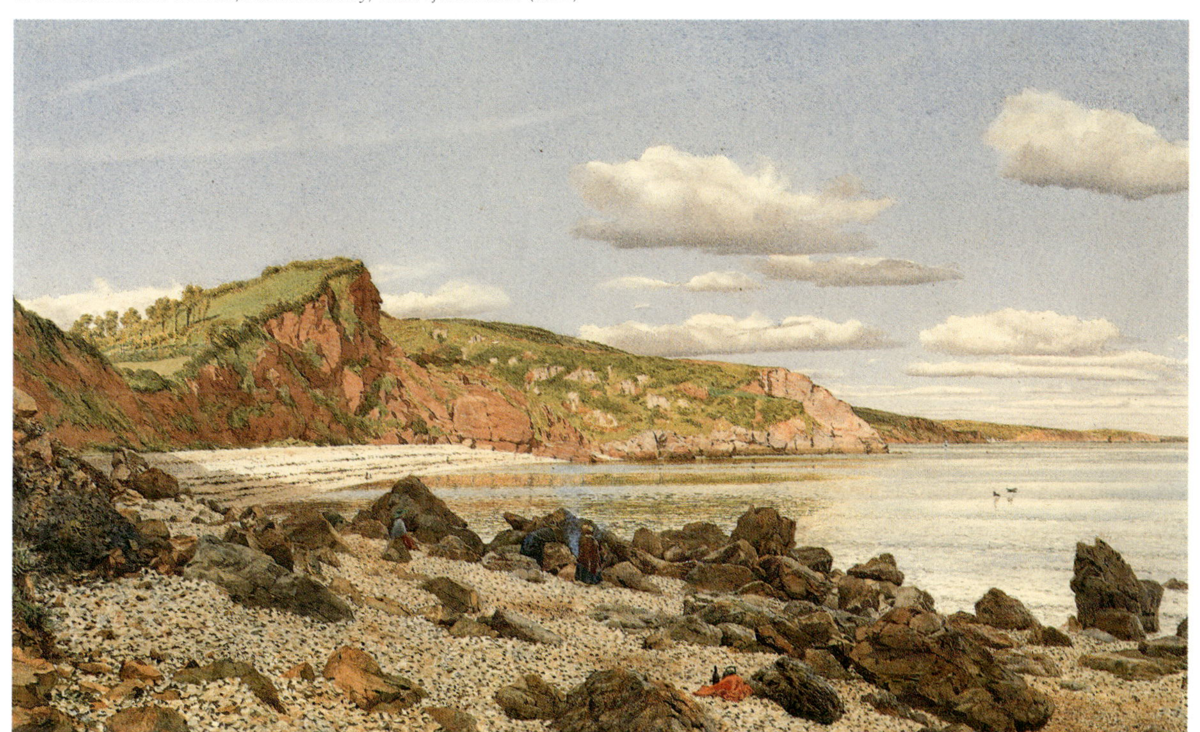

4. HENRY BRIGHT, *On the Borders of Dartmoor* (c.1840)

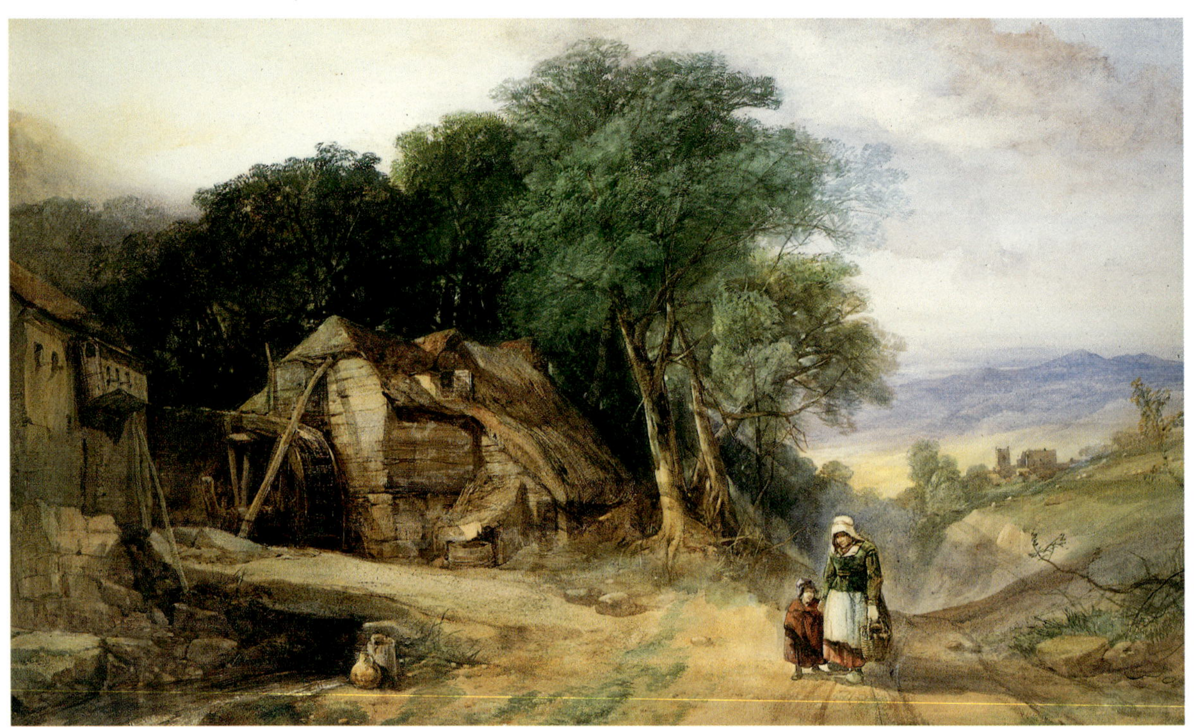

8. WILLIAM COLLINS, *Hartland Quay from the Warren* (1821)

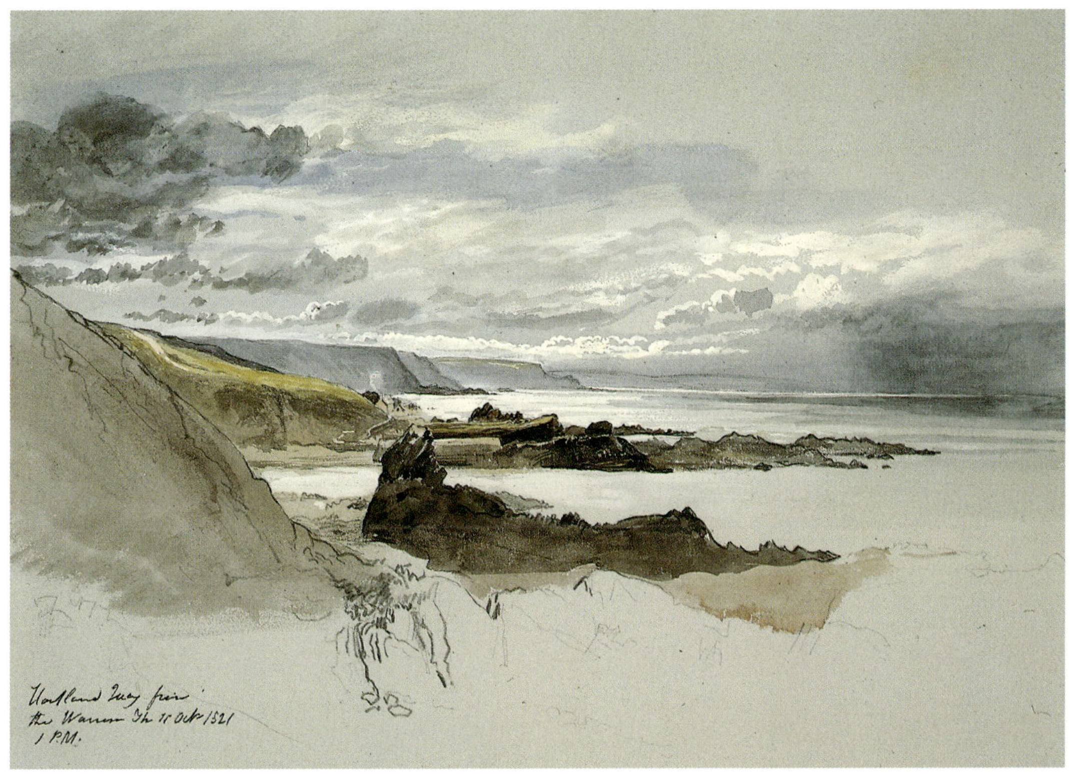

9. DAVID COX, *Lynmouth Pier* (1824)

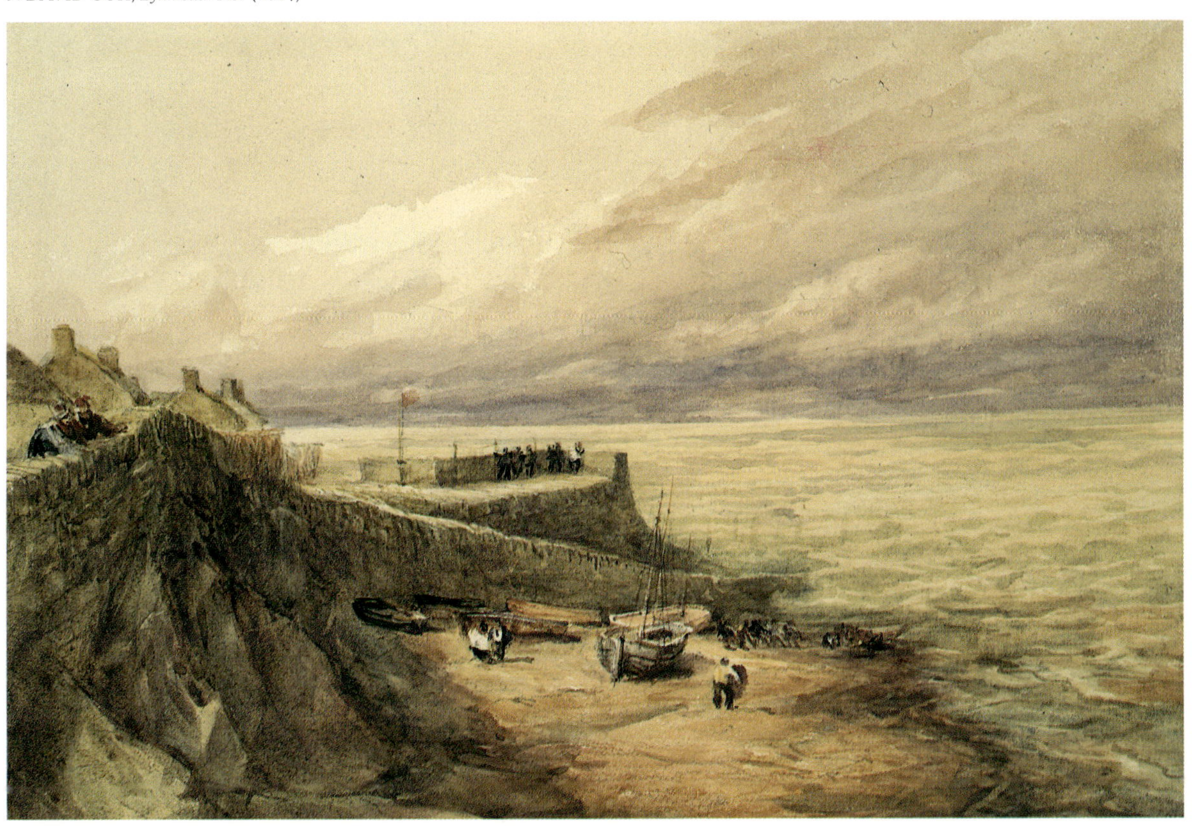

10. FRANCIS DANBY, *Dead Calm - Sunset at the Bight of Exmouth* (1855)

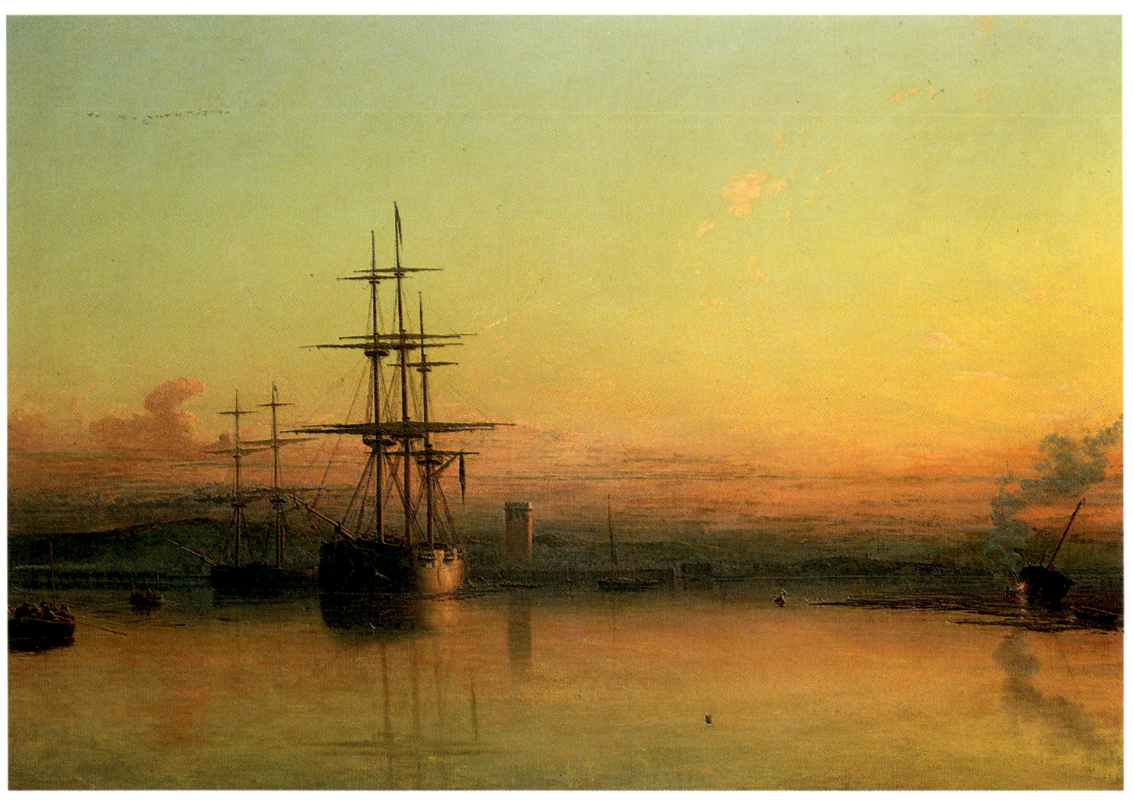

12. FRANCIS DANBY, *Sunset through Trees* (c.1855)

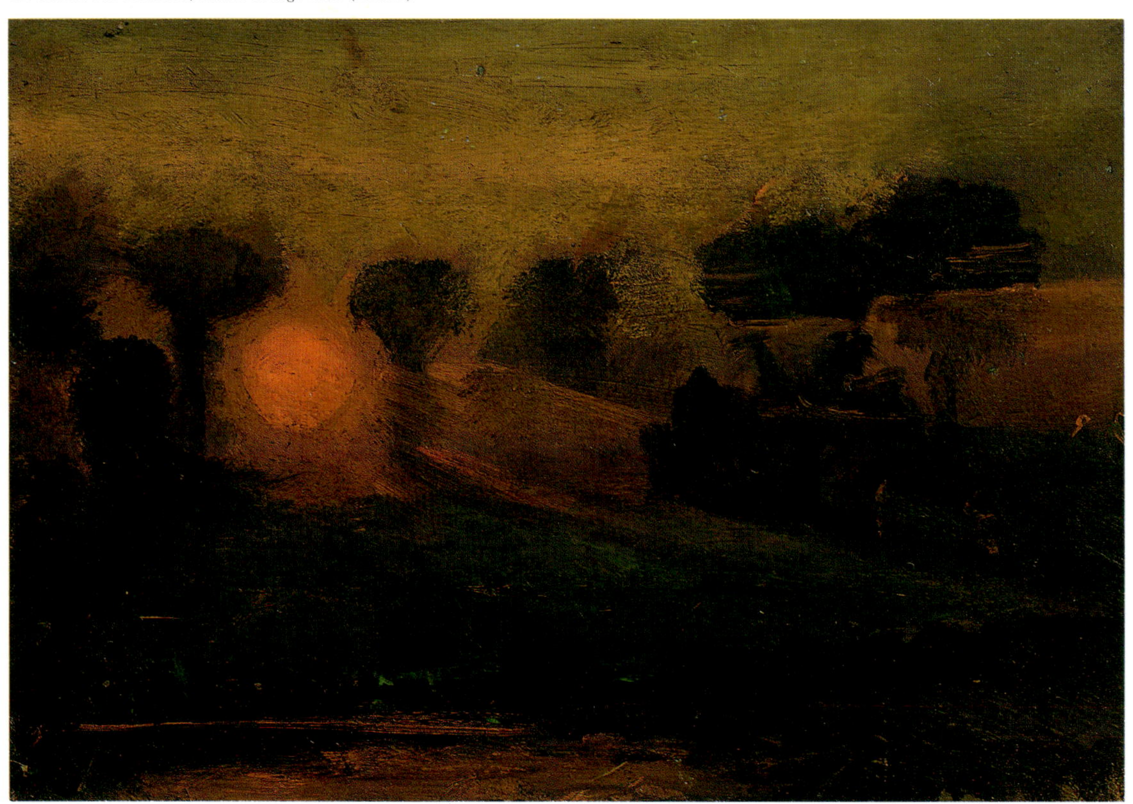

5. FRANCIS CHANTREY, *(? Berry Pomeroy Castle) and Near Dartmouth* (1821)

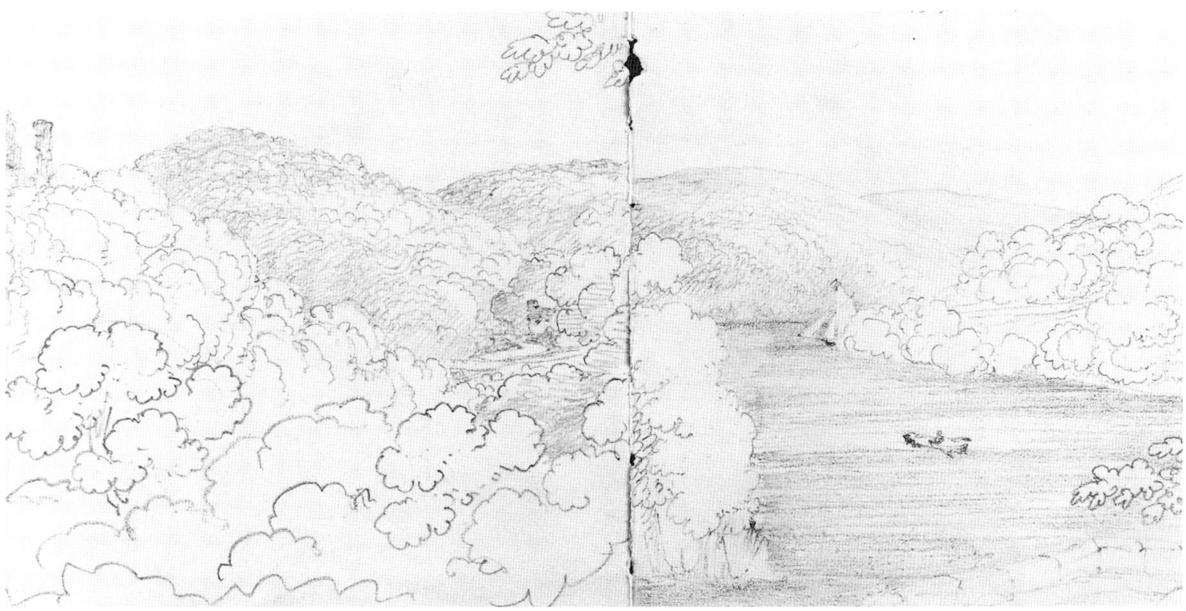

6. FRANCIS CHANTREY, *Clovelly from the Pier* (1821)

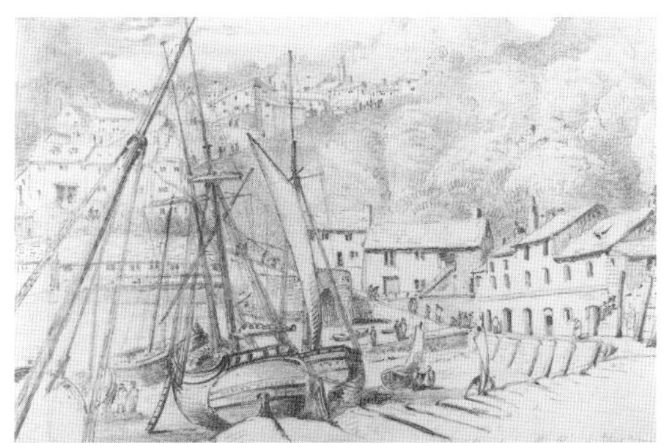

West Country in 1840) painted a companion picture
of a rocky coast scene at Polperro.[2]
Between 1841 and 1844 he exhibited scenes in north
Devon, at Clovelly and Lynmouth, and on the River
Lydd and on Dartmoor, as well as a few from
Cornwall.[3]
In 1843 his *Scene in North Devon* was considered 'the
most general favourite' in the exhibition of the New
Society of Watercolour Painters.[4] The following year
Thackeray was critical of Bright's too evident
dexterity - 'too much dash, skurry, and sharp
cleverness of execution.' Two more modest and unsold
pictures by another exhibitor, John Absalon, of
Dartmoor Turf Cutters and *The Devonshire Cottage
Door* were recommended for their lack of affectation.[5]
Like Harding (q.v.) and William Callow, Bright
developed a fluent and sophisticated style of drawing,
which could tend to be slick, which attracted many

amateur sketchers who were keen to learn from their
example. (MP)

FRANCIS CHANTREY (1781-1841)

5. *(? Berry Pomeroy Castle)* and *Near Dartmouth* (1821)
Two pages from a sketchbook, pencil on paper, each
17 x 12 cm
Inscribed 'Near Dartmouth. Sept. 20'
(upper right of right hand page)
Sheffield City Art Galleries

6. *Clovelly from the Pier* (1821)
Pencil on paper, 21 x 31.5 cm
Inscribed 'Clovelly from the Pier 29th Sepr 1821 11
A.M.' (lower right)
Sheffield City Art Galleries

Chantrey was the leading portrait sculptor in England
in the first half of the nineteenth century and was
much in demand.[1] Although he made large and
impressive portrait drawings for his sculptural busts it
was for his own pleasure that he regularly sketched on
his journeys out of London. Some of his scenic
sketches of the Peak District and Dovedale were
engraved in the 1820s and when they were re-issued
in the 1880s 'the old fashioned manner of Chantrey's
pencilling' was remarked upon.[2] The same can be said
about his Devon sketches made in September 1821.
From the collection of drawings now in Sheffield we
can plot Chantrey's excursion from Sidmouth on
September 7 to Clovelly on September 29. Between
these dates he was at Teignmouth, Dartmouth and
Plymouth, after which he went on to Looe and

7. WILLIAM COLLINS, *Salcombe, Devonshire* (?1819) [Here illustrated by E. Finden's engraving from *Picturesque Views on the Southern Coast of England* (1824)]

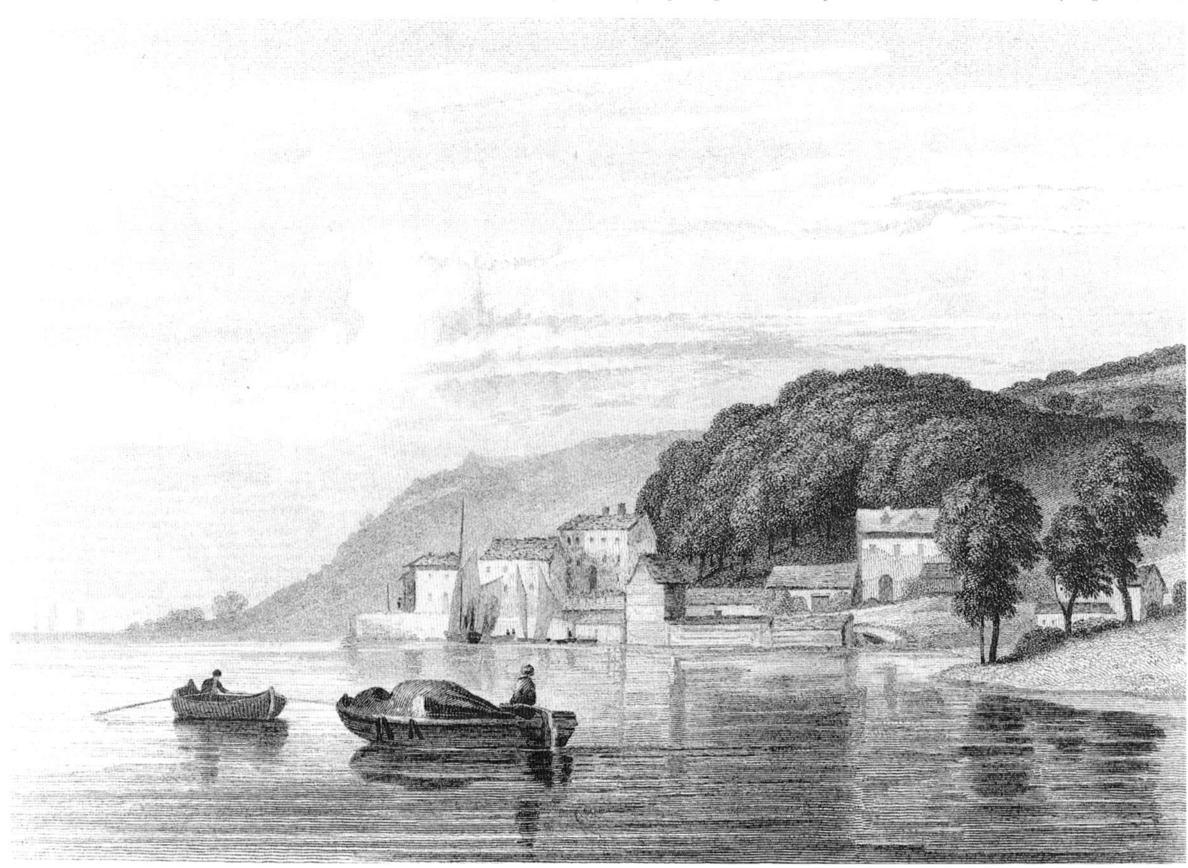

Falmouth and up to Bideford.

The diary of Henry Woolcombe mentions meeting 'the great sculptor' in Plymouth on September 13. According to a local newspaper Chantrey was on his way to Cornwall to investigate its geology, looking out for appropriate stone for sculpture. In Plymouth he visited Mount Edgcumbe, the Breakwater and Staddon Heights and was 'highly gratified with the matchless beauty of the neighbourhood.'[3] Chantrey returned to Devon at least once on sculptural commissions, in 1841 when supervising the installation of his memorial to James Northcote in Exeter Cathedral.[4] That he retained an interest in the region is shown by his subscribing to F.C. Lewis's Exe etchings of 1827. (MP)

WILLIAM COLLINS (1788-1847)

7. *Salcombe, Devonshire* (?1819)
Watercolour on paper, 10 x 13.7 cm
The Board of Trustees of the
Victoria and Albert Museum, London

8. *Hartland Quay from the Warren* (1821)
(Illustrated in colour on p.45)
Watercolour with graphite on grey paper, 20.7 x 31.0 cm

Inscribed 'Hartland Quay from the Warren Th 11 Octr. 1821 1 p.m.' lower left
Trustees of The British Museum

Collins made three sketching tours to Devon, in 1819, 1821 and 1845, and was highly impressed with what he found. Writing to his brother in 1829 he enthuses over the landscapes of south Devon and to David Wilkie in 1836 he remembers north Devon as having 'perhaps the finest scenery in England.'[1] He first visited Devon in August and September 1819, making a sketching tour to Dartmouth, Plymouth, the river Dart again, Torquay, Babbacombe, Teignmouth, Dawlish and Sidmouth. He found the vale scenery of Devon 'exceedingly beautiful'[2] and depicted it in a picture submitted to the Royal Academy in 1820, *A River Scene - Cottage Girl buying Fish*. A second subject from this tour, *Dartmouth, Devon* was exhibited at the Royal Academy in 1821.[3] It is likely that *Salcombe, Devonshire* (cat.no.7) also dates from this tour. It was engraved for Cooke's *Picturesque Views on the Southern Coast of England* in 1824.[4]

In 1821 he made an extensive autumn tour to Devon. He was in Plymouth in early September, for Henry Woollcombe records meeting him then, and returned to London about eight weeks later when Constable noted 'Collins... speaks in raptures of his tour.'[5] He seems to have divided his time between the Bastards' houses at Ashburton, Sharpham (on the Dart) and Kitley (on the Yealm), William Elford at Bickham and the Leaches of Spitchwick, Widecombe. Then, at the beginning of October he travelled into north Devon. From Bideford he wrote to his mother on October 7th. '..we heard the most afflicting account of the loss of upwards of *forty fishermen*, who have perished in the gale of Thursday evening last, (all inhabitants of Clovelly and its neighbourhood.) With feelings of the deepest melancholy shall I to-morrow set out, please God, for this spot, the scene of so much affliction...' On Monday October 8th, in Clovelly, he wrote again. '... the misery the accident has caused here can never be forgotten. I have this day seen some of the remains of the boats, torn to pieces in a way one would hardly have supposed possible. Going down the village, I saw a crowd assembled before a door; they were singing a psalm over the body of one of their comrades. Not above one half of the corpses have been found... Clovelly certainly presents the finest scenery I ever beheld; but as the days are now so short and cold, I must use dispatch, particularly as I have yet many other places to visit...'[6]

Hartland Quay from the Warren (cat.no.8) was painted three days later in one of the most isolated spots on the Devon coast, about six miles from Clovelly as the crow flies. There are signs of life here, chimney smoke directs our gaze to a small group of cottages huddled under the cliff, but the overall impression is one of bleak and savage grandeur. Only the silvery band of light on the horizon relieves this subdued, grey landscape, with jagged rocks pushing out into the surf and a rain squall lowering threateningly in the distance.[7] As Collins's letter to his mother indicates, even in the most harrowing of circumstances he could still appreciate the sublimity of the north Devon coast but, equally, that appreciation was now tempered by the knowledge that the sea could kill.

Collins's third trip to Devon in September and October 1845 was confined to the neighbourhood of Torquay, which he visited on his doctor's advice. His failing health did not respond but from his sketches he completed two final pictures, *Mede-foot Bay* and *Hall Sands* which were exhibited at the Royal Academy in 1846.[8] (SS)

DAVID COX (1783-1859)

9. *Lynmouth Pier* (1824)
(Illustrated in colour on p.45)
Watercolour on paper, 26.2 x 37.5 cm
Birmingham Museums and Art Gallery

David Cox was born in Birmingham and learned his craft in that town. He visited Devon in the late 1810s, certainly in 1819 and probably earlier as well. Evidence for the earlier tour comes from his account book which lists a drawing of *Berry Pomeroy* which he sold to Messrs S. & J. Fuller on February 18th, 1818, for £1-5-0.[1] A watercolour of *St Mary's Church, Teignmouth* (Laing Art Gallery) should presumably be ascribed to this tour, as should the subjects of three steel engravings of south Devon scenes: *Teignmouth, Torquay* and *The Tor, Devonshire.*[2]

Solly records that Cox 'made a journey by himself into north Devon' in 1819 but, frustratingly, gives no more information about this second tour.[3] Further material from the trip is scant; Cox exhibited *Comb Martin, North Devon* at the Society of Painters in Water Colours in 1821 and a watercolour of *The New Inn, Lynmouth* was once in Gillott's collection.[4] This exhibit is possibly the watercolour of *Lynmouth Pier* commissioned by the Parisian publisher and art dealer, Ostervald, in the summer of 1824 and worked up from an 1819 sketch.[5]

Cox had produced a number of drawing manuals by the time he worked on this painting and hints as to his intentions may be taken from them.
'The great merit of a picture depends on the most appropriate Effect given to each scene... A flat country on the marshy banks of a winding river should be seen beneath a grey-coloured sky. The transient effect adapted to such a landscape is provided by the fleeting lights of the sunbeams struggling between the interstices of the blowing clouds...'[6]

Cox is painting a grander scene than flat, marshy country but he adopts a similar procedure, following his own advice that 'it ought to be fully explained, that these observations must be understood as by no means intended to confine the exertions of the Student entirely to the particular subjects which have been chosen for illustration... Students will find subjects very different, equally adapted to this purpose.'[7] Rather than responding to the picturesque qualities of Lynmouth harbour and its romantic position at the base of the cliffs he is preoccupied with the effect of diffuse light in the rolling clouds and its reflection moving over the sea. The density and richness of effect is produced by a wonderfully complex surface, where a variety of small touches of colour are woven together over an armature of broadly washed tone. Closer inspection reveals that this fresh, wind-blown scene is studded with human incident: the couple to our left gaze at the goings on as idly as we, the group on the pier seem to have spotted something out to sea and a team of fishermen strain to beach a boat on the shore below us. (SS)

FRANCIS DANBY (1793-1861)

10. *Dead Calm - Sunset at the Bight of Exmouth* (1855)
(Illustrated in colour on p.46)
Oil on canvas, 77.4 x 107.0 cm
Signed and dated 'F. Danby 1855' (lower right)
Royal Albert Memorial Museum, Exeter

11. *Shore scene with Breakwater and Hulk
at Low Tide* (c.1855)
(Illustrated in colour on p.55)
Oil on white ground on card
8.5 x 14.4 cm
Bristol Museums and Art Gallery

12. *Sunset through Trees* (c.1855)
(Illustrated in colour on p.46)
Oil on card
12.6 x 17.8 cm
Bristol Museums and Art Gallery

Francis Danby, born near Wexford in Ireland in 1793, is perhaps best known today for his links with the art scene in Bristol where he settled in 1813. He moved to London in the mid 1820s and then spent a decade abroad from 1829-39 in France, Belgium, Germany and Switzerland. After a few years in London he moved to Exmouth in 1846 and lived there for fifteen years until his death in 1861.

It seems that he made several sketching trips to the Exe in the 1820s and he was an original subscriber to F.C.Lewis' *Scenery of the River Exe* published in 1827, the year that he may also have sketched at Lynmouth and on the Dart.[1] The Exe was to inspire some of his best pictures of his later years including *Dead Calm - Sunset at the Bight of Exmouth* (cat.no.10), exhibited at the Royal Academy in 1855. The setting is that of his first known Devon scene of c.1820, a panoramic watercolour *View of Star Cross from Exmouth.*[2]

If the colour of *Dead Calm* appears exaggerated it is only because such effects are seldom seen. But it is quite likely that Danby was only notching up his poetic fancy a few points, as witness the text accompanying the view of Exmouth in William Daniell's *Voyage Round Great Britain*, published in 1825:
'Among other circumstances it has been remarked, that the "sun seems to shine brighter and longer here than in most parts of England, especially towards evening, when the sky frequently assumes an Italian lustre."[3]

The text suggests that this was a 'far-fetched and fanciful' comparison but Danby makes it seem very real and Richard Ford, then living in Heavitree, Exeter, is another witness of precisely this phenomenon in April, 1845.

'Arrived at Exmouth I again wander on the lonely shore and watch the sunsets, which are transcendental, the heaven and the earth all crimson.'[4]

Since the death of Turner in 1851 Danby had been seen as the sole remaining original exponent of 'poetic' landscape, even if his two sons Thomas and James were, to some extent, continuing in his path:
'It is rarely that talent in Art is hereditary, - but we find a case in the two sons of Mr Danby. Now that England has lost her great chief in landscape painting, Turner, - Mr. Danby, the father, stands unquestionably at the head of the poetical landscape painters of his day. While following the same branch of art with the deceased master, the points of dissimilitude between the two are yet as great as can be conceived. Mr. Turner's art was more creative and more suggestive - rather arresting the imagination by the force of its ensemble than gratifying the reason in the analytic examination of its details. Mr Danby is less excursive in his range, and contents himself with more positive phenomena and special effects in nature, produced with greater care and elaboration.'[5]

This last remark certainly relates to *Dead Calm* which was bought by Thomas Miller of Preston, an art collector, 'one of a knot of gentlemen all residing near each other, many of whom have been enriched by manufacture and all distinguished by their manifest patronage of Art'. The picture was well described in the *Art Journal* in 1857 in an article on Miller's collection, housed in a special top-lit gallery:
'Twilight is here closing over an estuary in which, in the nearer section, is a ship at anchor. Both sky and water are enriched with the fading lines of what has been a glorious sunset. But the sentiment of the picture is perfect tranquility and so fully is this realised that the spectator is sensibly affected by the voiceless stillness of the scene.'[6]

In 1946 the picture was sold at Christie's by a descendant of the original owner. It had become dingy and lacklustre but it attracted the attention of Geoffrey Grigson, who laconically detailed his acquisition of it for next to nothing:
'A big solemn seascape, darkened, in need of cleaning, varnishing, re-stretching; and sadly in need of a reputation. Four bids. Fourteen guineas.'[7]

Grigson helped to put Danby back on the map. His own analysis of the picture's 'careful arrangement' is worth quoting:
'A train with a smoke trail (is seen) moving out to the left, smoke curling out to the right, and in between an intricacy of horizontals and verticals, masts and spars, the square tower of a church, doubled and made more intricate by their reflections in the water. And this formality enforces the wide, melancholy, meditative impact of the picture.'[8]

The centrally placed tower is not, in fact, a church but the tower of a pumping station on Brunel's atmospheric railway which is still there today, if in truncated form. By the time that Danby painted his picture the short-lived experiment to propel trains by atmospheric pressure had come to a less than glorious end.[9] There is a surprising amount of activity going on in Danby's tranquil scene: a boat being caulked; two boatloads of passengers being ferried between Starcross and Exmouth; a moving train on its way towards Dawlish; floating logs being moved by the side of the larger vessel; sails being furled on the more distant one; gulls skimming over the water, and a 'V' formation of over-flying birds on their passage out of the picture upper left. Sound and silence and melancholy transcience come together in this remarkable picture which is also an accurate reflection of what Danby would regularly have witnessed. This is confirmed in a local guidebook's account of Exmouth: 'Vessels frequenting this port usually lie at anchor just within the Warren (a long, low sand bank), and opposite Exmouth, in an expansive natural basin called the Bight, to wait for the tide, &c., ere they can proceed farther, and many of them discharge their cargoes there. The coal and coasting trades are at present the most considerable that are carried on, and occasionally vessels from the Baltic and America, with timber.'[10]

The increase of alluvial mud was already impeding navigation and a rail-road was suggested as a much more convenient way to conduct goods 'more cheaply and expeditiously' on 'the fine level track that spreads along the whole of the right bank of the stream below the city (of Exeter).' This is just what happened during Danby's years as a local resident.

More of Danby's pictures painted in his years at Exmouth have come to light recently including examples of his small oil studies from nature like the two exhibits here from Bristol City Art Gallery (cat.nos.11,12). As well as coastal and estuary scenes inspired by his surroundings Danby also painted quite different works like the now lost *Blackberry Pickers: a Lane in Devonshire*, exhibited at the Royal Academy in 1847 and described as small and miniature-like in execution. It depicted a scene between two rows of trees at sunset.[11]

Danby enjoyed not only painting but building and sailing his own boats, the names of two of which are known, the *Chase* and the *Dragon Fly*. He informed his good friend and patron John Gibbons that he 'lived like a bird in the fields, or on the sands all summer, for this pleasure is what I most care for in life, and I am content to fag all winter.'[12] He even talked about his paintings in boat-building terms: 'I have now more work ordered and cut out than I ever had, but I wish to put yours on the stocks first.'[13] His life, however, was not unencumbered with 'most unhappy events and deepest family affliction.' A letter from Exmouth on February 13, 1853 tells of the death of two of his sons within a period of five months. Coming so soon after the death of Gibbons, Danby reckoned he had lost nearly two years in his professional pursuits, but was now back at work painting again. He regretted losing the opportunity of sending works to Ghent, Antwerp and Dublin so living at the seaside had not reduced him to a provincial outlook.[14] Judging by a report in the *Western Luminary* for April 7, 1857, he was keen to spread an enthusiasm for art among the local populace, no fewer than six hundred of whom 'of all ranks' turned up at Suggs' Assembly Rooms at Exmouth to hear him talk to the Mutual Improvement Association on the 'Progress and Retardation of Art in England.' After dealing with the history of art 'the lecturer then dwelt on the arts of music, poetry, &c., which might in a great measure enlighten and instruct the mind as well as the art of painting.' He remarked on the 'great demand' for photography which nevertheless had 'no comparison to the beautiful art of landscape painting.'

'The lecturer, in conclusion, urged on everyone to possess himself while young of everything that may tend to cultivate the mind or enlarge the ideas on the subject of fine arts, so that not only Devonshire may send forth some of the first artists, but that Exmouth may stand high in society as regards art and inventive skill.'[15]

Danby's own qualities as a painter and the inspiration he drew from his surroundings were noted by the writer of a feature on Danby in the *Art Journal* in 1855: 'Time has not dimmed his eyes to the perception of the beautiful, nor palsied his hand to incapacitate him for the representation of nature in her most glorious aspects, which his residence, now and for some time past, in one of the most picturesque towns of Devonshire, and by the sea-side, affords him the most favourable opportunities of doing.'[16] (MP)

13. WILLIAM DANIELL, *Babbacombe* (1823)

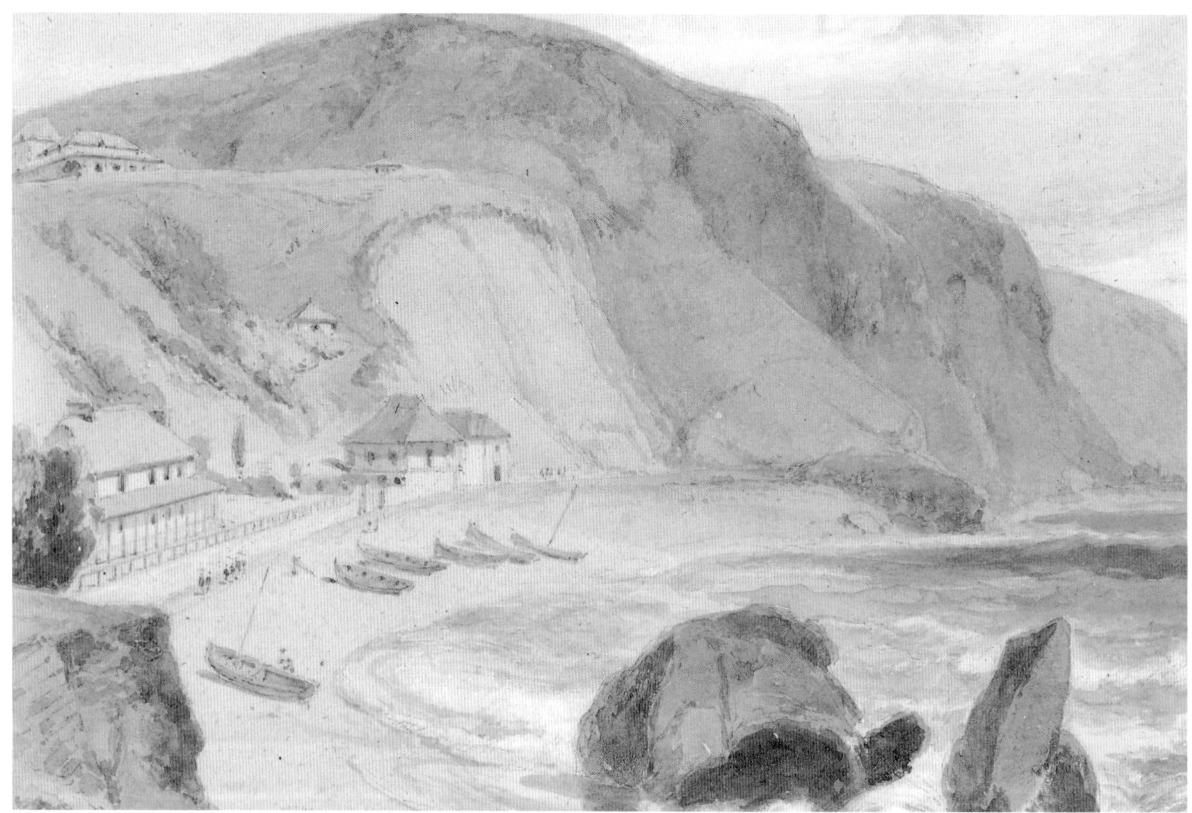

Fig.20. W. DANIELL *Babicome* (sic), *Devon*, aquatint, from *A Voyage round Great Britain*, vol. VIII, 1825.

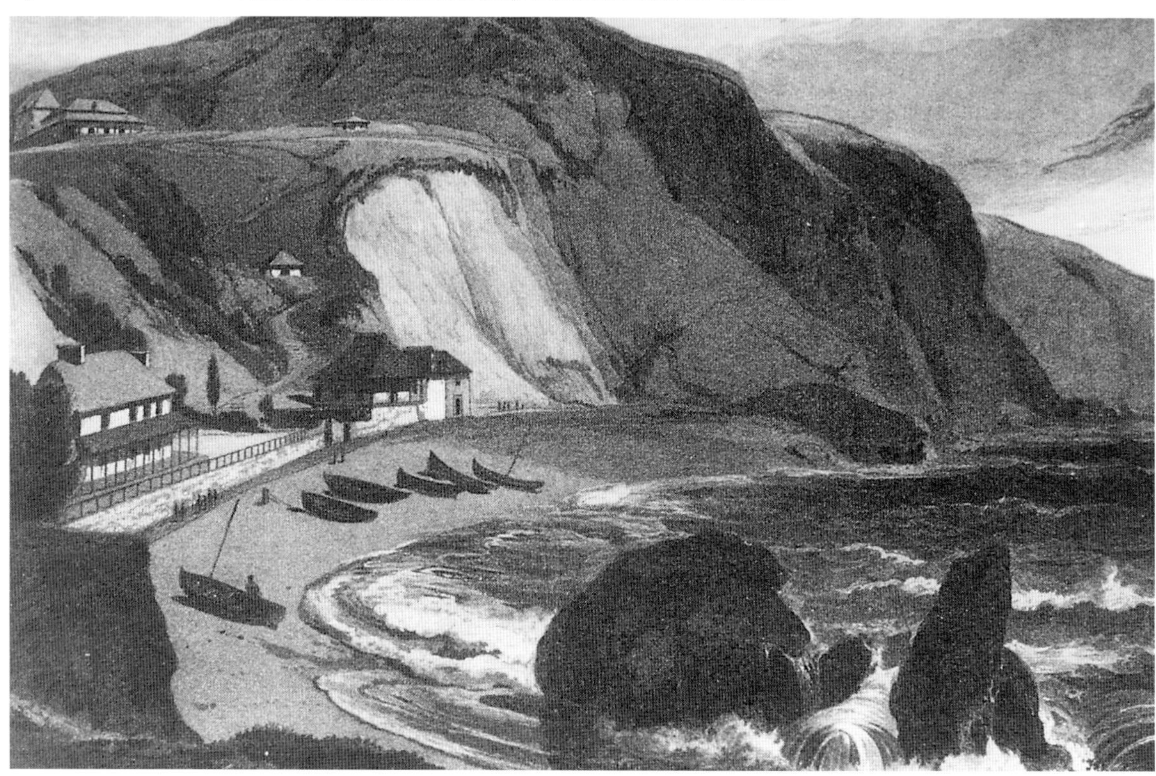

14. ANTHONY DEVIS, *Valley of Stones, Devon* (c.1779-80)

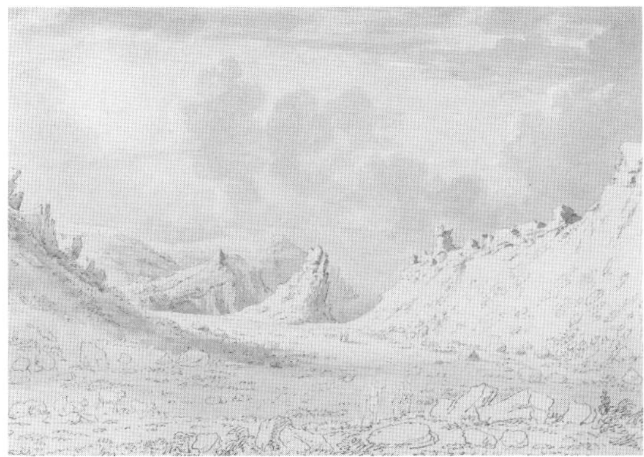

15. ANTHONY DEVIS, *Valley of Stones, Devon* (c.1779-80)

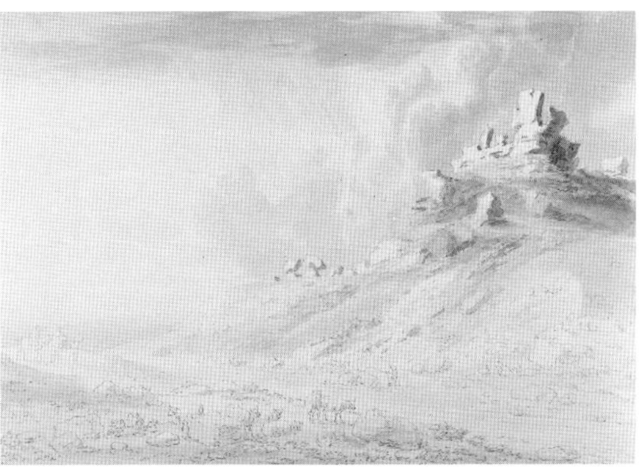

WILLIAM DANIELL (1769-1837)

13. *Babbacombe* (c.1823)
Sepia wash with white gouache on fawn-tinted paper,
16.1 x 23.5 cm
Royal Albert Memorial Museum, Exeter

Farington records that Daniell originally proposed
visiting Devon in the summer of 1812 to make studies
for his *Voyage Round Great Britain*.[1] The
circumnavigation began at Lands End in 1813 and
was eventually completed in 1823; the work was
eventually published between 1814 and 1825.[2]
Daniell's endeavour is a good example of the
increasingly ambitious topographical publications
produced in the early nineteenth century, with high
quality prints accompanying well researched texts. As
with much preparatory work for topography, initial
studies such as this seem almost too spirited and
somewhat crude in their notation, but the resultant
aquatints were highly refined images (fig.20). The
British Museum contains a drawing, *Harbour at
Hartland, Devon*, in the same style and technique
dated August 19 (1813). (SS)

ANTHONY DEVIS (1729-1816)

14. *Valley of Stones, Devon* (c.1779-80)
Pen and wash and watercolour on paper,
30.5 x 43.4 cm
Signed 'A.D.' (lower left)
Harris Museum and Art Gallery, Preston

15. *Valley of Stones, Devon* (c.1779-80)
Pen and wash and watercolour on paper,
30.3 x 43.2 cm
Signed 'A.D.' (lower left)
Harris Museum and Art Gallery, Preston

Anthony Devis was a topographical artist and the
younger half-brother of Arthur Devis, the portrait
painter. Born in Preston, he moved to London in 1742
and exhibited there between 1761 and 1781.[1] He
seems to have visited Devon in 1772 and again in
1779 or 1780. He exhibited a view of *Linton in
Devonshire* at the Royal Academy in 1781 so these two
drawings were presumably made on the later tour,
which probably also occasioned further watercolours
of Tapley (near Bideford),[2] Barnstaple,[3] Appledore,[4]
and an oil painting of Ilfracombe.[5]
Devis' drawings of the Valley of the Rocks at
Lynmouth are especially interesting insofar as they
pre-date the valley's 'discovery' by W.G. Maton in his
*Observations relative to… the Western Counties of
England* (1797), which book helped to draw tourists'
attention to the spectacular beauties of the north
Devon coast.
'Every step was on romantic ground. New features,
new embellishments, new combinations continually
rose into view.- Our rapture rendered us insensible to
fatigue, though we had long been obliged to follow on
foot a devious, indistinct tract that now sunk with
terrific steepness, now ascended with an almost
insurmountable perpendicularity... Vast fragments
overspread the valley, and, which way so ever we
turned our eyes, awful vestiges of convulsion and
desolation presented themselves, inspiring the most
sublime ideas.'[6]
Although Devis shows a few tourists enjoying this
spectacle of nature, in the late 1790s only a few
visitors made excursions to this most inaccessible spot,
among them Wordsworth, Coleridge and Southey.
It is not until 1804 that Lynton and Lynmouth begin
to generate widespread artistic interest, a taste
exemplified by T.H.Williams' eight etchings of the
location published in his *Picturesque Excursions in
Devonshire and Cornwall*. (SS)

17. PETER DE WINT, *On the Dart* (c.1848-9)

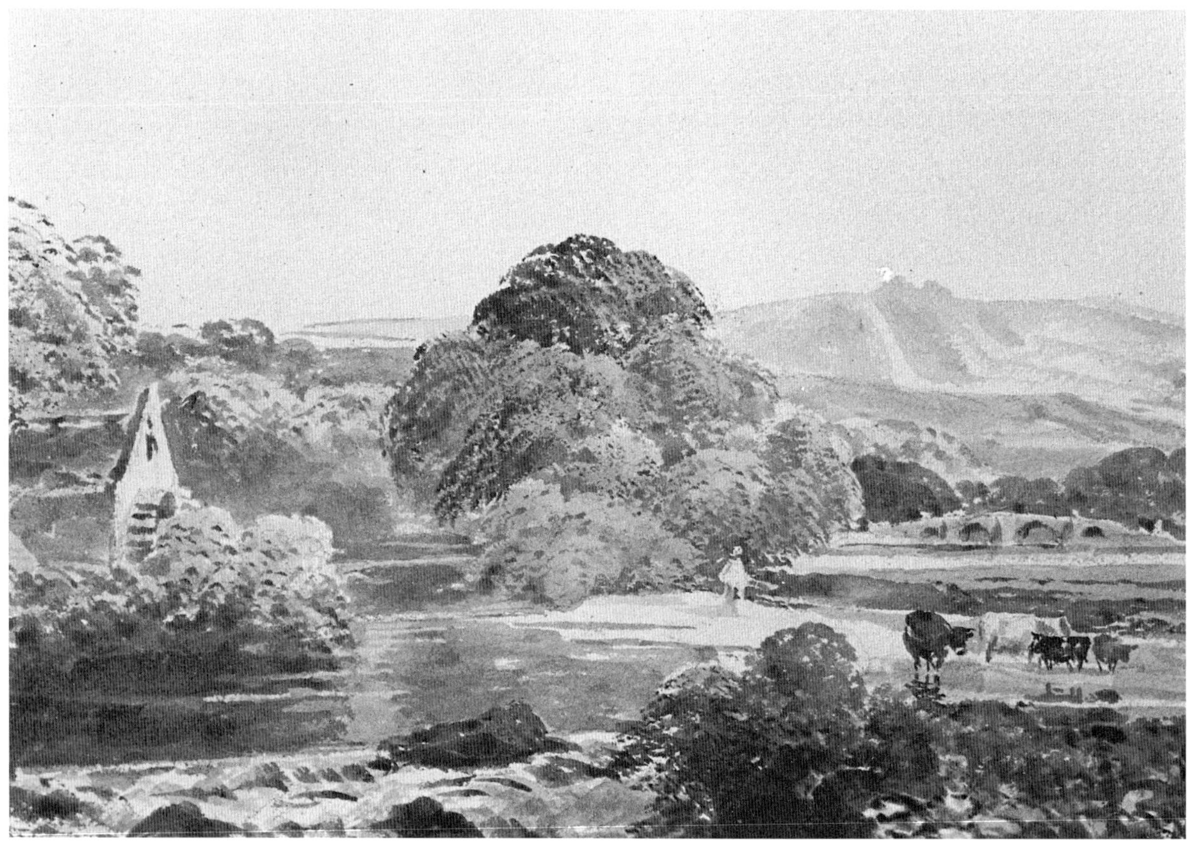

PETER DE WINT (1784-1849)

16. *View of Exeter* (1848-9)
(Illustrated in colour on p.55)
Watercolour on paper 31.2 x 98.1 cm
Prudential Corporation plc

During September 1848 De Wint visited Devon and sketched in Exeter and on the Dart. He was suffering from poor health having never fully recovered from a severe attack of bronchitis in 1845. The Devon climate did not prove very beneficial but it was nevertheless a productive visit and from his studies he painted two large compositions which he exhibited in 1849. One of these, *Exeter* (cat.no.16), is in this exhibition along with a preparatory sketch (cat.no.17) for his second Devon subject, which was entitled *View on the River Dart, Devonshire*. They were among the last important works he painted as he died in June 1849 aged 66. His widow Harriet's *Memoir* of her late husband is a useful source of information on his Devon trip, 'the last excursion he made':
'He had been some years previously into Somersetshire, and as far as Lynton in North Devon, with which he was much pleased (this was in 1841)...
He was ill the whole of the year 1848, and it was

hoped the country would be beneficial. The mild humid air of South Devon, however, did not suit him, although the few days he spent at Exeter he was better and was able to sketch a good deal, as he very much admired the city and its fine venerable cathedral.'[1]
From his on-the-spot sketches De Wint produced his large panoramic composition of the city seen from the river, dominated by the cathedral and Colleton Crescent. The foreground is enlivened by a few boats, figures and cattle which well demonstrate the artist's versatility in introducing picturesque elements without destroying an overall sense of spaciousness. Exeter compares favourably with De Wint's better known panoramas of the river and cathedral of Lincoln. The critic of the *Athenaeum* thought his works in 1849 were 'as remarkable for breadth and mastery of handling as any we have hitherto seen by him' and considered his style was seen at its best in 'the view of Lincoln from below the Lock (139) - or in Exeter (276). As we have before observed, the painter's style resembles that of Richard Wilson; and it has never been more fittingly employed than on this pair of cathedral cities.'[2]
De Wint's *Exeter* makes a good comparison with Turner's watercolour (cat.no.80) in which Colleton

11. FRANCIS DANBY, *Shore scene with Breakwater and Hulk at Low Tide* (c.1855)

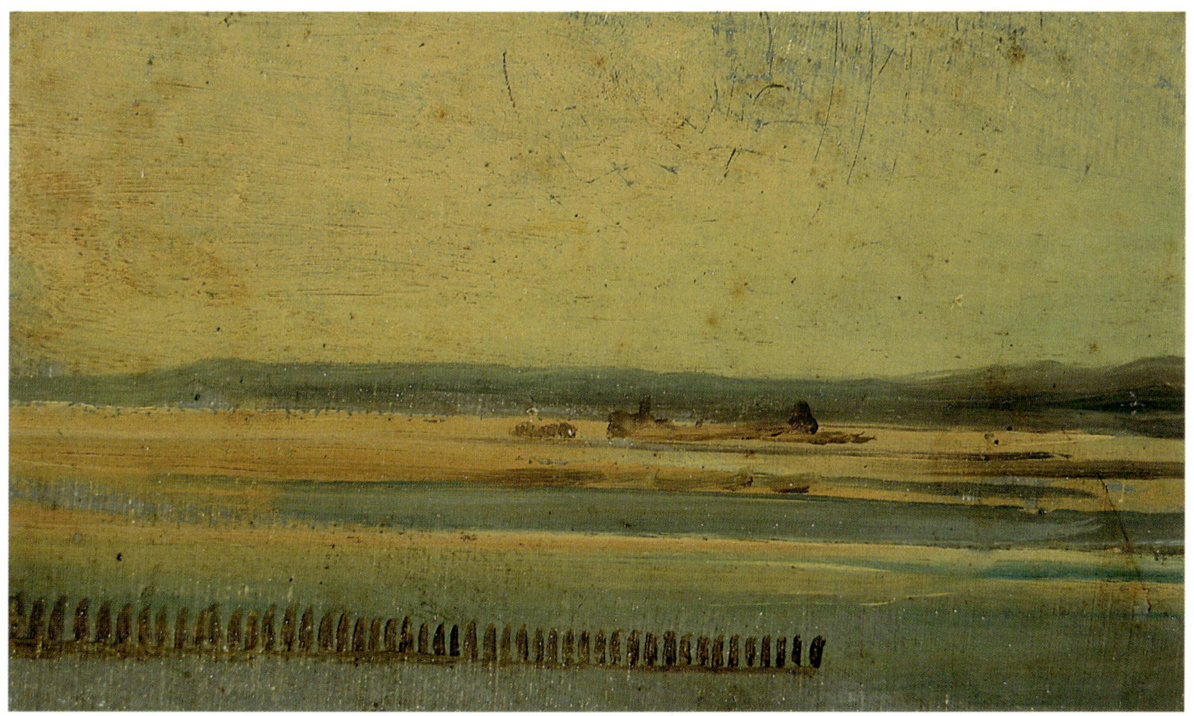

16. PETER DE WINT, *View of Exeter* (1848-9)

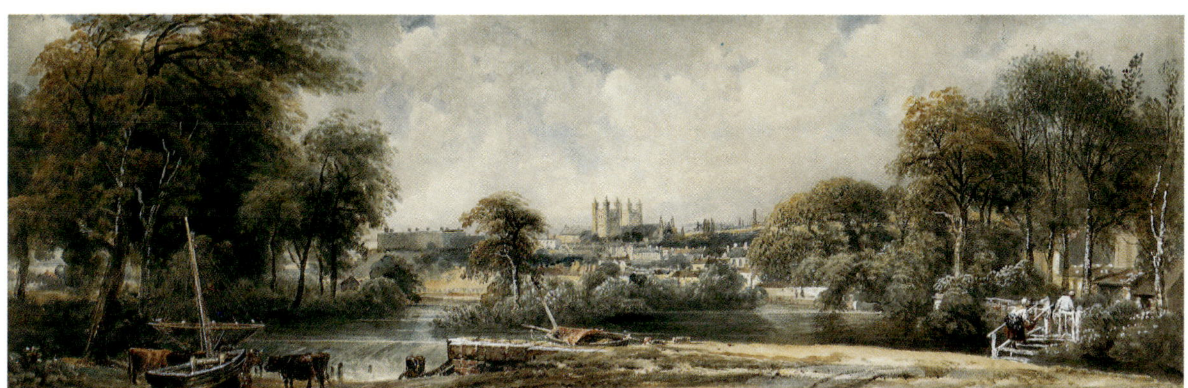

Crescent is much more dominant. It is worth considering the problems artists encountered in composing such scenes in which topographical accuracy needed to be combined with the demands of picture making.

17. *On the Dart* (c.1848-9)
Blue grey wash with traces of sepia on paper,
19.0 x 30.3 cm
Lincolnshire County Council: Usher Gallery, Lincoln

This is a study in two tones of wash for one of De Wint's last major works, *View on the River Dart, Devonshire*, exhibited at the watercolour Society in 1849, along with *Exeter*. His initial watercolour study from nature is inscribed 'Holme Chase on the River Dart, Devonshire. 9th Sept. 1848.' The artist's Devon itinerary and the state of his failing health are described in Harriet De Wint's *Memoir*:
'From Exeter he went to Totnes, where he was taken worse, having fatigued himself by walking all day to explore this new scenery, which always excited him. On the following day he went to visit Mr Champernowne at Dartington, where he remained nearly a fortnight, and from whence he visited the River Dart, where he made his last finished sketch. He was very, very ill, almost unable to move, but the beauty of the scene seemed to inspire him, although when he reached the house he was completely exhausted and found he must not attempt to sketch again. Dartington House is one of those lovely romantic places which once seen can never be forgotten. There De Wint would have found abundant scope for his pencil had it pleased God to have restored his health, but this was not to be, and he was compelled to return to London to obtain medical advice. To Mr Champernowne's kindness he ever referred with great thankfulness, and his bereaved wife feels she owes that gentleman a debt of gratitude which she can never repay.'[3]
The study from nature and the exhibited picture are in the Fitzwilliam Museum, Cambridge, together with yet another study for it. We therefore possess very full documentation about De Wint's methods of developing a sketch into a fully elaborated composition.[4] The wash study from Lincoln exhibited here is the smallest of the studies and in it De Wint is both adding features to his first study from nature and balancing the light and shade. The water mill on the left, the bridge on the right, as well as the cattle and the diminutive figure have all been added to the study from nature. These were further re-arranged in the final composition in which the foreground was carefully elaborated and a greater sense of depth achieved. It is quite possible that De Wint knew F.C. Lewis' *Rivers of Devon*, the text of which comes close

to putting into words what De Wint does here in his transforming of nature. Lewis had sought to bring 'to bear upon his transcripts from nature the principles of Art.' Art, wrote Lewis, 'appeals to our higher faculties - to the mind, the imagination through the eye, but not to the eye alone. A picture ought to delight us more than actual scenery for it is the human mind, in addition to external scenery.'[5] (MP)

REVEREND JOHN EAGLES (1783-1855)

18. *A View of the River above Lynmouth* (1832)
(Illustrated in colour on p.58)
Watercolour and bodycolour on paper, 36.0 x 53.2 cm
signed 'John Eagles' and inscribed 'Lymouth 5 July 183(2)' (lower left)
Bristol Museums and Art Gallery

Eagles was a friend of Müller's (q.v.) and is associated with the Bristol School of artists, with whom he sketched from nature in and around Bristol and from imagination in their evening gatherings. He had a highly poetical view of nature and wrote against the early nineteenth-century tendency towards naturalism in landscape painting.
This exhibit is one of a group of watercolours of Lynmouth produced in June and July 1832.[1] Eagles visited Lynmouth on frequent occasions and evoked its beauties in a series of lengthy and enthusiastic descriptions of sketching tours there. These were first published in *Blackwood's Magazine* in the early 1830s and then collected together as *The Sketcher* in 1856. He considered the river Lynn to be 'as exquisitely beautiful a mountain river as I had ever seen'[2] and of his numerous effusions on it one will have to suffice:
'... The true admirer, who looks into Nature's retirements for the poetry she lavishly throws around her, will descend from the path, which he can do without much difficulty, to the water's edge; and among the larger stones he will find full employment for his pencil, and the whole power of his colours, whichever way he may look. The deep brown pools of refuge, and the water with all its variety of silvery green, grey, and brown, circling, loitering, hastening - and the falls from above (edged with sunshine, and thereby showing their depth of colour) seen amid boughs and fragments of moss-brown rocks, will delight him many an hour in a spot so sheltered, as if Silence had lingered there, and ever after charmed the turbulence of the water into gentle music.'[3]
Eagles was in two minds about the development of Linton and Lynmouth as their fame grew. He disliked the introduction of new villas and hotels, yet acknowledged their need and was even prepared to sanction the removal of obstacles which hindered tourists from exploring the scenery in reasonable comfort and safety.[4] (SS)

19. HENRY EDRIDGE, *Berry Pomeroy Castle* (1818)

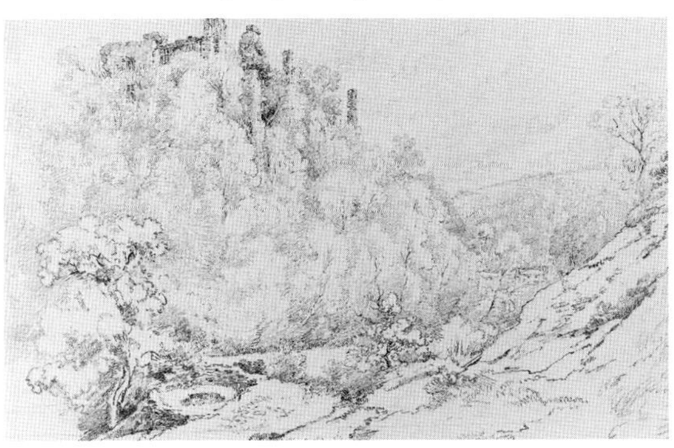

20. JOSEPH FARINGTON, *Houses near Exeter Quay* (1809)

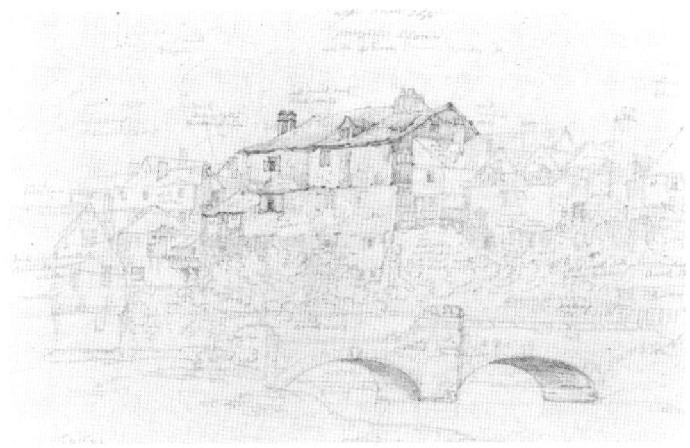

HENRY EDRIDGE (1769-1821)

19. *Berry Pomeroy Castle* (1818)
Pencil on paper, 31.4 x 44.8 cm
Inscribed 'Berry Pomeroy Castle Sep. 19 1818'
(lower left)
Royal Albert Memorial Museum, Exeter

Edridge may have first toured Devon in 1817, for there
are drawings of Sidmouth and Dawlish in a
sketchbook of that date in the British Museum. His
1818 trip seems to have been prompted by medical
concerns, as recorded by Joseph Farington that spring.
'Edridge called in the eveng., and informed me that
tomorrow He shd. take His son to Devonshire to try
what the air wd. do for Him. He spoke of it being very
uncertain whether He will recover or not. - I described
to Him several situations in Devon and Cornwall.'[1]
In the event the trip seems to have been postponed to
the autumn (we have no information on what
happened to Edridge's son). If Farington's advice on
'situations' was aesthetic rather than medical he
would surely have recommended Berry Pomeroy as his
own drawing of it was first engraved c.1818 before its
eventual publication in the Lysons's *Magna Britannia*.[2]
Although rather fussy, Edridge's drawing style owes a
marked debt to Girtin whom he had worked alongside
on at least one occasion, for the British Museum
contains a drawing by Edridge of the younger artist at
work. Other drawings from this tour in public
collections include a view at Dawlish in the
Whitworth Art Gallery, Manchester, a sketch of the
Exe estuary dated August 13, 1818, in the collection
of the British Museum, and a sketch of Salcombe
dated September 2, 1818 in Nottingham Castle
Museum.[3] (SS)

JOSEPH FARINGTON (1747-1821)

20. *Houses near Exeter Quay* (1809)
Pencil on paper, 21 x 33.7 cm
Numerous inscriptions and dated 'September 22, 1809'
Royal Albert Memorial Museum, Exeter

21. Page from Sketchbook (1810)
Pencil and watercolour on paper, 20 x 13 cm
Numerous inscriptions and dated 'Oct. 24 1810
afternoon 4 o'clock' (top left)
The Board of Trustees of the
Victoria and Albert Museum, London

Farington's two extended visits to the West Country
in 1809 and 1810 were recorded in detail by the artist
himself.[1] He visited north and south Devon to draw
scenes for Lysons's *Magna Britannia*.[2] Much of his time
was spent in Exeter, sketching and socialising. He
much admired the city's rich array of old buildings,
bridges and quaint thoroughfares. They reminded him
of the pictures of Canaletto whom he refers to twice
on the exhibited drawing, made on the morning of
September 22, 1809. (cat.no.20). On September 21
he had reconnoitred for possible subjects and viewed
the city from three vantage points:
'Proceeding through the narrow streets and passages (I)
saw a succession of groupes of old Houses, with small
bridges, and water, the most picturesque combination
of this kind that I recollected to have seen.'[3]
On his second visit in 1810 he made a further study in
his small sketchbook which contains many other
studies in pencil, pen and ink and watercolour.
Farington duly noted the light effects at four o'clock
in the afternoon of October 24, 1810 and followed his
observations when he coloured his sketch: 'sun on the
windows glittering in points like bright naples yellow
touches' (cat.no.21).
For many weeks, weather permitting, he drew the
city's ancient structures, sometimes from inside
convenient premises which afforded him good views
and greater comfort. He found 'excellent matter for
study both for form and colour.'[4] (fig.21) His
dedication to detail and accuracy is clear in some of
his comments:
'I passed the day till 5 o'Clock in studying the
Colouring &c of the picturesque subjects I sketched
the last year among the Old buildings of the City & in
making notes for the completion of them.'[5]

18. REVEREND JOHN EAGLES, *A View of the River above Lynmouth* (1832)

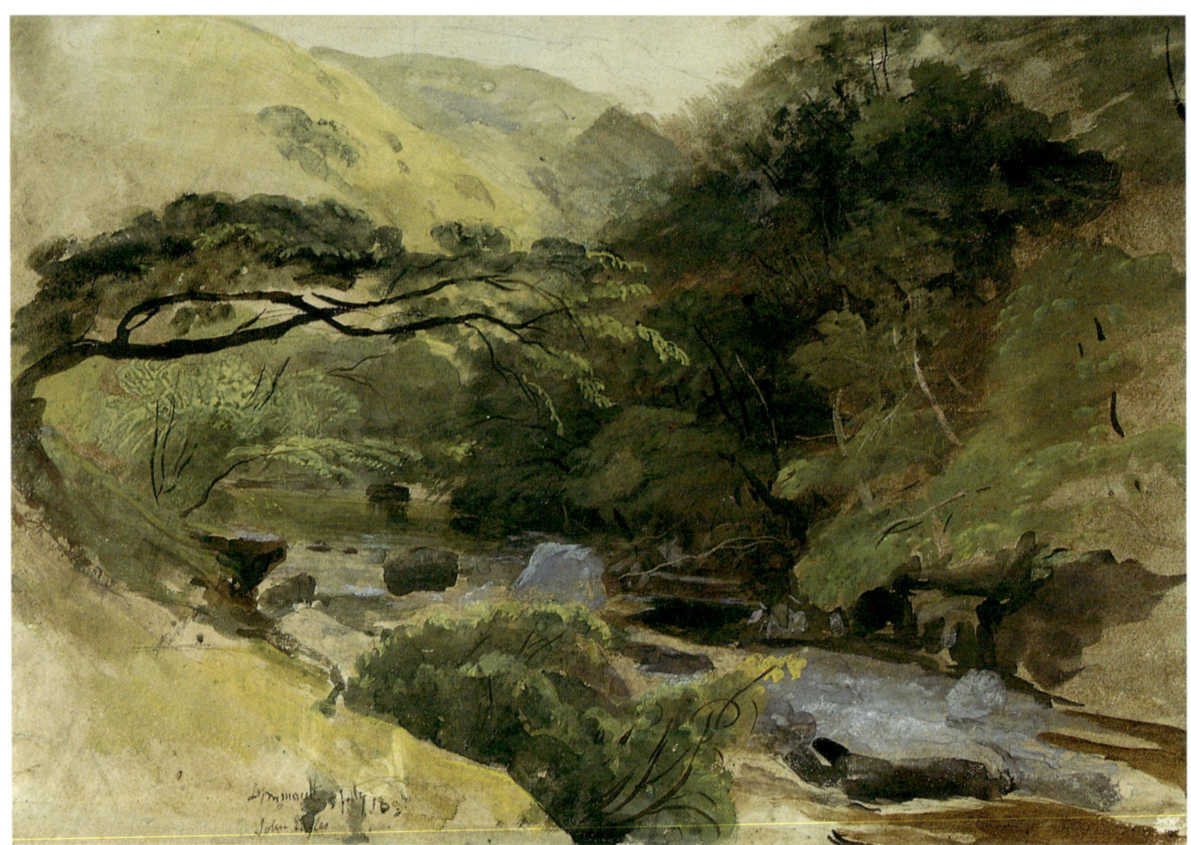

22. MYLES BIRKET FOSTER, *A Dell in Devonshire*

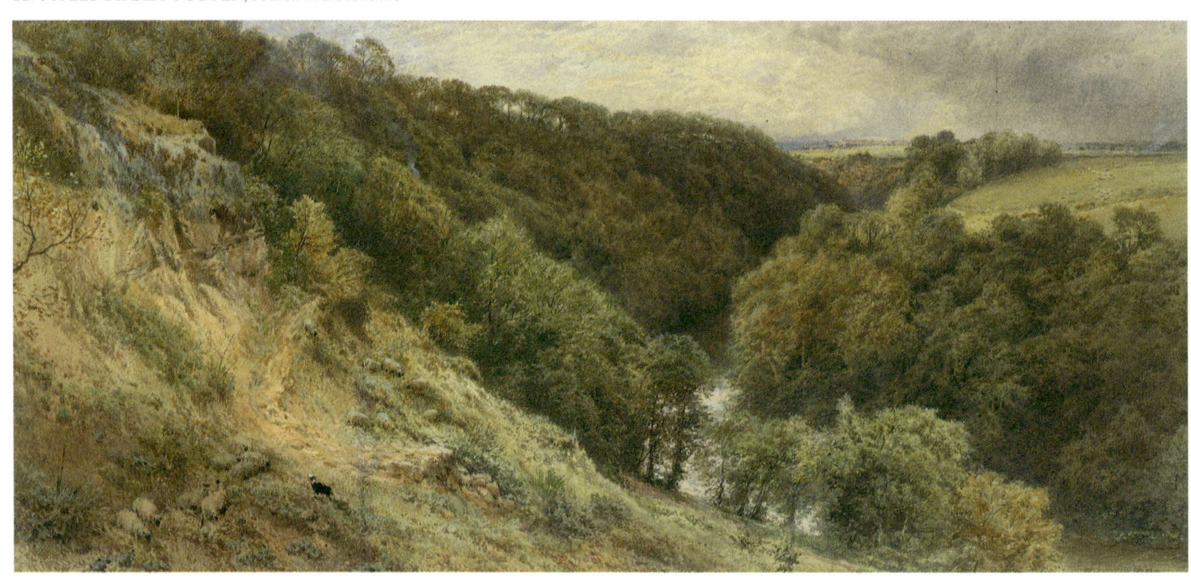

23. HENRY GASTINEAU , *Near the Waters Meet, Lynton* (c.1850s)

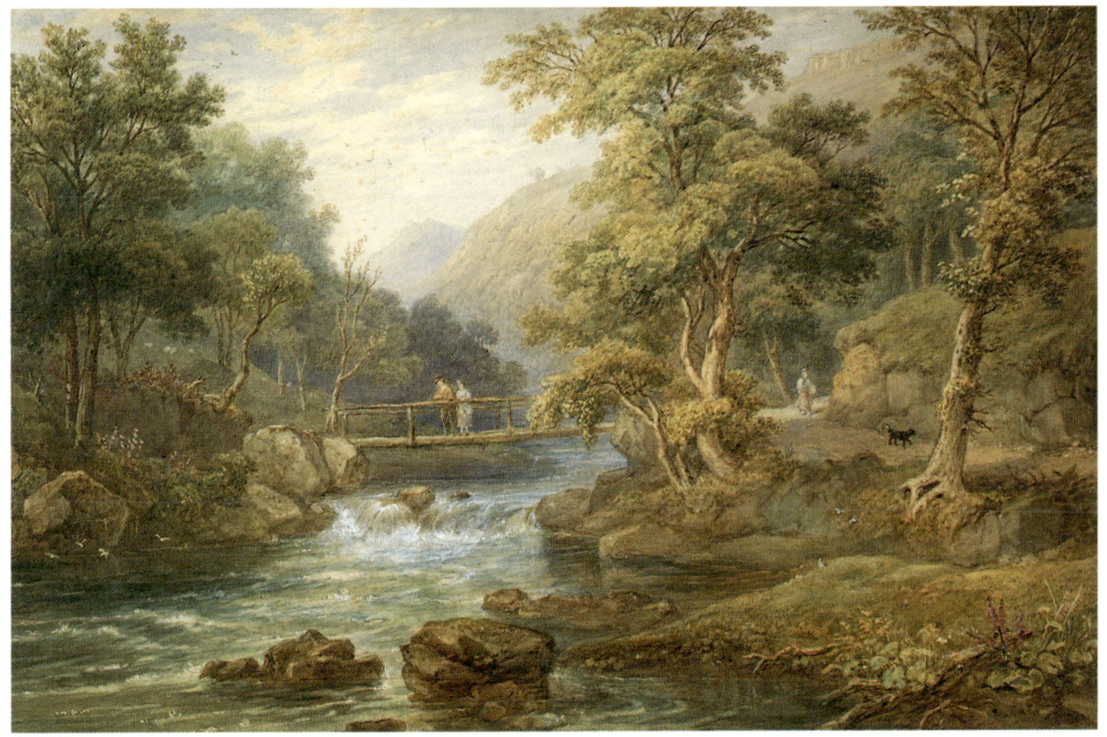

25. THOMAS GIRTIN, *Exeter from Trew's Weir* (c. 1799)

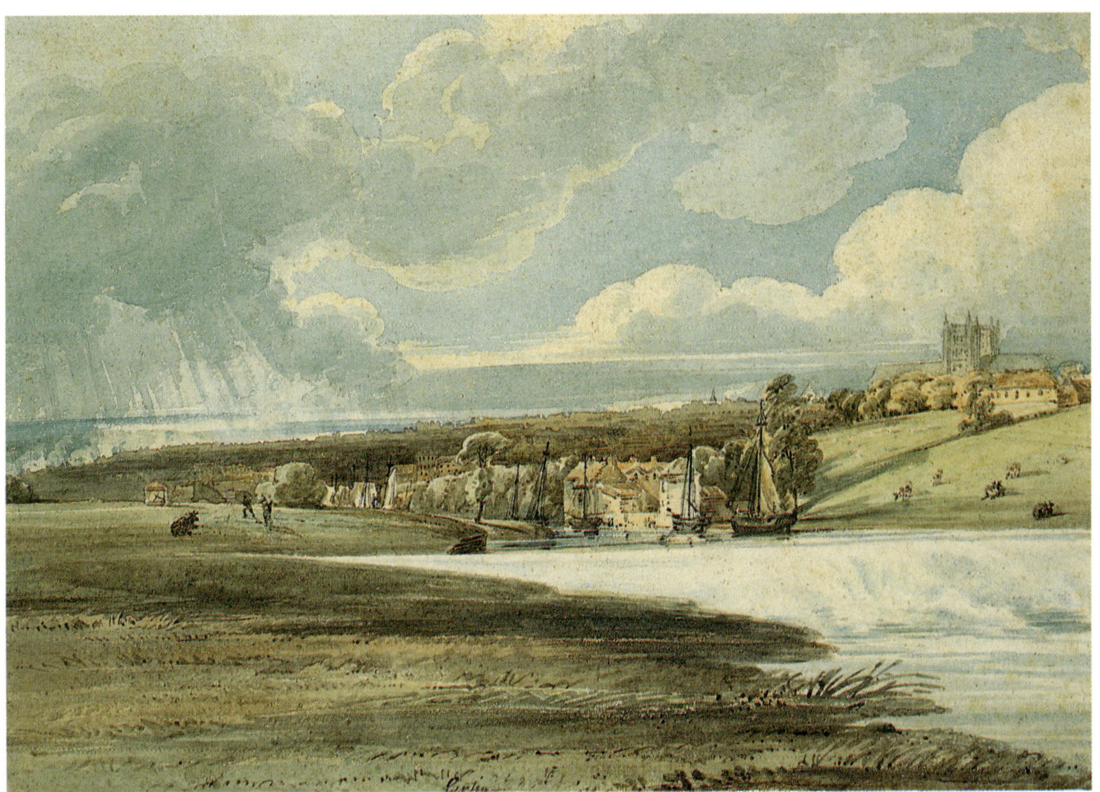

21. JOSEPH FARINGTON, Page from Sketchbook (1810)

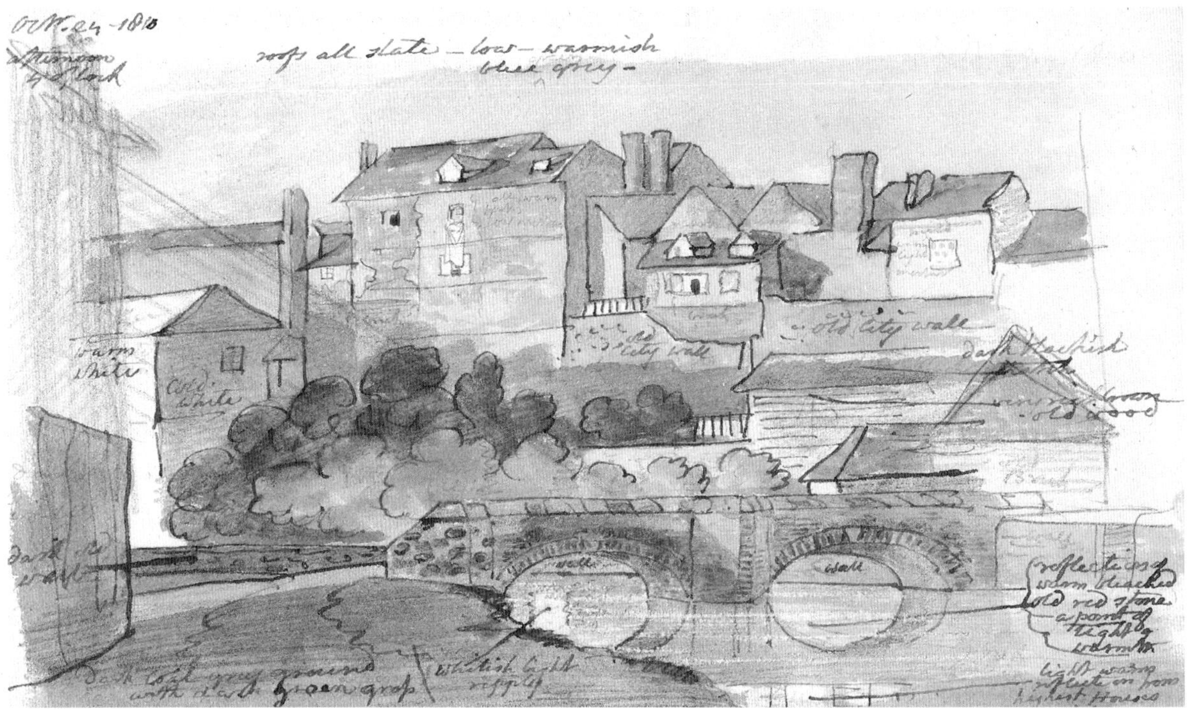

Fig.21. JOSEPH FARINGTON Page from Sketchbook (1810), The Board of Trustees of the Victoria and Albert Museum, London

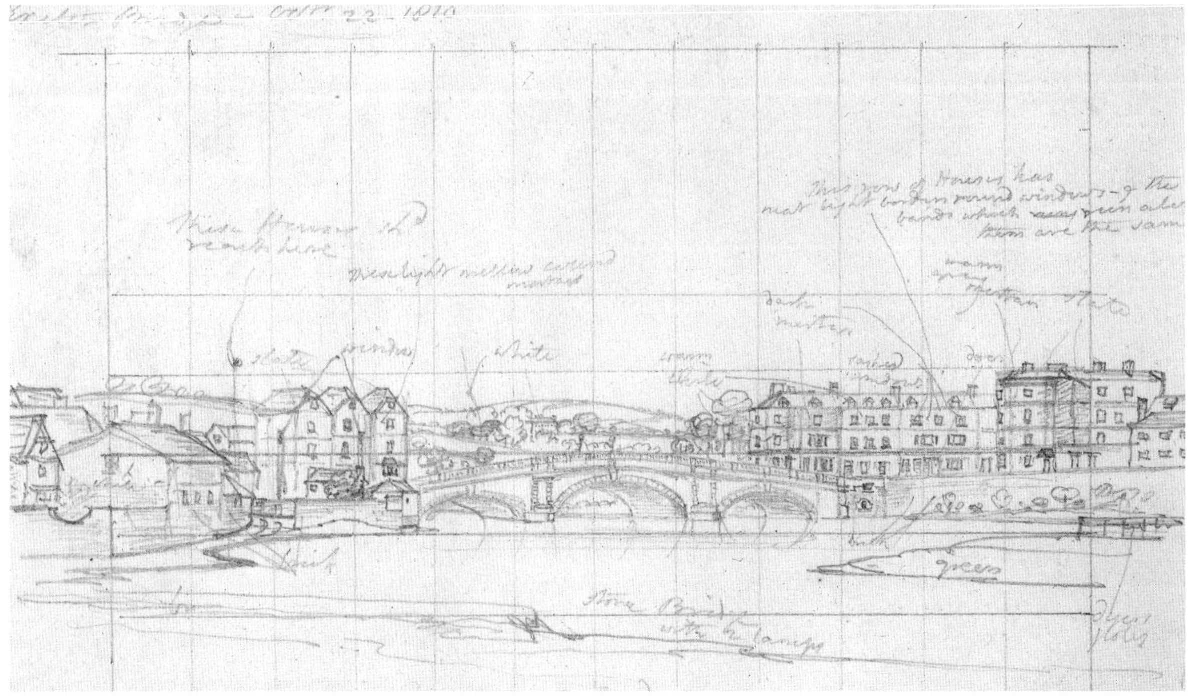

Farington's 1810 West Country tour (including Cornwall) kept him away from London for three and a half months during which he celebrated his sixty-fourth birthday in Exeter on December 3. He felt sure that a 'good drawing master' was much wanted. 'Such a one would find much employment in the town and in the neighbourhood.'[6] (MP)

MYLES BIRKET FOSTER (1825-1899)

22. *A Dell in Devonshire*
(Illustrated in colour on p.58)
Watercolour on paper, 24.2 x 50.8 cm
Signed 'BF' (bottom left)
The Board of Trustees of the
Victoria and Albert Museum, London

This watercolour, with its general title, seems
nevertheless to be very specific in its depiction of an
actual site. Foster's extraordinarily refined handling of
watercolour gained him many admirers. The
wonderful range of greens and blues are offset by well-
placed touches of subdued purple and yellow, and
pinky greys and lilac. His friend Tom Taylor expressed
a generally felt view when he wrote: 'It is one of the
mysteries of Mr. Foster's art how he manages to
conciliate such finish with such breadth of effect.' He
had 'carried suavity and grace to the very highest
point to which they can be carried without falling
into effeminacy, as he has pushed delicacy of
execution to a pitch beyond which it seems impossible
to go without pettiness and loss of unity.'[1]
At the other end of the scale to this watercolour is a
tiny view of Exeter cathedral seen from the river.[2]
Foster also made a series of Devon coastal resorts
which were engraved in the *Illustrated London News*
under the heading 'Watering Places of Devon.' They
included views of Exmouth from Starcross, Budleigh
Salterton, Sidmouth, Teignmouth and Torquay.[3] (MP)

HENRY GASTINEAU (1791-1876)

23. *Near the Waters Meet, Lynton* (c.1850s)
(Illustrated in colour on p.59)
Watercolour on paper, 62 x 93 cm.
Birmingham Museums and Art Gallery

Gastineau had a wide practice as a drawing master,
exhibited from 1815 to 1875 and showed over 1,300
works at the Old Water Colour Society alone, yet he
tends to be overlooked in histories of watercolour
painting and has been perhaps unjustly neglected. He
travelled widely and produced a number of studies of
coastal scenery in Devon and Cornwall, many of
which were exhibited in the 1860s.[1] He may have
visited Lynton and Lynmouth in the late 1850s as
The Road from Lynton to Lynmouth was shown at the
Old Water Colour Society in 1860.[2] This picture is
especially interesting insofar as it shows the extent to
which Lynton and Lynmouth had been 'tamed' in the
interests of tourists, with smooth paths on moderate
gradients allowing easy access to celebrated beauty

spots like this one. Although Eagles (q.v.) had
recommended judicious alterations it is unlikely that
he meant anything quite so obvious. (Henry James
was amused by a similar over-management at
Ilfracombe).[3] Yet despite this rather manicured
experience, Gastineau manages to give the scene a
poetic quality, even if Eagles' romantic idyll had
disappeared. The watercolour vies with oil painting in
the boldness of its handling and its large size, and its
rather overblown picturesque sensibility is comparable
to the image of Devon in mid-century oils by Thomas
Creswick and Frederick Richard Lee. (SS)

THOMAS GIRTIN (1775-1802)

Girtin's first tour to Devon probably took place in
1797, when he travelled from Weymouth in Dorset to
Plymouth, sketching castles and coastal views. Four
watercolours derived from this tour were exhibited at
the Royal Academy in 1798, including *Inside of Exeter
Cathedral* and *Berry Pomeroy Castle*.[1] Other known
Devon subjects from this visit include *An Overshot
Mill in Devon*,[2] *Exeter*,[3] *Star Cross, Totnes*,[4] *Kingswear*,[5]
Teignmouth and *Okehampton Castle*.[6] This list of
subjects indicates that Girtin kept to a fairly
conventional route, sketching on the rivers and
estuaries and making some studies of the major towns
and antiquities.
One of Girtin's patrons was the antiquary James
Moore who had privately published *A List of the
Abbies, Priories and other Religious Houses, Castles, etc.
In England and Wales* in 1786 and was working on a
revised public edition at the time of Girtin's tour.
Girtin had already made drawings of *Exeter Cathedral*
and *Okehampton Castle* after Moore's 1791 sketches
and it is possible that Moore gave Girtin advice on
what to visit in 1797.[7] He purchased Girtin's *Exeter
Cathedral* from the Royal Academy exhibition in
1798, so we know they were still in communication
then. Yet Moore's antiquarian interests were
insufficient for Girtin's imagination and it is his
developing understanding of landscape which marks
the trip.
Girtin had at least three West Country patrons, the
Bluett family of Holcombe Court, near Cullompton,
the Bastard family of Kitley, near Plymouth, who also
owned Sharpham House on the Dart, and the artist
Edward Calvert's father in Appledore (after whom
Girtin's son was christened Thomas Calvert in 1801).[8]
It is worth speculating that Girtin met local artists in
Devon as well, for the name of a Plymouth artist,
Ambrose Johns, appears on the mount of one version
of *The White House, Chelsea*.[9]

24. THOMAS GIRTIN, *Appledore, North Devon* (1798)

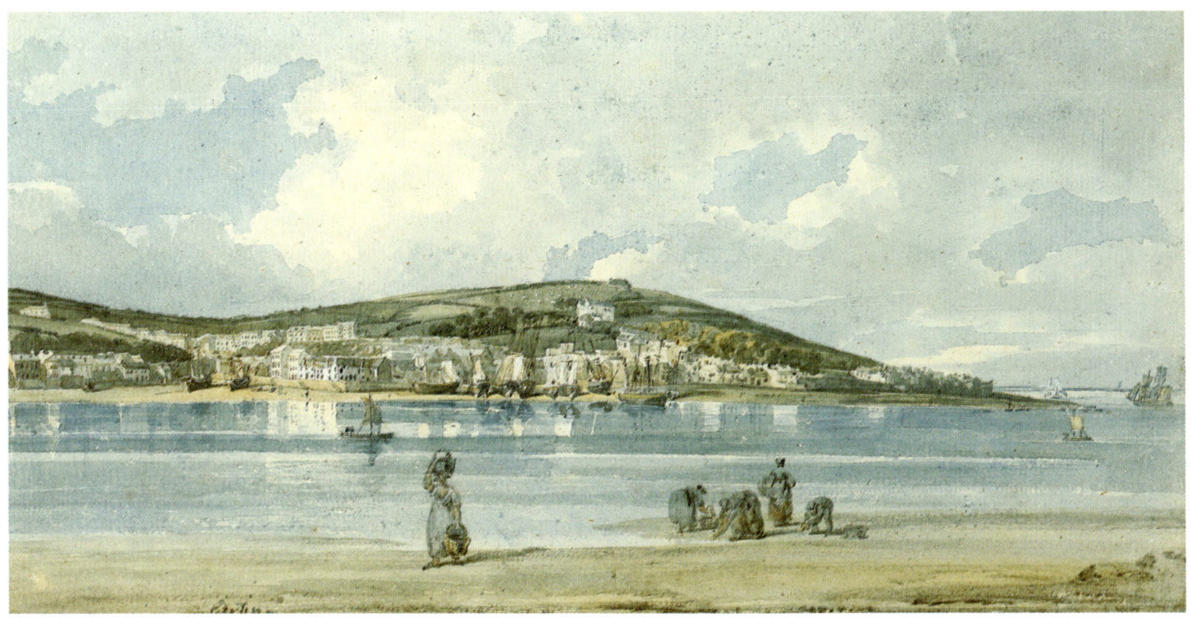

24. *Appledore, North Devon* (1798)
Watercolour on paper, 24.5 x 47.2 cm
Signed 'Girtin' (bottom centre)
Courtauld Institute Galleries, London (Witt Bequest)

The most accomplished of all the 1797 subjects is
surely this picture which has been seen as anticipating
Girtin's famous *The White House, Chelsea* (1800)
(Tate Gallery) in its rendering of atmosphere and
controlled use of colour.[10] Girtin's development of
watercolour as a medium is readily apparent here,
moving away from the eighteenth century's
characteristic tinted drawing style, as seen in
Wheatley's *Ilfracombe* (cat.no.85), and allowing tone
and colour to structure the composition. This results
in a much more subtle and expressive use of light and
colour and a more dynamic image overall. The warm
tones of the sand in the foreground are carried over
into the beach on the farther shore where the
reflections in the water and the patch of sunshine on
the hill behind seem to be enveloped in the same
humid, light-drenched atmosphere. The sunlit clouds
in particular owe much to the colour of the cartridge
paper which orchestrates the overall tonality of the
image.
Appledore itself had established a modest reputation
at the close of the eighteenth century as a small
watering-place for health cures, with some limited
facilities for tourists, as had Instow on the opposite
side of the Torridge estuary which is Girtin's vantage
point here. Girtin was in Appledore presumably to
enjoy the patronage of the Calverts, which would also
explain two later watercolours of this area.[11]

25. *Exeter from Trew's Weir* (c. 1799)
(Illustrated in colour on p.59)
Watercolour on paper, 32.0 x 44.4 cm
Signed 'Girtin' bottom centre
Royal Albert Memorial Museum, Exeter

Girtin shows Exeter from the banks of the river Exe
below Trew's Weir, looking back towards the
Cathedral and the south and west quarters of the city.
The masts in the middle distance indicate the
direction of the river and help to provide a sense of
scale. The nearer houses are well defined but beyond
them the city is reduced to a pattern of different
tones, washed in with long horizontal sweeps of the
brush, with only the most cursory indication of
architectural form. This patterning helps to establish
the sense of fast-moving shadows raking over Exeter as
the rain clouds to the left advance across the town.
The tumult of the weir to our right balances the storm
to our left, leaving the cathedral serenely illuminated
against the more placid cloud formations behind it.
As with *Appledore*, Girtin uses the cartridge paper
itself for the lights in the clouds and the rush of water
over the weir.
This image might be compared with De Wint's
(cat.no.16), who took his view from about three
quarters of a mile further downstream, and with
Turner's (cat.no.80) who probably took his from the
promontory on the left in front of us, close to the
entrance to the canal.

26. THOMAS GIRTIN, *Rainbow - a Scene on the River Exe*

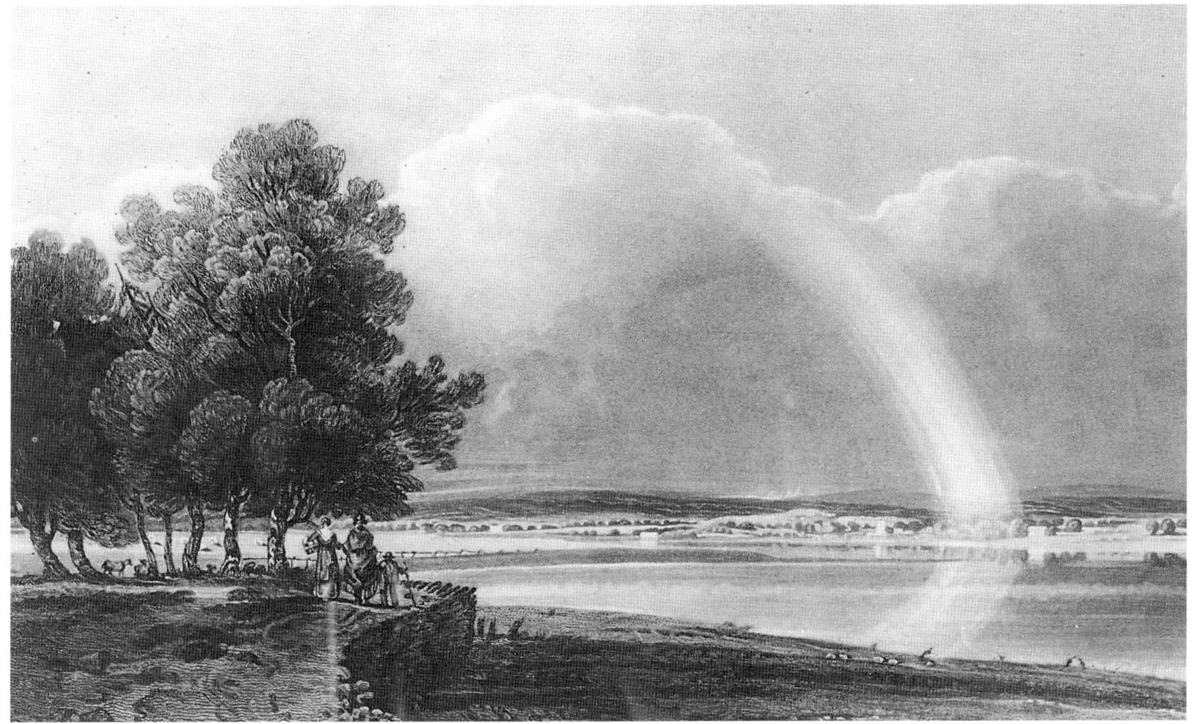

26. *Rainbow - a Scene on the River Exe*
Etching and aquatint, 14.0 x 22.8 cm
Engraved by Charles Turner
Published W.B. Cooke, May 1st, 1823 as Plate 4
of *Gems of Art.*

The original watercolour for this engraving is dated
1800 and is now in the Henry E. Huntington Library
and Art Gallery. In 1823 it was engraved in mezzotint
by S.W. Reynolds in his *Girtin's Liber Naturae* and in
etching and aquatint by Charles Turner, the print
shown here.
Girtin's style was developing rapidly in this period
towards an even more austere and rarified vision. It is
hard to tell whether or not watercolours in this
mature style are merely the result of him working up
1797 sketches at a later date or whether they
represent the results of further tours. Nevertheless,
even though his movements are difficult to trace it is
probable that Girtin returned to Devon around 1800
or 1801. The *Shepherd Sketchbook* (1799-1801)[12]
contains a reference to Mount Edgcumbe and there
are views of Plymouth and Devonport dated 1801.[13]
The recently discovered *Lydford Castle, Devon*
(PrivateCollection) is signed and dated 1800[14] and

The Estuary of the River Taw (Yale Center for British
Art) has been ascribed to 1801.[15] It is possible,
therefore, that this image too is also derived from
Girtin's second tour to Devon.
The broad expanse of the river Exe is seen from a
viewpoint near Powderham Church looking upriver
towards Exton. The estuary's placid surface acts like a
mirror for the enormous rainbow which irradiates the
further shore and contrasts dramatically with the
darkness of the sky. The upper edges of the clouds are
highlighted and further bright accents are found in
the four buildings glimpsed in the distance. As with
Appledore, but now even more abstractly, we are
presented essentially with an exploration of light and
atmosphere, using differences of tone to structure the
composition. Conventionally picturesque qualities
give way here to a rigorous control of the pictorial
medium in the interests of a unified expression,
undistracted by detail.
Three other engraved subjects after Girtin's work in
Devon are known: *Marine Barracks at Stonehouse,
Kingswear* and *Totnes*,[16] which were published in
Walker's *Copper Plate Magazine* and re-issued in
The Itinerant[17] All of these, however, are pedestrian
topography in comparison with this composition. (SS)

JOHN GLOVER (1767-1849)

27. *The Teign near Drewsteignton, Devonshire* (1829)
(Illustrated in colour on p.69)
watercolour on paper, 26.7 x 42.8 cm
Dated on reverse
The Board of Trustees of the
Victoria and Albert Museum, London

When T.H. Williams made his tour of Devon in the very early nineteenth century he had heard that 'the scenery in the vicinity of Drewsteignton' had been 'celebrated by tourists as grand and magnificent.' Even 'making the usual allowance for descriptions which were sullied with much of the common cant of affected taste' he was expecting to be impressed.[1] Unlike John Glover, who made this very successful interpretation of the scene before him, Williams could find 'no very interesting scenes which would form pictures' giving as his reason the fact that the hills had 'a sameness of appearance, a family likeness with each other, which excite no pleasurable emotion.' There were bold features and the hills had dignity, many being 'enriched with coppice wood,' but he tried in vain to find a view 'that with strict propriety could be classed as being eminently of a picturesque character.'[2] Glover's near monochrome is mainly in tones of grey with the palest grey blue in the sky. There are just enough man-made features to give a sense of habitation and scale and the solitary silhouetted animal is placed with a masterly touch. Glover was well known for using a split-brush technique to convey texture and in this work he uses it sparingly and to good effect. Like Payne (q.v.) from whom he had lessons, his finished exhibition pictures can seem stilted and lifeless, just too 'professional'. His sketches show him in a much better light. He was a prolific exhibitor but only six of his works were of Devon subjects, three of these being of Bradley Mill, near Newton Abbot.[3] The other three show that he must have travelled to the north and south coasts of Devon. On his 1810 visit to Exeter, Farington had heard that Glover intended coming to the city for a period of time to set up his son as a drawing master.[4] (MP)

JAMES DUFFIELD HARDING (1797-1863)

28. *Lynmouth* (1859)
(Illustrated in colour on p.68)
Watercolour and bodycolour over pencil on paper,
30.7 x 55.5 cm
Lent by the Syndics of the Fitzwilliam Museum,
Cambridge

29. *View of Lynmouth* (1859)
Pencil and wash on paper, 24.5 x 34.8 cm
Inscribed 'Lynmouth 5.9.59' (lower right)

Lent by the Syndics of the Fitzwilliam Museum,
Cambridge

Harding's first exhibits at the British Institution in 1827 had all been of Lynmouth which he must have visited in 1826 on his first documented tour to the west country.[1] The two examples of Harding's Devon views exhibited here are also of Lynmouth and represent a further trip to Devon in 1859. This was probably his third and last tour of the county; in September 1858 he had sketched in south Devon too.[2] It is instructive to note how Harding's watercolour offers a more composed view than the immediacy of his sketch from nature.

Although we have no information on Harding at Lynmouth, Anna Bray gives us some details of the artist's response to the scenery around Tavistock which she enthused over to all her artist visitors: 'When our friend Mr. Harding, the landscape artist, was here, Mr Bray set off to guide him to the Virtuous Lady, but Harding, who, like most men of genius, is a great enthusiast, was so enchanted with the scenery through which he had to pass in his way thither, that he could never get to the place of destination; and he sat down near the Goat Rock (as we call it), took out his pencil, and I saw no more of Mr. Bray and his guest till they were driven home by the approach of evening.'[3]

The Virtuous Lady, it should be said, was a cave and mine set in such dramatic scenery that 'the pencil alone could attempt to portray, so as to give any distinct idea of its character.' She records Harding's comments on Mary Tavy Rock ('covered with ivy, lichens, and every sort of rock plant... found in Devon') that it 'would in itself furnish many subjects for a painter.' In common with practically everyone who visited them Harding sketched the water mill belonging to the Rev. Bray, and also painted an oil of some cottages. But he was unfortunate, according to Mrs. Bray, in 'chancing to come hither during the long drought of 1826, for there was so little water in the rivers and streams, that he lost sight of them in all their beauty.'[4]

Harding made good use of some of his Devon sketches when he lithographed some for inclusion in his *Sketches at Home and Abroad* of 1836 and in his *Picturesque Selections* of 1861, a volume also containing British and foreign subjects.[5] His best known links with Devon scenes are his contributions to Finden's *Ports and Harbours*, published in 1842 and consisting of a fine series of steel engravings (fig.22). All six of his Devon views are credited to Harding from sketches by 'Jendle.' This is a mis-spelling of John Gendall, the Exeter artist who had provided the original sketches. It was not uncommon for well known metropolitan artists to work up the sketches of

29. JAMES DUFFIELD HARDING, *View of Lynmouth* (1859)

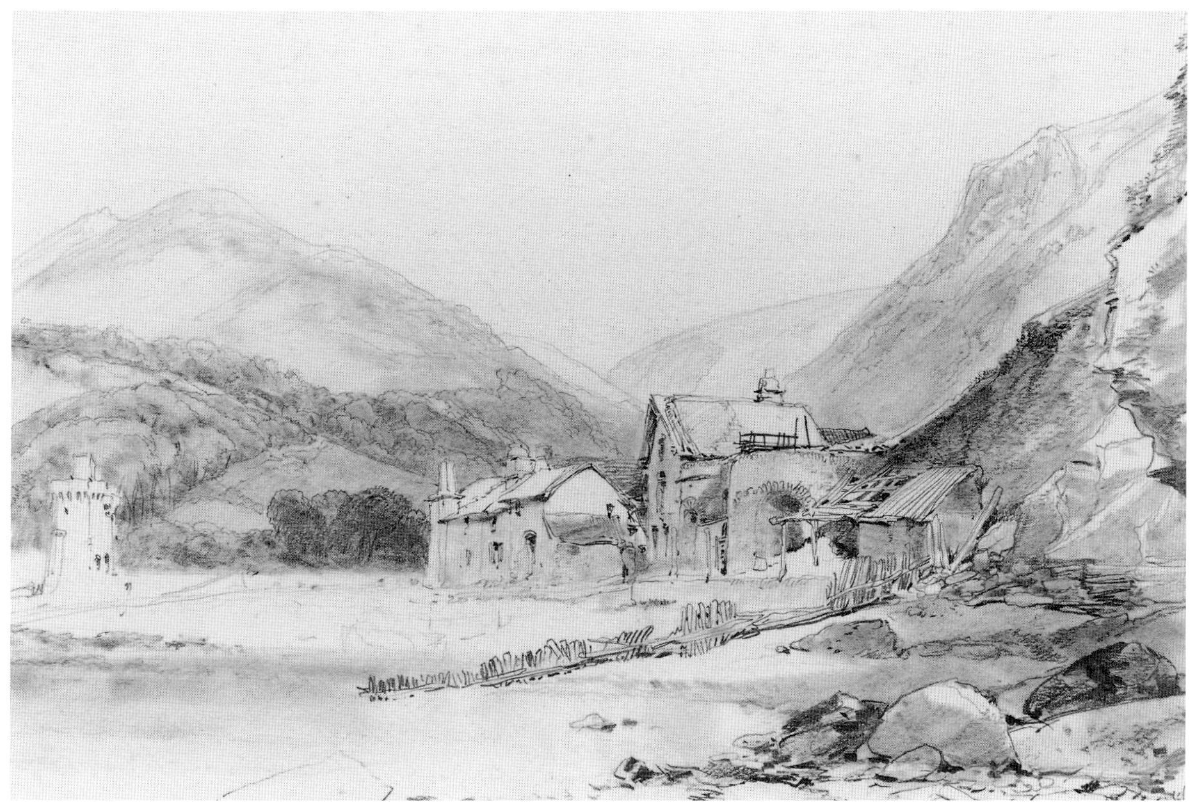

Fig.22. J.D. HARDING, from a sketch by Jendle (J.Gendall), engraved E. Finden, *View from the Beach at Sidmouth looking towards the South-West*, from William and Edward F. Finden *Views of Ports and Harbours, Watering Places, Fishing Villages and Other Picturesque Objects on the English Coast*, London, 1838.

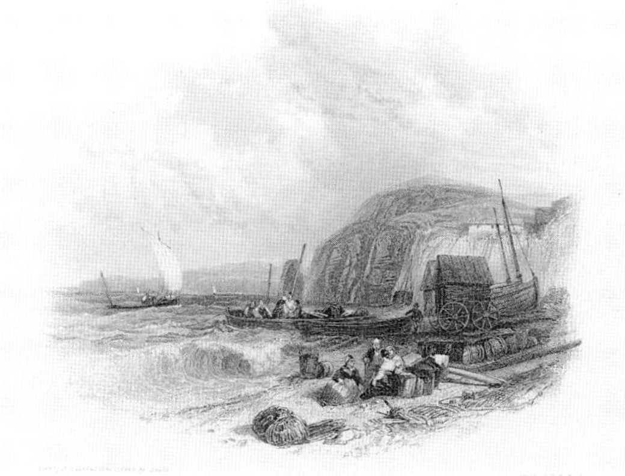

their lesser known provincial counterparts in this way. Although most of the hard work (and travelling) had been undertaken by Gendall he gets no credit at all in the list of artists which prefaces the volume.[6] Harding's invention of a particular kind of sketching paper marketed under his name is discussed in the essay on sketching. (MP)

CHARLES NAPIER HEMY (1841-1917)

30. *Among the Shingle at Clovelly* (1864)
(Illustrated in colour on p.67)
Oil on canvas, 43.5 x 72.1 cm
Signed 'CNH. 1864' (lower right)
Laing Art Gallery, Newcastle upon Tyne
(Tyne and Wear Museums)

31. *Evening Grey* (1866-68)
(Illustrated in colour on p.67)
Oil on canvas, 57.1 x 91.4 cm
Tate Gallery, London

Among the Shingle at Clovelly is recognised as Hemy's youthful masterpeice.[1] It was painted when he was in his early twenties and exhibited at the Royal Academy in 1865. It makes an interestring comparison with John White Abbot's watercolour of 1811 (fig.23). Little seems to have changed in half a century. Hemy's picture is unusually detailed and has, not surprisingly, been associated with other Pre-Raphaelite inspired pictures of the late 1850s, particularly William Dyce's *Pegwell Bay*.[2] It is probably just as relevant to see a link with Boyce's *Babbacombe Bay* (cat.no.3) and a connection with the pious strain of nature study which P.H. Gosse had inspired.

Fig.23.J.W. ABBOTT, *Clovelly*, watercolour, 18.3 x 27.0 cm, inscribed 'Augt. 20, 1811'. Royal Albert Memorial Museum, Exeter.

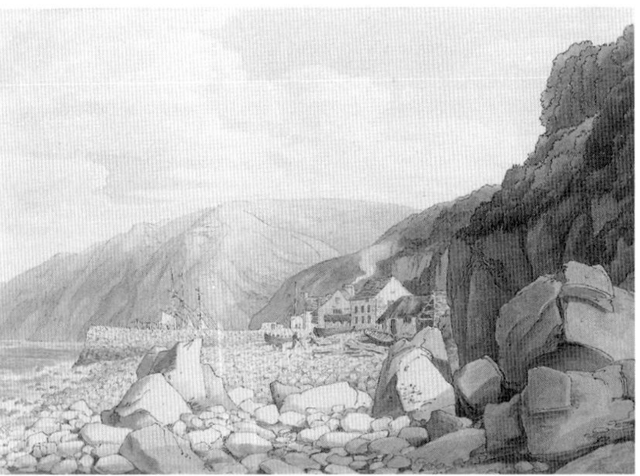

32. HOPKINS HORSLEY HOBDAY HORSLEY, *Bishopsteignton* (1847)

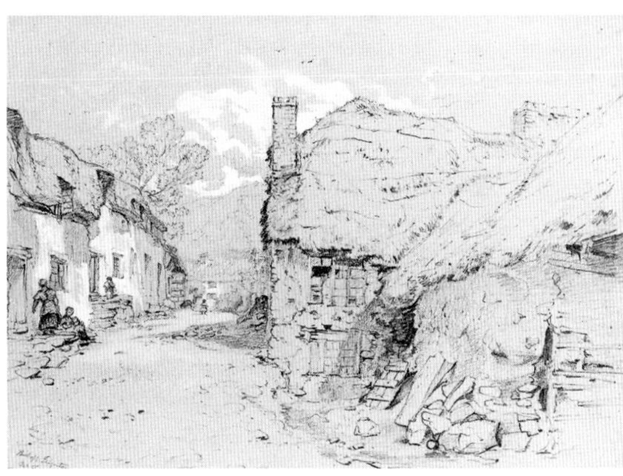

His name had already been conjured up by the critics when discussing pictures of north Devon. In 1859, for example, the painter Henry Moore had been singled out as 'an easy first for power of observation' and his *Oak Coppice, Clovelly* called 'a treasure of beautiful and skillful painting... all as true and beautiful as one of Mr. Gosse's descriptions.'[3] Reviewers of Gosse's writings always remarked on his 'comprehensive and minute' descriptions over which was 'breathed a spirit of piety so pure and fervent' that one could not fail to see the 'associations with the great Author of all.'[4] Hemy was a devout Catholic who very nearly became a Dominican priest so it is fair to assume that his almost photographic clarity is intended to reveal a close inspection of God's handiwork, not merely a surface reflection. It is one of the few landscapes of the period which has the power to make the spectator ponder on actual and geological time, on the momentary and the timeless.

In the mid 1860s when Hemy was painting at Clovelly the place was already associated in the minds of most people with one artist in particular. James Clarke Hook had become 'the acknowledged painter of Devonshire life.'[5] Even the aforementioned Henry Moore was said in 1858 to be 'trespassing a little on Mr. Hook's Devonshire ground, for artists will run in packs.'[6] Hook concentrated largely on fishermen and their families and invented a genre that was to be developed and further sentimentalized by the artists of the Newlyn School as artists found Cornwall increasingly promising and easier to get to.[7]

Hemy's second picture painted at Clovelly (cat. no.31) is entirely different from his first being self-consciously gloomy in mood. A heavy air of stillness and melancholy pervades the figure, deep in contemplation, and the surrounding landscape. *Evening Grey* was exhibited in 1868 and shows the new influence of G.J. Pinwell, a watercolourist and draughtsman who, with J.W. North (q.v.) and Fred

Walker (see *Sketching from Nature*), was a leading book-illustrator. Hemy's 'morbid melancholy' and interest in 'the study of nature' had been noticed in 1867 when he exhibited *The Cottage Garden*, a theme taken up in *Evening Grey*.[8] (MP)

HOPKINS HORSLEY HOBDAY HORSLEY (1806-92)

32. *Bishopsteignton* (1847)
Pencil and gouache on paper, 27.5 x 36.2 cm
Inscribed 'Bishops Teignton, near Teignmouth, May, 1847' (lower left)
Birmingham Museums and Art Gallery

Horsley's rather complicated name is explained by his taking his mother's name in 1832 on inheriting money from his aunt. He was first apprenticed to a Birmingham *papier-mâché* painter and by 1830 had already achieved a high standard of competence as a draughtsman and watercolourist.[1] Like S.H. Baker (q.v.) he was an important contributor to the Birmingham Society of Arts, especially in respect of the watercolour exhibitions held from 1866.[2] He exhibited in London from 1832-66 at the Royal Academy, British Institution and Society of British Artists.

His first tour to Devon was probably in 1847, the date of this sketch, for *Mill at East Ogwell, Devon*, exhibited at the British Institution in 1848, was his only Devon subject shown there. Bishopsteignton lies just north of the Teign estuary, while East Ogwell is close to Newton Abbot which suggests that Horsley was sketching in and around the Teign valley.[3] The South Devon Railway had opened a station at Newton Abbot in December 1846 and it is feasible that Horsley took advantage of this for his sketching tour the following year, taking the train to its westernmost destination and working in that area.[4] In this drawing the artist has explored a motif very much in emulation of Samuel Prout's earlier *Views of Rural Cottages* (cat.nos.60,61),

30. CHARLES NAPIER HEMY, *Among the Shingle at Clovelly* (1864)

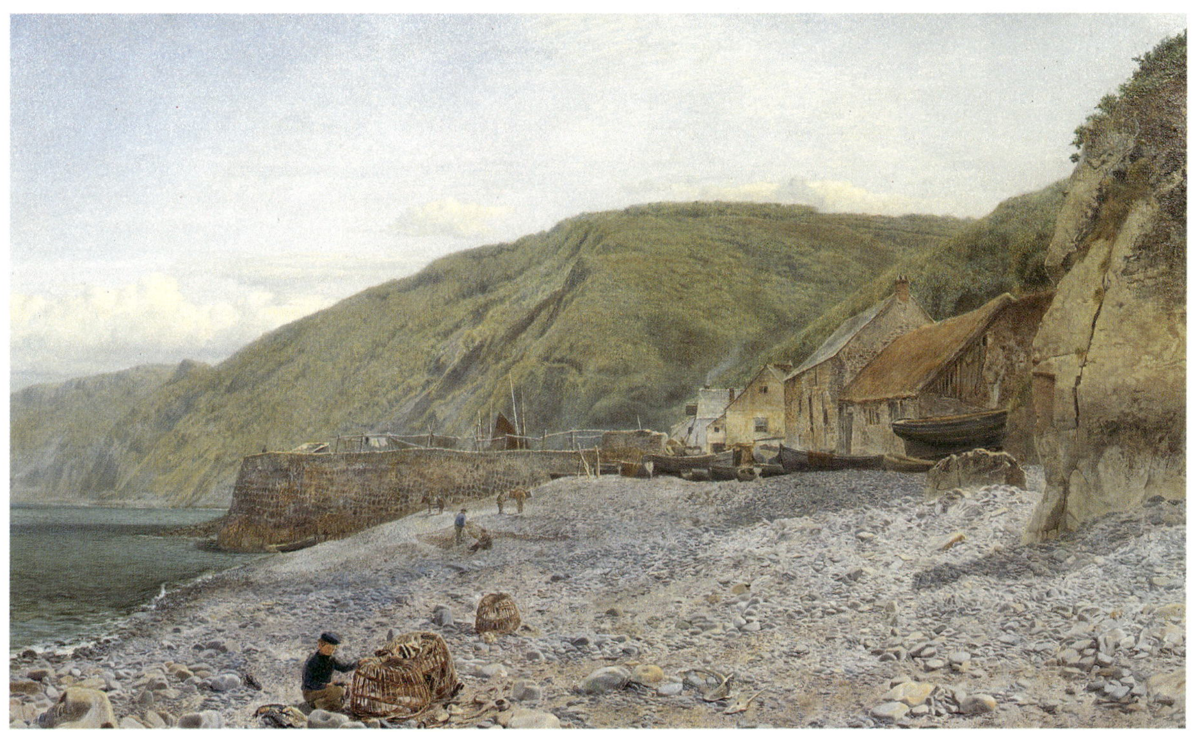

31. CHARLES NAPIER HEMY, *Evening Grey* (1866-68)

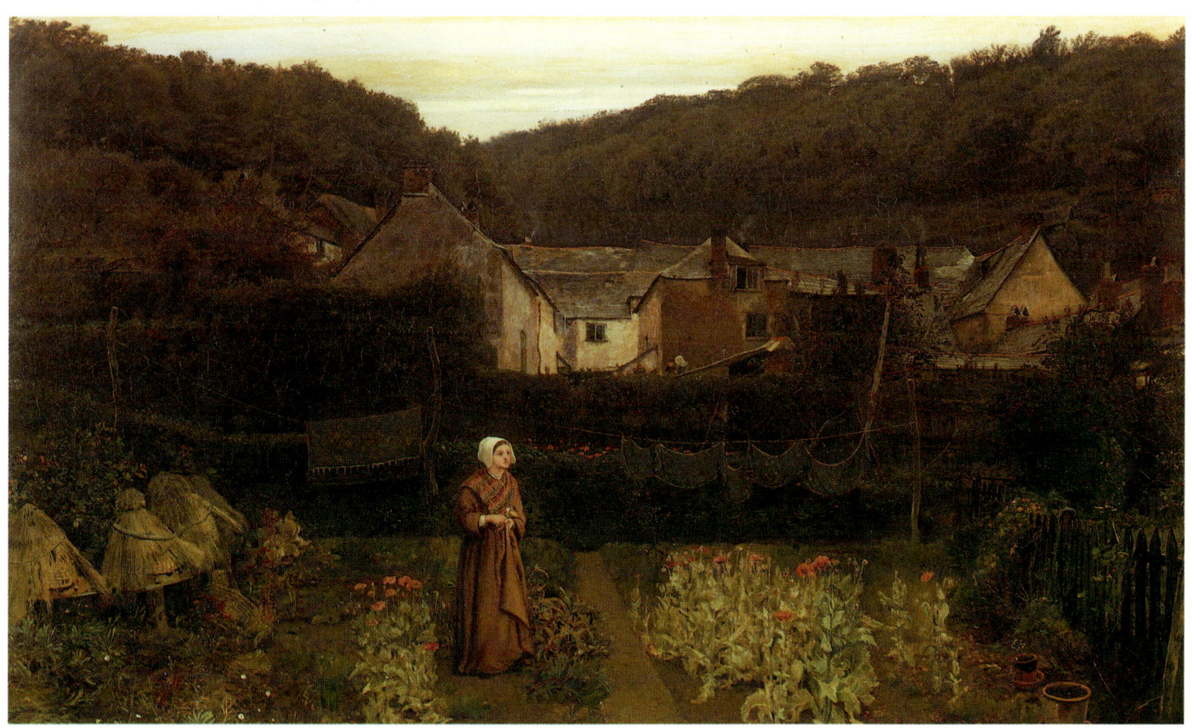

28. JAMES DUFFIELD HARDING, Lynmouth (1859)

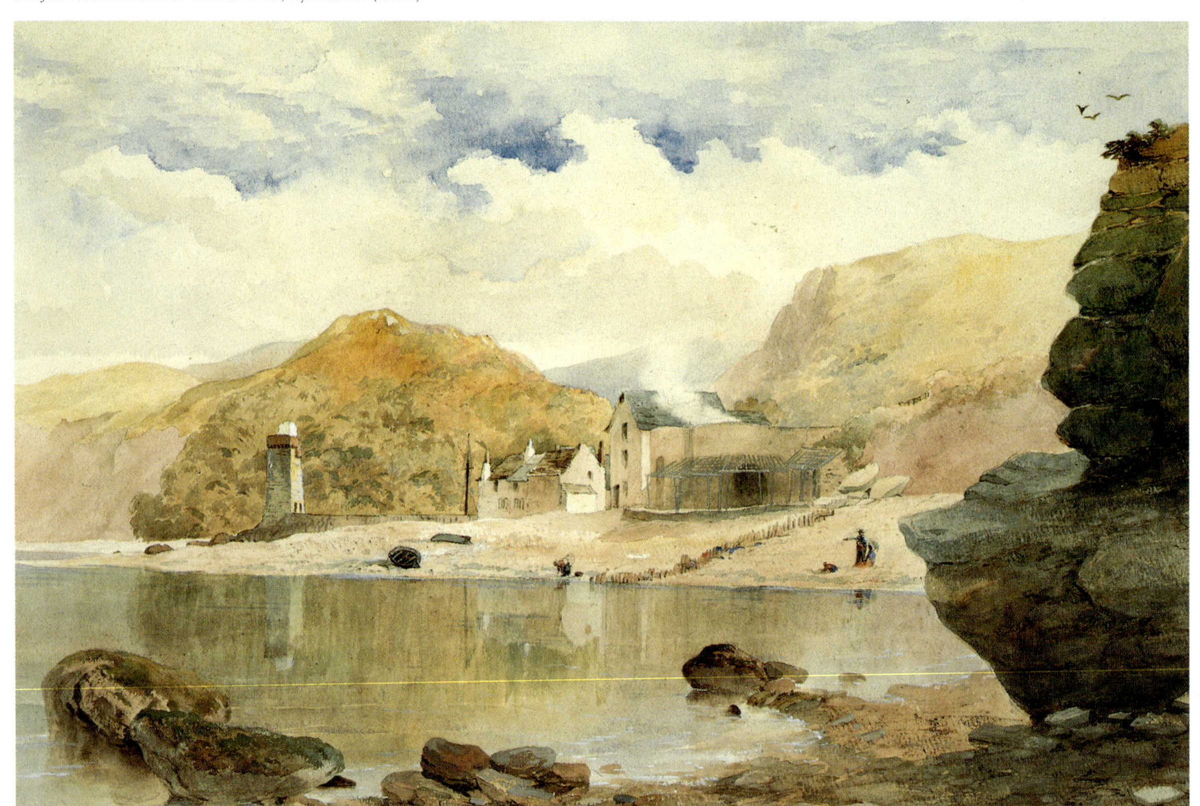

27. JOHN GLOVER, *The Teign near Drewsteignton, Devonshire* (1829)

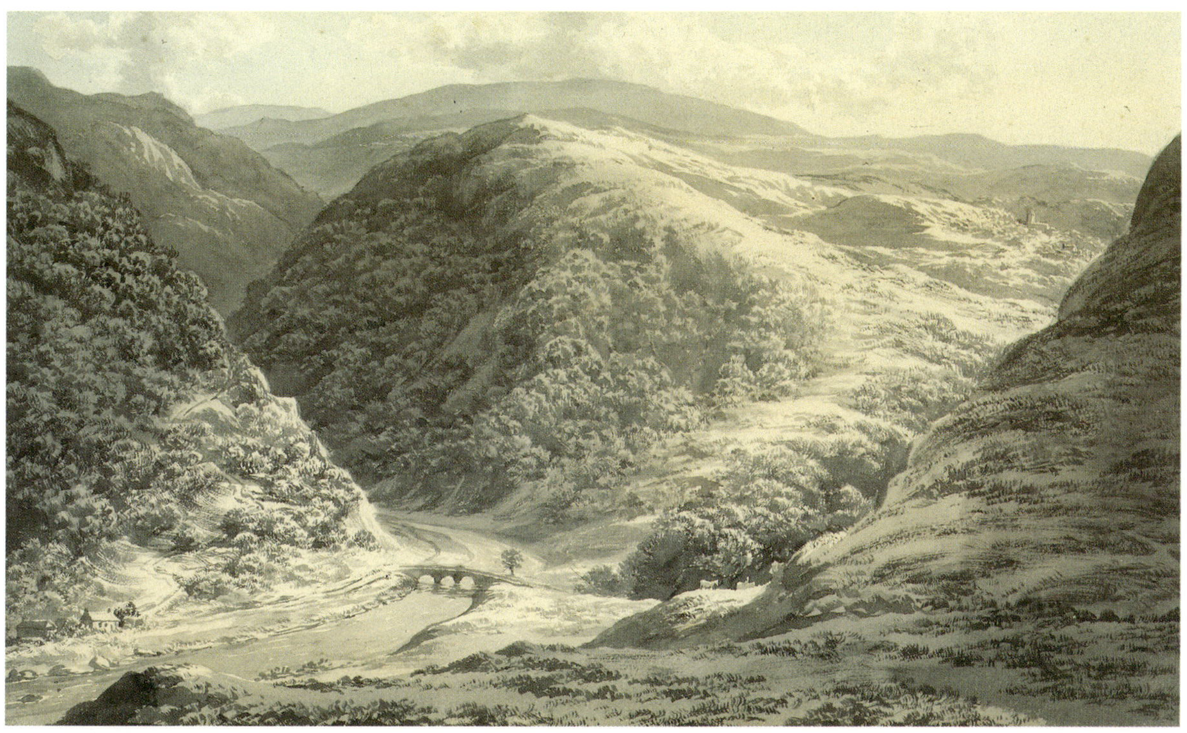

33. JOHN WILLIAM INCHBOLD, *The moorland (Dewar-stone, Dartmoor)* (1854)

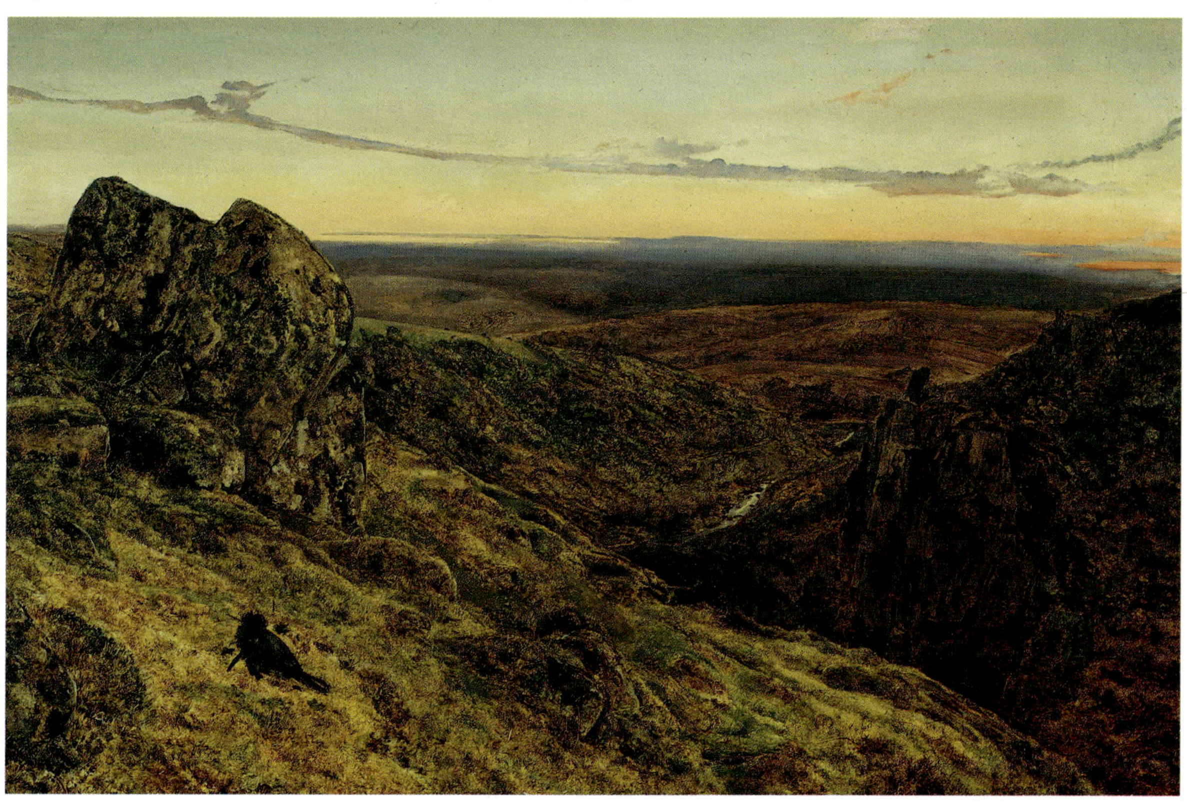

34. JOHN WILLIAM INCHBOLD, *Westward Ho!* (1862)

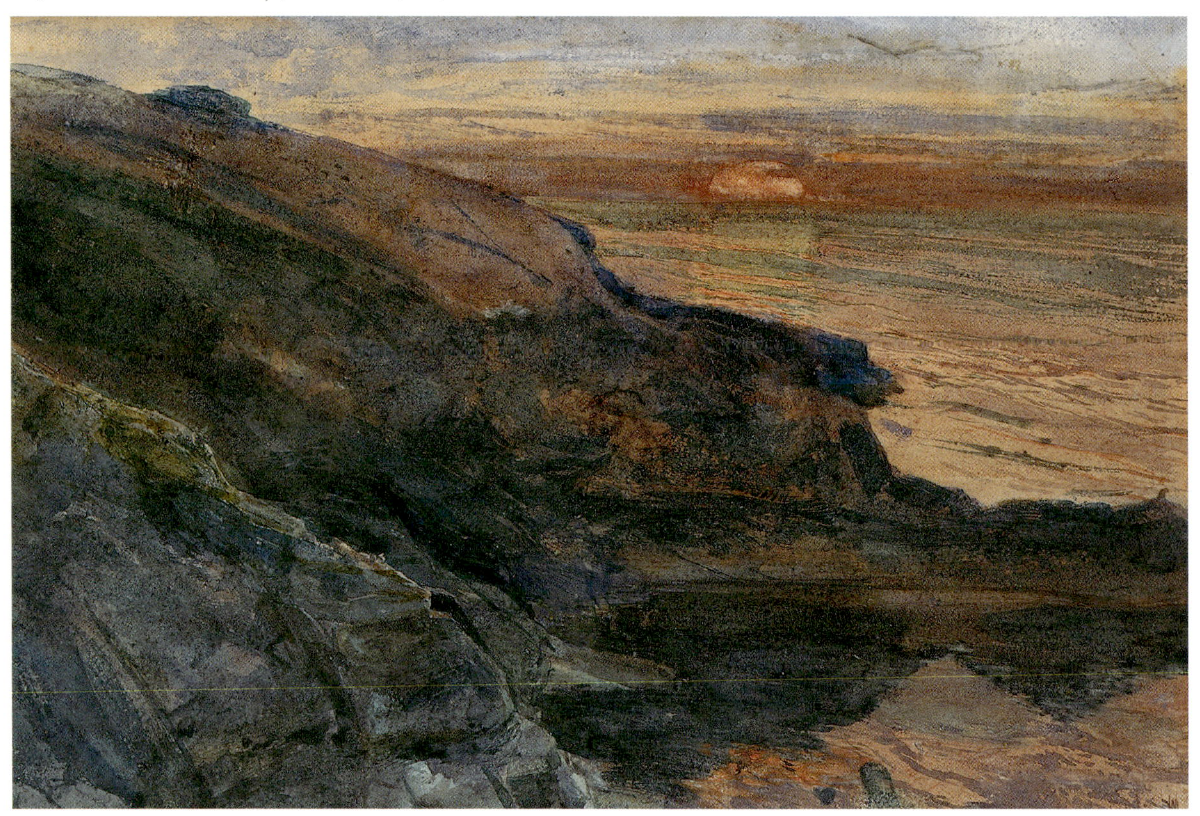

detailing the crooked irregularity of these old dwellings.[5] The neat architecture and white stucco of the early nineteenth-century houses in Bishopsteignton are, naturally, nowhere to be seen. (SS)

JOHN WILLIAM INCHBOLD (1830-1888)

33. *The moorland (Dewar-stone, Dartmoor)* (1854)
(Illustrated in colour on p.69)
Oil on canvas 356 x 533 cm
Signed and dated 'Inchbold 1854' (lower right)
inscribed with the title 'The moorland (Dewar stone)'
and signed in ink on the stretcher.
Tate Gallery, London

Inchbold's association with Devon dates from about 1850, at the very beginning of his career, when he sent two watercolours of Dartmoor to the Society of British Artists, one of which showed the Dewar Stone and was subtitled 'the favourite haunt of the poet Carrington'. It has recently been suggested that this picture may be a reworking of that watercolour.[1] Inchbold exhibited a painting entitled *"The Moorland" - Tennyson* at the Royal Academy in 1855 which excited Ruskin's admiration for its painting of lichenous rock but it is unclear whether this is the same painting.[2] His Devon masterpiece, *Anstey's Cove* (Fitzwilliam Museum, Cambridge), also dates from this period and Millais and Ruskin both protested at its rejection by the Royal Academy selection committee in 1854. As has been noted, George Price Boyce (q.v.) was also working in Devon in the summer of 1853 and it is possible that both artists were travelling together.[3] At the end of the decade Inchbold painted a third major Devon oil, *Furze blossom from Devonshire* (1858-9; private collection), which was shown at Liverpool (1860) and the Royal Academy (1861) and an oil and watercolour of *Cornwood* (both 1860).[4]
The Moorland presents Dartmoor as a bleak and cheerless expanse whose sky is as wan as the landscape it covers and the solitary crow seems to have been included to highlight the sense of desolation. By 1854 Inchbold was close to the Pre-Raphaelites and *Anstey's Cove* shows his ability to paint in their manner. *The Moorland* lacks that picture's most minute attention to detail but it is still something of a tour de force in its subtle use of a narrow colour range and its nicely discriminated representation of the different textures of rock and vegetation.
Inchbold's picture captures a new interest in Dartmoor's wilderness. Explorations of Dartmoor before the 1840s are not numerous, although there are some significant exceptions in the case of Prout, F.C. Lewis, Turner and the Rev. and Mrs. Bray. None

the less, in 1828 Henry Carrington, the poet's son, had grumbled that:
'Very few of the numerous strangers who resort during the summer months to Plymouth and Devonport think of visiting the romantic wastes of Dartmoor. The truth is, it is generally imagined to be a region dreary, monotonous, and wholly devoid of attraction...'[5]
The impact of N. T. Carrington's *Dartmoor - a descriptive poem* (1826) can be traced in the local guide-books, newspaper articles and a growing aesthetic interest in the moor during the 1830s. The publication in 1848 of Samuel Rowe's extensive topographical guide, *A Perambulation of the Antient and Royal Forest of Dartmoor*, consolidated Dartmoor as a tourist destination;[6] henceforth no trip to Devon was complete without a visit. Despite its desolate appearance, Inchbold was working in one of the most accessible and popular Dartmoor sketching grounds, lying just above Shaugh Bridge, and the beginning of the ascent to it forms the background to Turner's 1813 oil sketch (cat.no.75).

34. *Westward Ho!* (1862)
(Illustrated in colour on p.70)
Watercolour on paper, 17.5 x 25.3 cm
Inscribed 'Westward ho! 1862 JWI' (lower right)
Royal Institution of Cornwall,
Royal Cornwall Museum, Truro

This painting must date to early in 1862 as Inchbold was in Venice by mid-summer and did not return to England until 1866. The watercolour shows the evening sky, looking out to sea from an elevated position, but it is unlikely that the title refers to a location, for the resort of that name was not operational until 1865. If the title is Inchbold's rather than James Leathart's, its original owner, we must understand it as a meditation on that scene in the spirit of Kingsley's novel, perhaps painted from recollection rather than from life. Certainly in 1860 Inchbold had been prepared to see Tintagel with reference to Malory and Tennyson[7] and tourists in north Devon were attracted to that coastline precisely because of the romance of Kingsley's book.
Inchbold's consistent interest in atmospheric effects is very evident here and contrasts markedly with the more minute handling of *The Moorland*. The deep twilight at the base of the cliff, the molten reflections in the water below us and the richness of the sunset itself give the picture a sumptuous, yet sombre effect and look forward to investigations of similar phenomena in some of his work of the 1870s. (SS)

35. SAMUEL PHILLIPS JACKSON, *The Hamoaze from Morice Town, with the Torpoint Ferry*

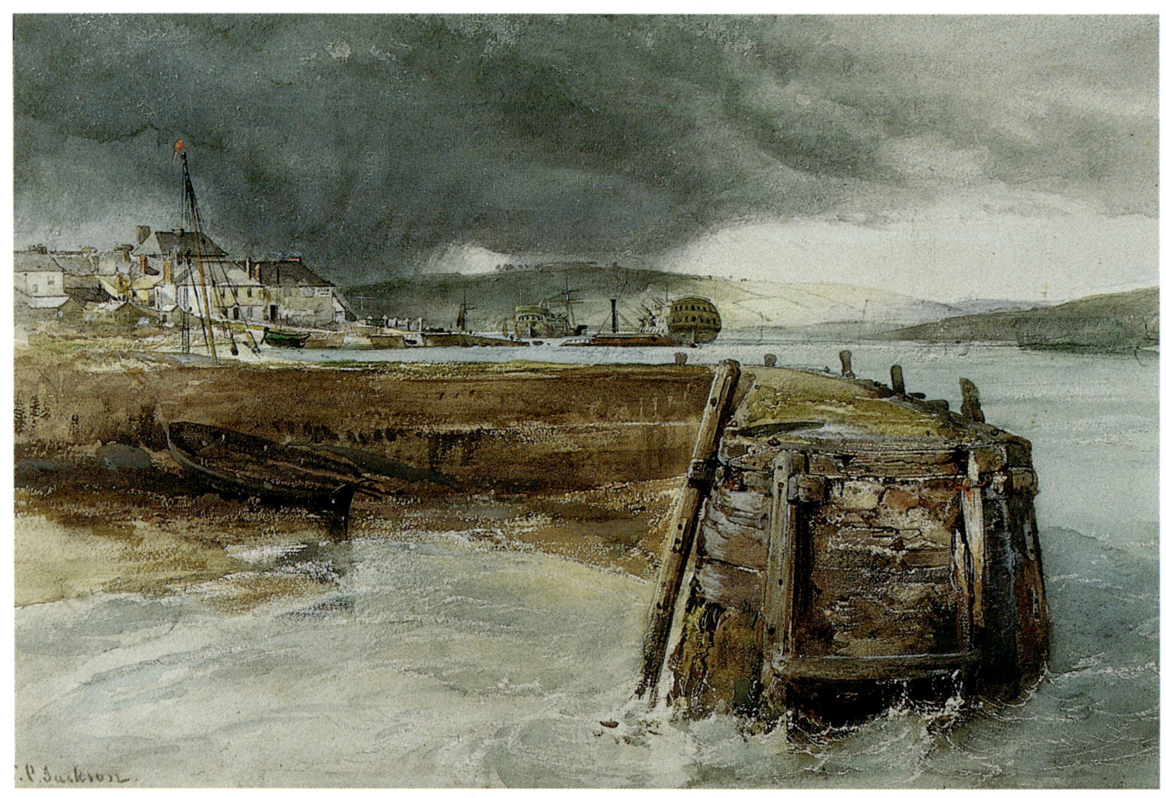

36. SAMUEL PHILLIPS JACKSON, *On the Hamoaze, Plymouth*

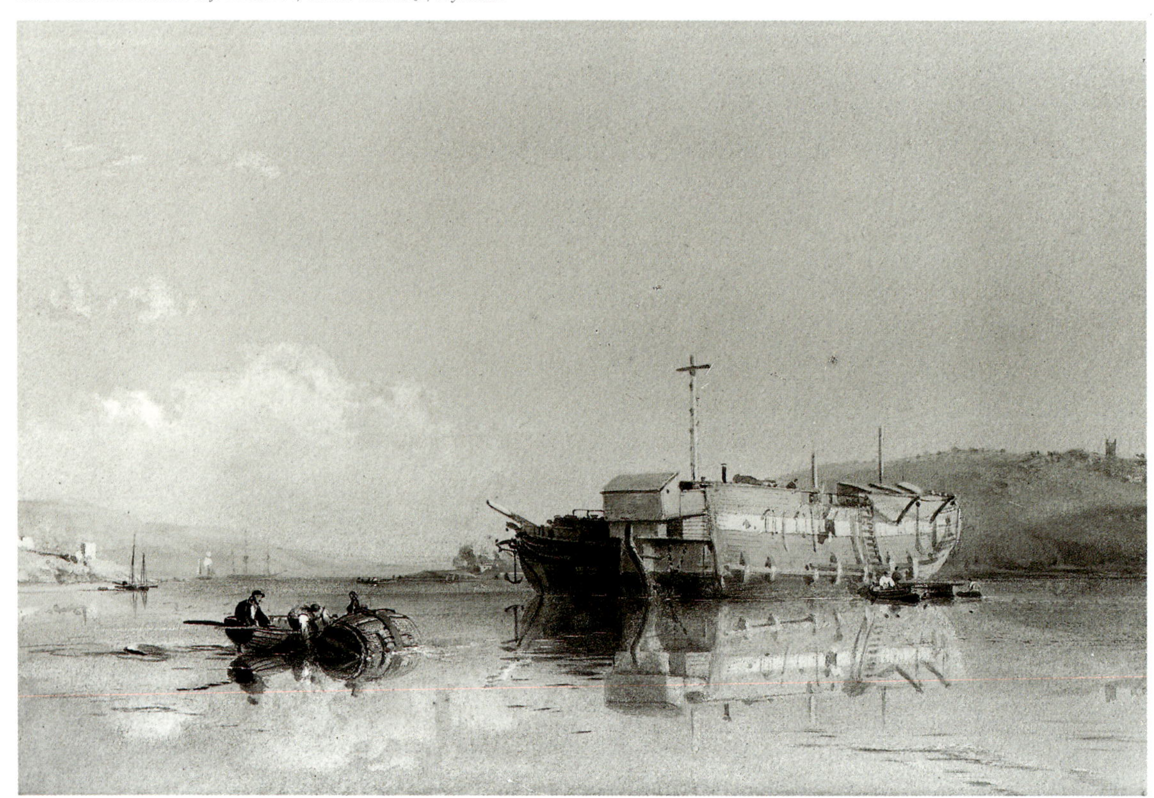

37. SAMUEL PHILLIPS JACKSON, *An Old Hulk at Teignmouth* (1851; reworked 1891)

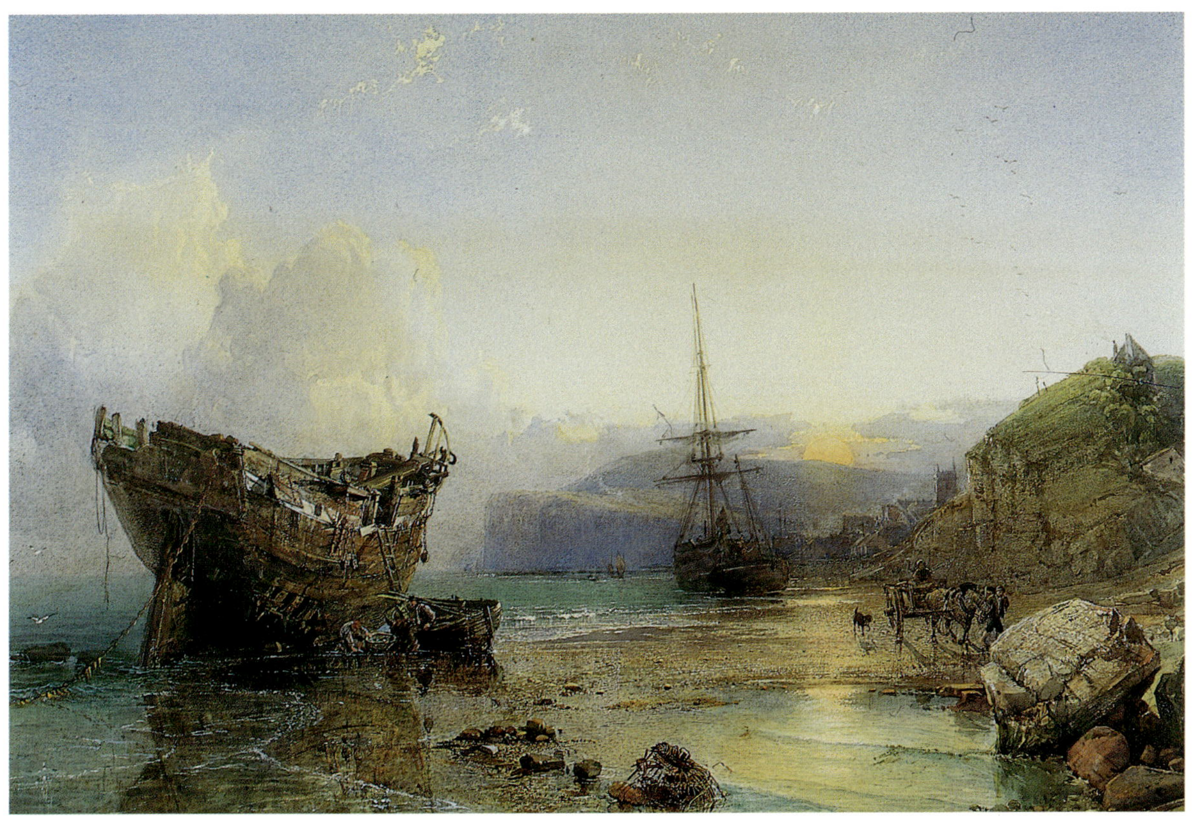

SAMUEL PHILLIPS JACKSON
(1830-1904)

35. *The Hamoaze from Morice Town,*
with the Torpoint Ferry
(Illustrated in colour on p.72)
Watercolour, with touches of bodycolour on
paper 34.3 x 50.8 cm
Signed 'S.P. Jackson' (lower left)
Bristol Museums and Art Gallery

36. *On the Hamoaze, Plymouth*
Watercolour on paper, 26 x 37.5 cm
Signed 'S.P. Jackson' (lower right)
The Board of Trustees of the
Victoria and Albert Museum, London

Jackson was born in Bristol, the son of Samuel
Jackson, one of the more notable members of the
Bristol school of artists. His early work was chiefly of
Devon and Cornwall coast scenes, exemplified by
Hazy Morning on the Coast of Devon (1853) and *On the
Hamoaze* (cat.no.36), both in the Victoria and Albert
Museum and the two pictures from Bristol exhibited
here. Both watercolours of the Hamoaze show men of
war lying 'in ordinary' (i.e. without rigging). In
cat.no.36 Jackson is concerned to capture the

tranquility of a still, summer's day with brilliant
reflections in the water. The Bristol watercolour
(cat.no.35) is a more animated composition and
includes J.M. Rendel's Floating Bridge, a steam driven
chain ferry which linked Devonport to Torpoint,
plying back and forth in the middle distance.[1] On one
of the houses can be seen the letters JAGO which
identifies it as Mary Jago's beer house in Charlotte
Street, Morice Town, close to the landing stage.[2] This
prosaic scene's matter of factness is emphasised by
Jackson's concentration on the foreground jetty, the
choppy water and the lowering sky, a far less typical
image of Devon than his other compositions.

37. *An Old Hulk at Teignmouth* (1851; reworked 1891)
Watercolour and gouache on paper 52.1 x 76.2 cm
signed and dated 'S.P. Jackson.1851-91' (lower left)
Bristol Museums and Art Gallery

This watercolour dates to Jackson's early career but
appears to have been reworked towards the end of his
life. It shows the beach and town of Teignmouth in
the distance with a boat drawn up for repairs on the
sand. The subject matter and the luxuriant use of
colour seem to indicate a much more picturesque
approach to Devon than is evident in cat.no.35, and

39. FREDERICK CHRISTIAN LEWIS, *Berry Pomeroy Castle*

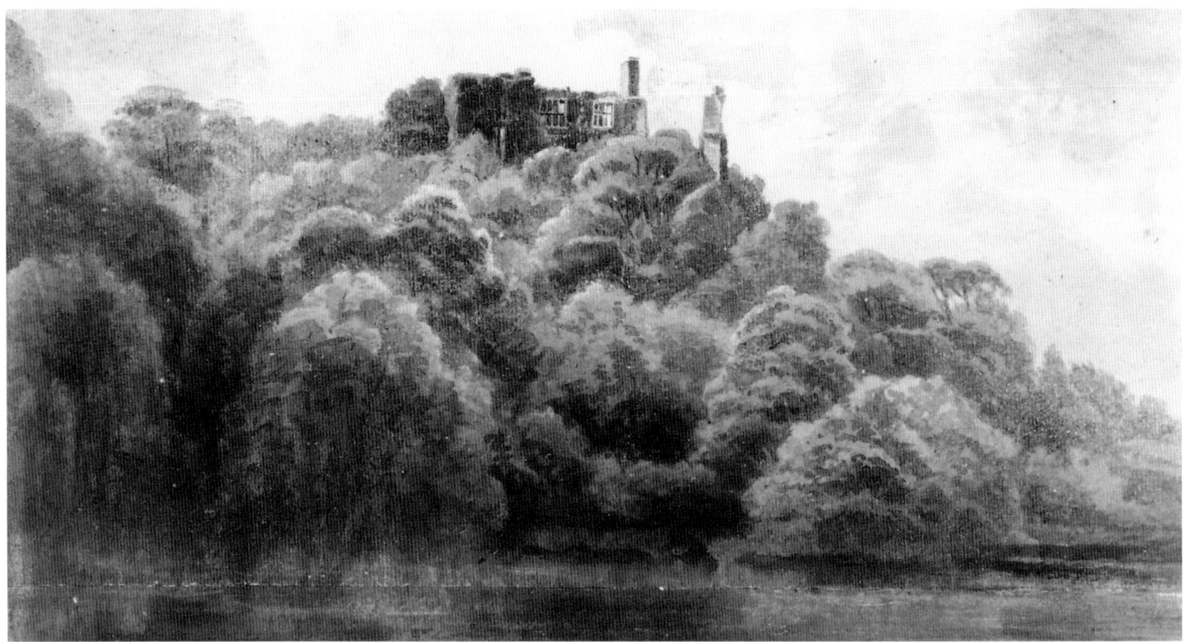

certainly one much more suitable to the image of Devon that was developing in the 1890s. Jackson's vantage point is strategic: the Great Western Railway follows the shoreline from Starcross to Teignmouth and is hidden in a cutting at this point as it approaches the town. Unlike his earlier inclusion of a modern steam ferry (cat.no.35) or Danby (q.v.) who had no qualms about including a train within a poetic evocation of tranquility, Jackson's later work seems to be an entirely picturesque confection. (SS)

FREDERICK CHRISTIAN LEWIS
(1779-1856)

38. *Berry Pomeroy Castle*
(Illustrated in colour on p.76)
Watercolour on paper, 18.2 x 29.7 cm
The Board of Trustees of the
Victoria and Albert Museum, London

39. *Berry Pomeroy Castle*
Watercolour on paper, 22.3 x 40 cm
The Board of Trustees of the
Victoria and Albert Museum, London

Berry Pomeroy Castle was among the most illustrated of all Devon's picturesque sites. An 1802 guidebook on south Devon commented:
'The antiquary and the painter must here unite in admiration, and the latter might multiply his sketches *ad infinitum*, for, in every aspect, wheresoever he places himself, he will meet with some peculiar discriminated beauty.'[1]
Somers Cocks records nearly fifty prints of this subject ranging in date between 1734 and 1861.[2] And there are certainly more because he does not list those by F.C. Lewis who included two mixed method prints of Berry Pomeroy in his *Scenery of the Rivers of England*.[3] The two sketches exhibited are typical examples of Lewis's free style of sketching and colouring and his penchant for using dark, dull greens and broadly handled masses, with sometimes rather matt effects. His methods derive ultimately from Girtin (q.v.) whose sketching technique he had studied at first hand.
As another guidebook of 1817 remarked of Berry Pomeroy: 'The whole of the ruins are so finely mantled with ivy, and so beautifully interspersed with thick bushes, that they present a scene, perhaps unequalled.'[4] Among those who depicted the ruins were Girtin, Farington, Turner and Cox. (MP)

42. JOHN FREDERICK LEWIS, *Above Shaugh* (?1829)

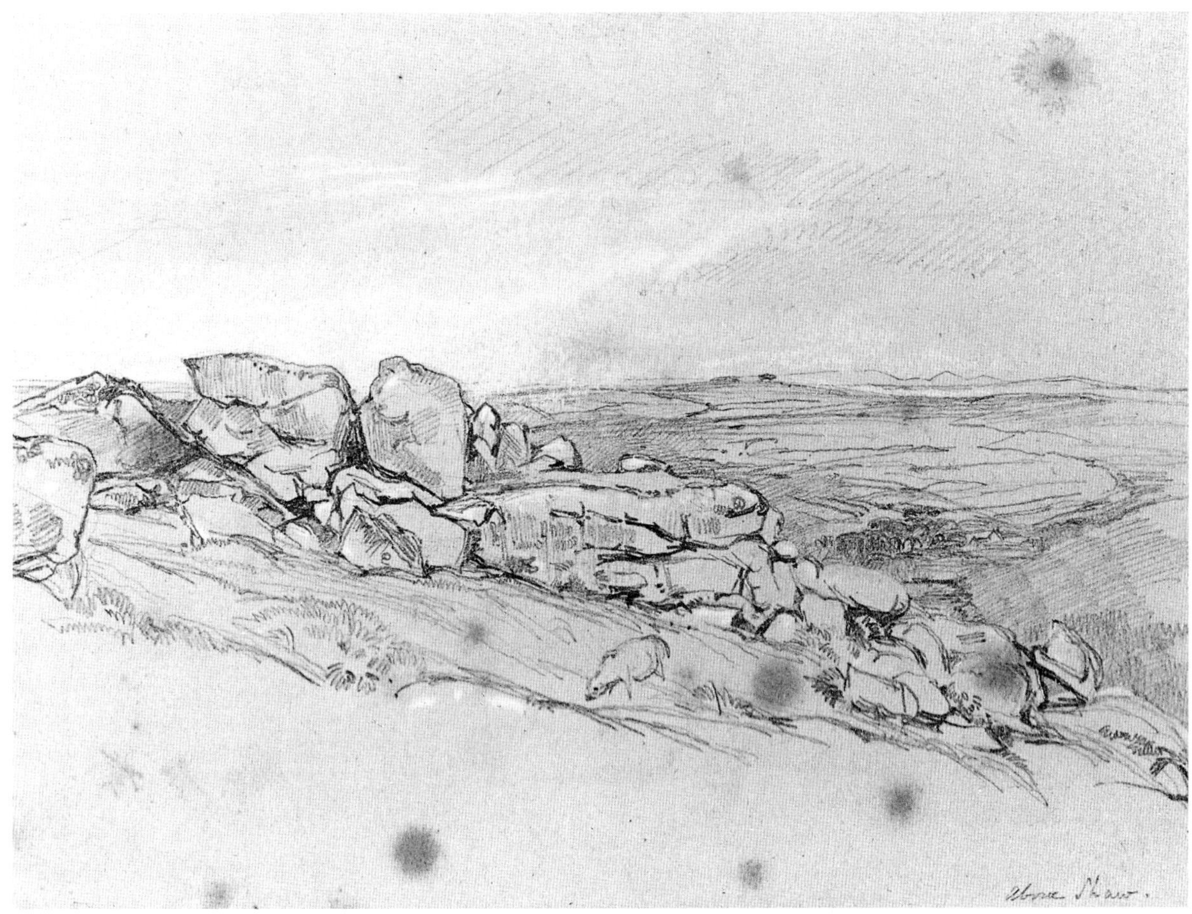

GEORGE ROBERT LEWIS
(1782-1871)

In his day Lewis was as well known for his figural subjects as his landscapes, most of which date from after 1850. He was a life-long friend of John Linnell and in the 1810s he shared Linnell's interest in naturalism, most notably in a group of paintings of harvest in Herefordshire, dated c.1815, now in the Tate Gallery. Although his brother, F.C. Lewis (q.v.), was heavily involved with the Devon landscape from the 1820s G.R. Lewis's investigation of it seems to have been more modest. Nevertheless, he exhibited three paintings of Ilfracombe at the Royal Academy in the early 1850s[1] which indicates that he visited the north Devon coast then. The tight, descriptive handling, allied to developments in Pre-Raphaelite landscape, in cat.no.40 and cat.no.41 further suggests that both of these watercolours should be dated c.1852-55.[2]

40. *Ilfracombe* (early 1850s)
(Illustrated in colour on p.76)
Watercolour and bodycolour on grey paper,
26.8 x 37.6cm

Inscribed 'At Larkstone Cove Ilfracombe G.R.Lewis' (bottom left)
Trustees of The British Museum

In this striking composition Lewis has emphasised the rock strata of the cliffs, especially at the left, a concern which echoes Ruskin's contemporary insistence on accuracy of notation and also chimes with the amateur geology practised by many tourists themselves.[3] This is very much a resort scene, with a bathing machine and animated groups of figures enlivening the beach. In the background a cart is being loaded with seaweed for use as fertilizer while a yacht sails off-shore. Numerous prints of Ilfracombe's bathing beaches were published from the 1840s to the 1860s and it is possible that Lewis was responding to their popularity in this image.

41. *Valley of the Rocks, Lynton* (early 1850s)
(Illustrated in colour on p.77)
Watercolour, 33.2 x 49.7 cm
Signed 'G.R.Lewis' (bottom left)
Trustees of The British Museum

38. FREDERICK CHRISTIAN LEWIS, *Berry Pomeroy Castle*

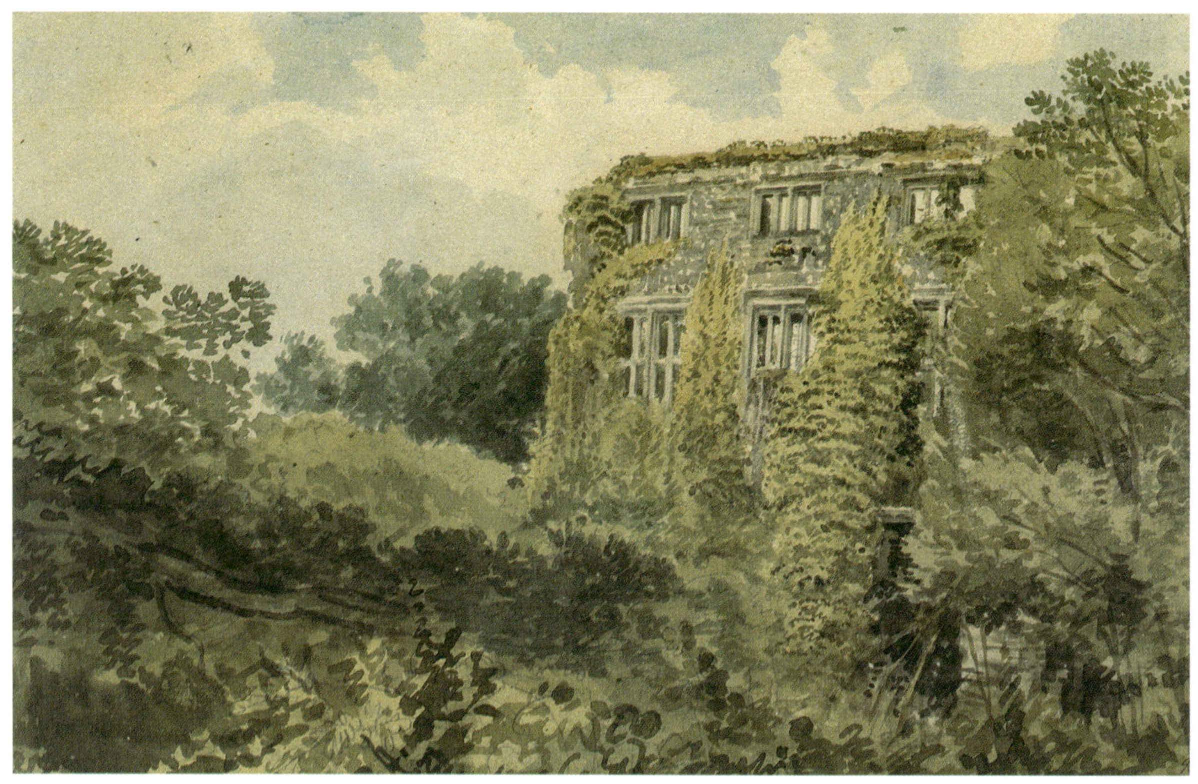

40. GEORGE ROBERT LEWIS, *Ilfracombe* (early 1850s)

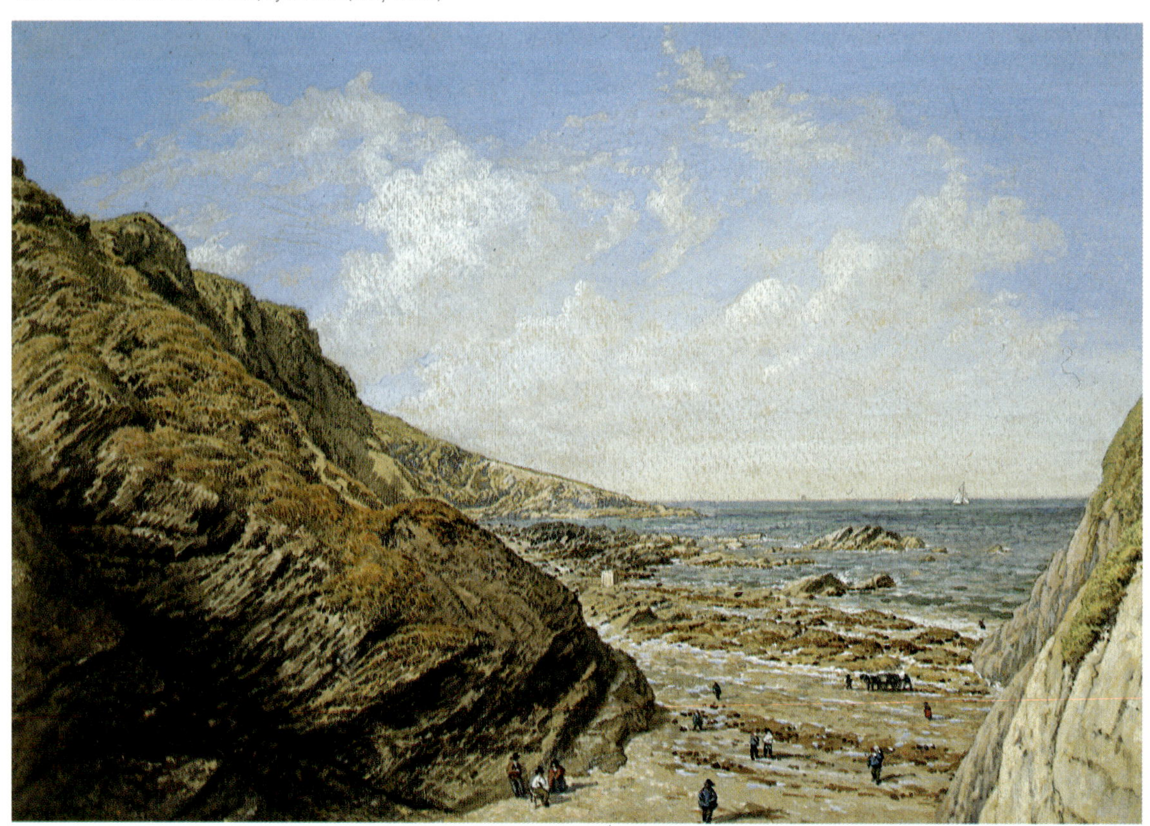

41. GEORGE ROBERT LEWIS, *Valley of the Rocks, Lynton* (early 1850s.)

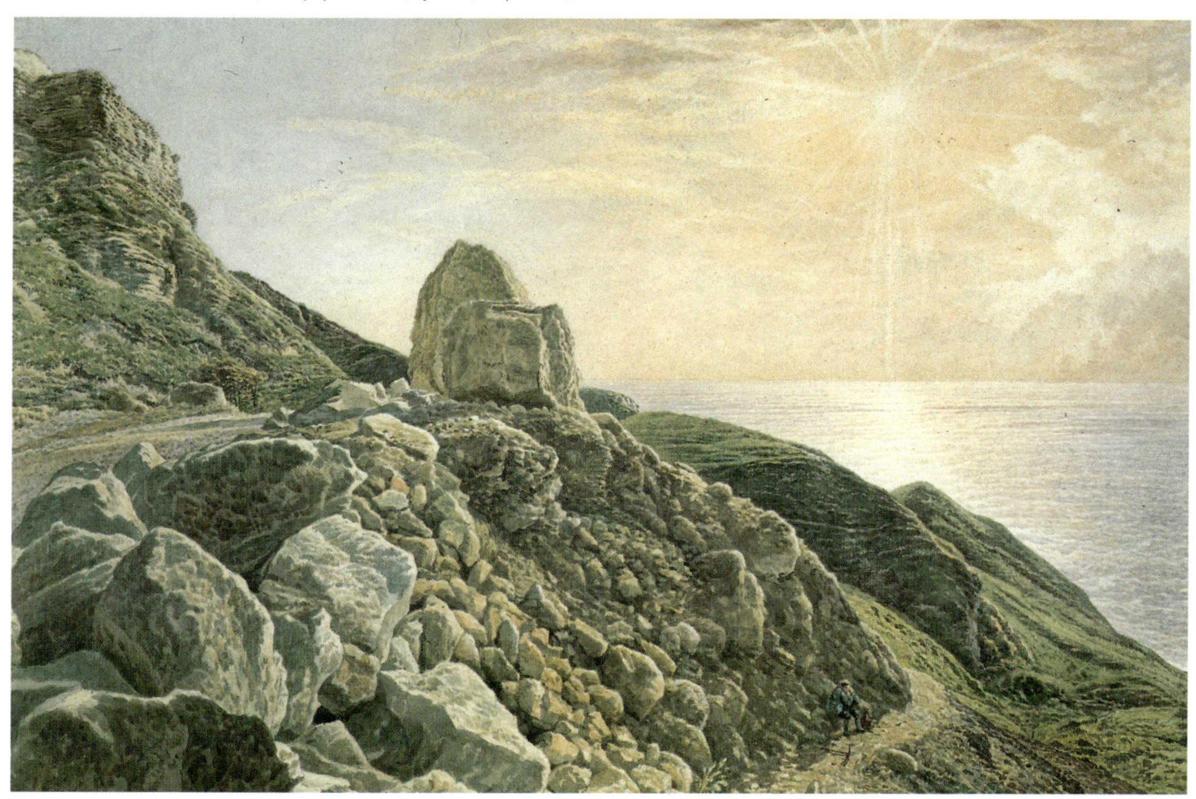

43. JOHN FREDERICK LEWIS, *Tavy* (?1829)

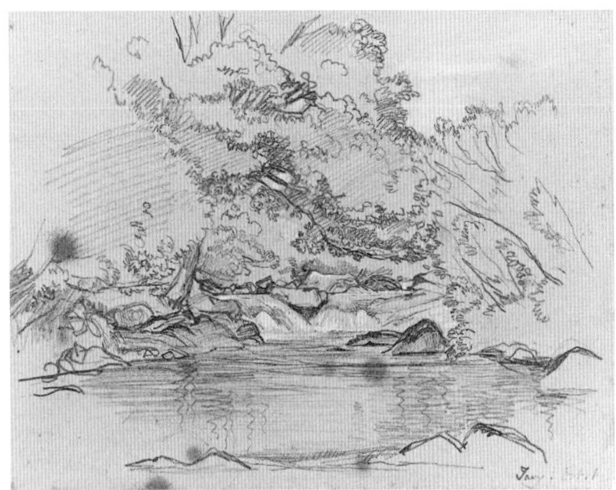

44. JOHN FREDERICK LEWIS, *Lynmouth* (?1829)

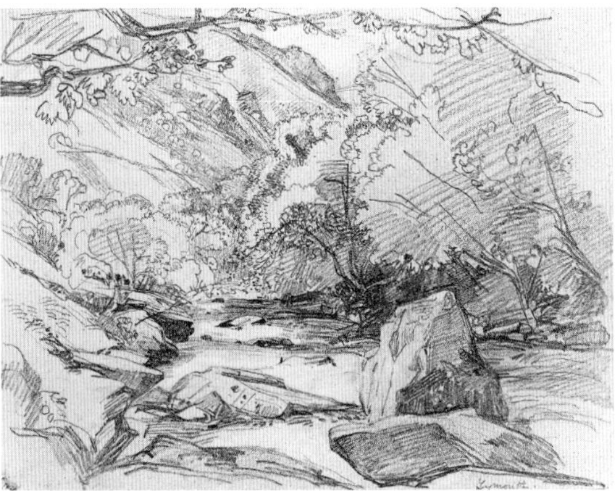

This impressive picture shows Lewis's qualities as a watercolour painter to their best effect. The handling of the foreground rocks is broad enough not to detain the eye's movement towards the centre of the composition, where the brightness of the declining sun and the reflected glare from the sea are brilliantly conveyed, dominating the painting's overall tonality. The massiveness of the foreground boulders is echoed in the almost architectural shapes of the rock formations on the hill above (whose size is indicated by the diminutive clump of trees below them) and the two huge outcrops which dominate the middle ground. Amidst the sublimity of nature Lewis has placed a stone-breaker, his head in his hands and his pick-axe discarded, sitting at the bottom of the rocky slope. The comparison between the magnitude of nature and the futility of the stone-breaker's labour could not be more exaggerated and as a result the heat and glare of the sun begin to take on a harsher aspect. (SS)

JOHN FREDERICK LEWIS (1805-1876)

42. *AboveShaugh* (?1829)
Pencil on paper, 11 x 14.2 cm
Inscribed 'above Shaw' (lower right)
Birmingham Museums and Art Gallery

43. *Tavy* (?1829)
Pencil on paper, 11.1 x 14.2 cm
Inscribed 'Tavy. Oct 1' (lower right)
Birmingham Museums and Art Gallery

44. *Lynmouth* (?1829)
Pencil on paper, 11.1 x 14.3 cm
Inscribed 'Lymouth' (lower right)
Birmingham Museums and Art Gallery

John Frederick Lewis is by far the best known of the Lewis family of artists and engravers. His father,

Frederick Christian Lewis (q.v.), was his teacher and it was probably with him that he visited Devon in 1829. By then John had already travelled abroad to Germany and Italy and it was with his foreign scenes that he was to go on to make his name, first with Spanish subjects (in the 1830s), and then with exotic subjects from the Middle East. George Robert Lewis (q.v.) was his uncle.

In 1830 John exhibited a group of Devon subjects at the Water Colour Society and it is reasonable to see cat.nos.42, 43 and 44 as sketches from the 1829 tour. The titles of these along with other known drawings and watercolours show that he visited north and south Devon.[1] An impressive watercolour merely called *The Glen* is almost certainly a depiction of The Glen at Chudleigh.[2] Another watercolour is of Lyneham near Plymouth.[3] A very picturesque scene of a water mill could be one of the 1830 exhibits and with its inclusion of a girl and some hens it has what Mrs Bray, in describing the mill at Tavistock which Lewis father and son both sketched, called 'the most animated accompaniments that a Morland or a Wilkie would have desired to complete their picture of rustic life.'[4] While staying with the Brays in 1829 John made drawings of Peter Tavy, a place his father pronounced 'unique in beauty and in subjects.'[5] (MP)

PHILIPPE JACQUES DE LOUTHERBOURG (1740-1812)

45. *Dartmouth Castle* (c.1786)
Pen and wash on paper, 12.9 x 19.2 cm
Inscribed 'Dartmouth Castle' (upper left)
National Library of Wales, Aberystwyth

De Loutherbourg trained as an artist in France and after some success there came to England in 1771. He became the principal scene painter for Garrick at Drury Lane and was elected to the Royal Academy in

45. PHILIPPE JACQUES DE LOUTHERBOURG, *Dartmouth Castle* (c.1786)

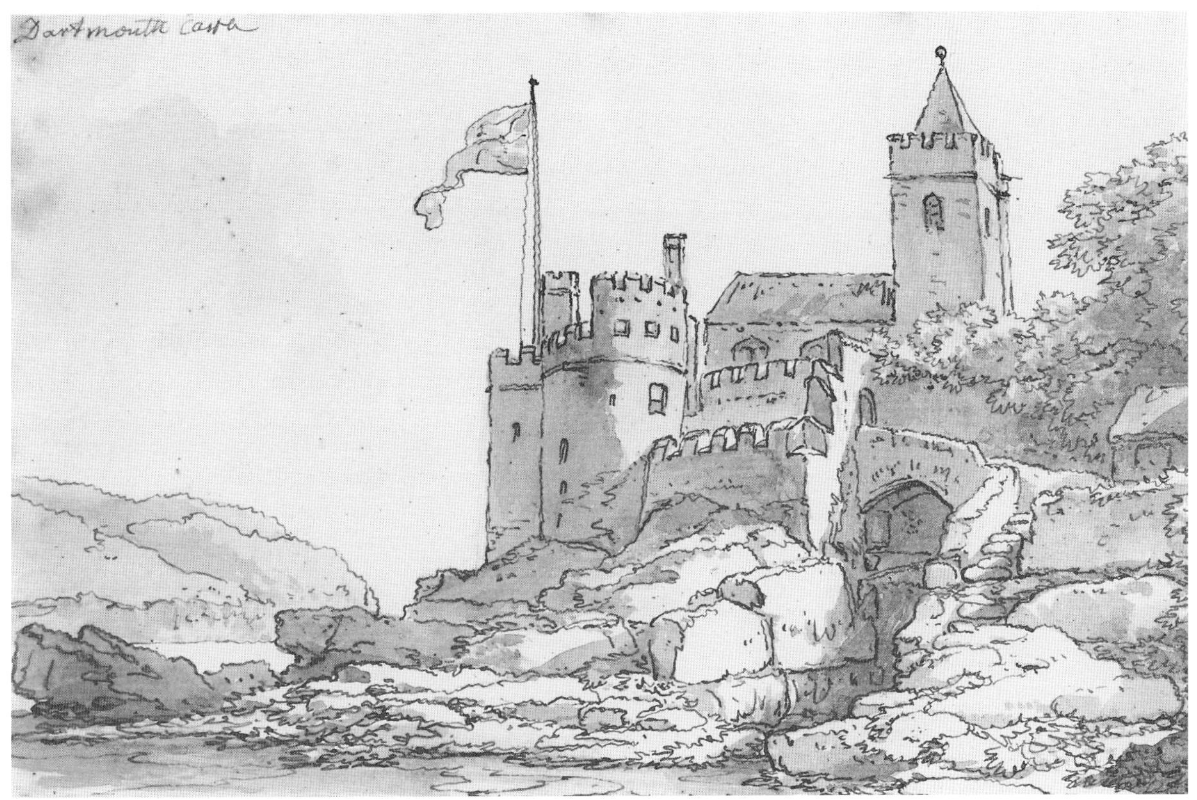

1781. Proficient as a history painter, he had won praise for his landscapes in France in the 1760s and maintained this interest in England, whose landscape he is credited as finding superior to continental examples.[1] He published *The Romantic and Picturesque Scenery of England and Wales* in 1805 and produced a number of landscapes in a style reminiscent of Ibbetson's.

De Loutherbourg's interest in British landscapes (and his tentative hold on English spelling) is indicated by the fact that this drawing comes from an album whose inscription lists various views of 'Devonshire Dorsetshire Barkshire Summersetshire Wilshire Oxfordshire Hamshire Glostershire.' His trip to Dorset and Devon should probably be dated to 1786, so making him one of the earliest artists to explore the county.[2] This is a good example of an artist looking out for picturesque subjects, positioning the castle for maximum effect by viewing it from below so that its outline breaks the skyline. The descriptive line is designed to exploit the massing of rocks and masonry without excessive detail cluttering the overall effect. Unassuming though it is, this drawing might stand for many similar notations produced by artists on picturesque tours in the late eighteenth century. W.G. Maton's description of Dartmouth itemises the site's picturesque appeal.

'The scenery of Dartmouth certainly presents a most exquisite treat to a landscape painter. The view towards the mouth of the harbour, in particular, exhibits such a happy assemblage of objects for a picture that it is perhaps scarcely to be exceeded. A rocky knoll projecting from the shore makes an admirable foreground. One of the side-screens is formed by the picturesque castle with the adjoining church, just emerging from a fine wood which enriches the right-hand side;- the other a high promontory, with a small fort at its feet;- whilst the main sea appears in front through a narrow opening, and leaves nothing for the imagination to wish for in the composition.'[3] (SS)

46. JOHN MIDDLETON, *Sunshine and Shade, Ivybridge* (c.1853-5)

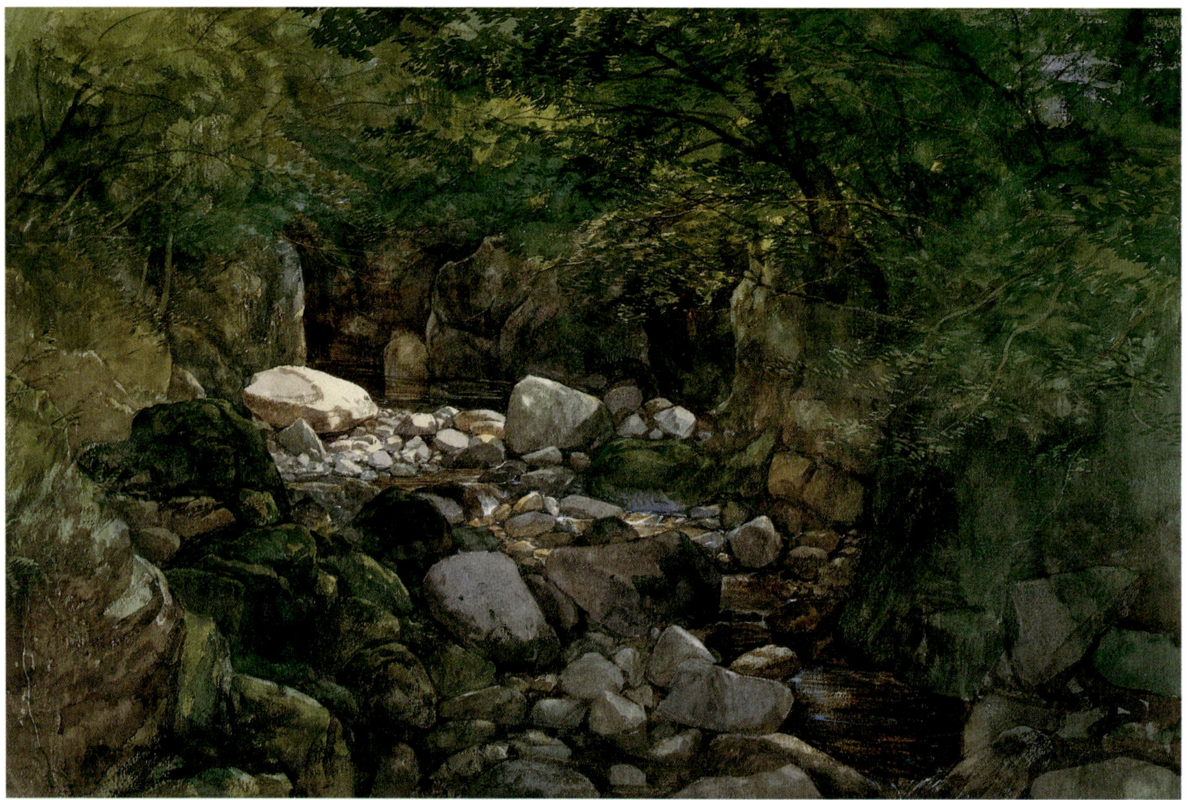

JOHN MIDDLETON (1827-1856)

46. *Sunshine and Shade, Ivybridge* (c.1853-5)
Watercolour heightened with bodycolour on paper,
32.9 x 48.5 cm
Norfolk Museums Service (Norwich Castle Museum)

John Middleton was a pupil in Norwich of Henry
Bright (q.v.). The fresh and direct style of sketching
from nature which is such a characteristic feature of
his best works was soon noticed in the art press.
Indeed he seems to have inspired his own teacher to
make less contrived studies when they went sketching
together. At times Middleton's style is also close to
Müller's (q.v.), whose skills as a sketcher were widely
admired:
'There is nothing we have ever seen in Water-Colour
art like his Welsh and Devonshire sketches - and he
was one of the few who understood the difference
between studies and pictures.'[1]
This quality Müller shared with Middleton, and in
each case their promising careers were cut tragically
short. Middleton died from consumption when he was
only twenty nine. He had already become a keen
photographer, and this kind of boulder-strewn river
bed with dappled light filtering through overhanging
trees was to become something of a favourite motif

with photographers in the 1850s. It was also in vogue
with drawing masters.
The dates of Middleton's trip(s) to Devon are not
recorded but he is known to have visited Lynmouth as
well as Ivy Bridge.[2] (MP)

WILLIAM JAMES MÜLLER (1812-1845)

Müller travelled to north Devon in the summer of
1844, shortly after his return to Bristol from Lycia in
Turkey and already suffering from the heart condition
which would kill him untimely in the following year.
Writing from Paris, on his way home, he speaks of his
intentions: 'I do not want to begin painting till
September or October. The Thames, about Windsor,
or the rivers of Devonshire will furnish my subjects.'[1]
He must have felt less fatigued than he anticipated for
he visited Lynmouth in July and remained there till
early September. He stayed at Highland Cottage,
accompanied by his brother and a fellow landscape
painter from Bristol, William West.[2] His biographer
Solly records that he made 'four or five oil-pictures,
painted entirely out of doors from nature, and two
dozen or more sketches and drawings in water-colour;
and his brother informs me that neither the oils nor
water-colours were ever touched or worked upon
afterwards.'[3] Writing from Lynmouth in August,

47. WILLIAM JAMES MÜLLER, *Rocky Stream at Lynmouth* (1844)

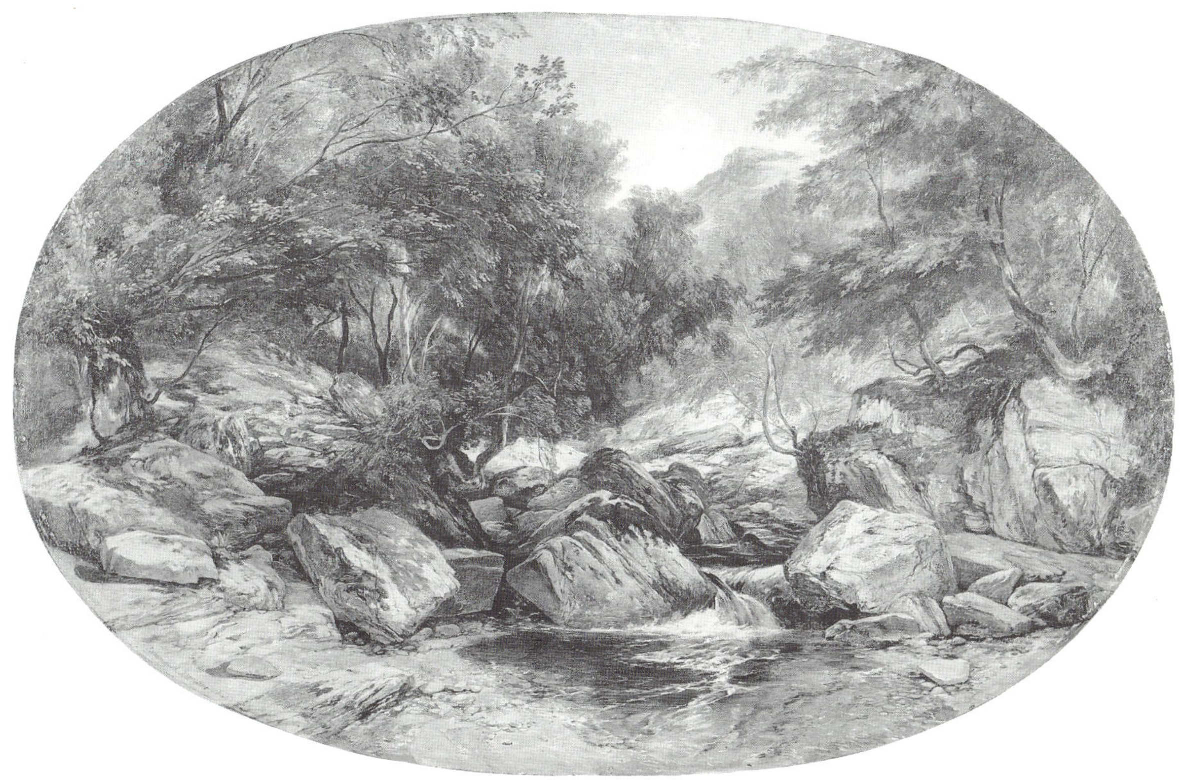

48. WILLIAM JAMES MÜLLER, *The Stag's Hollow, Lynmouth* (1844)

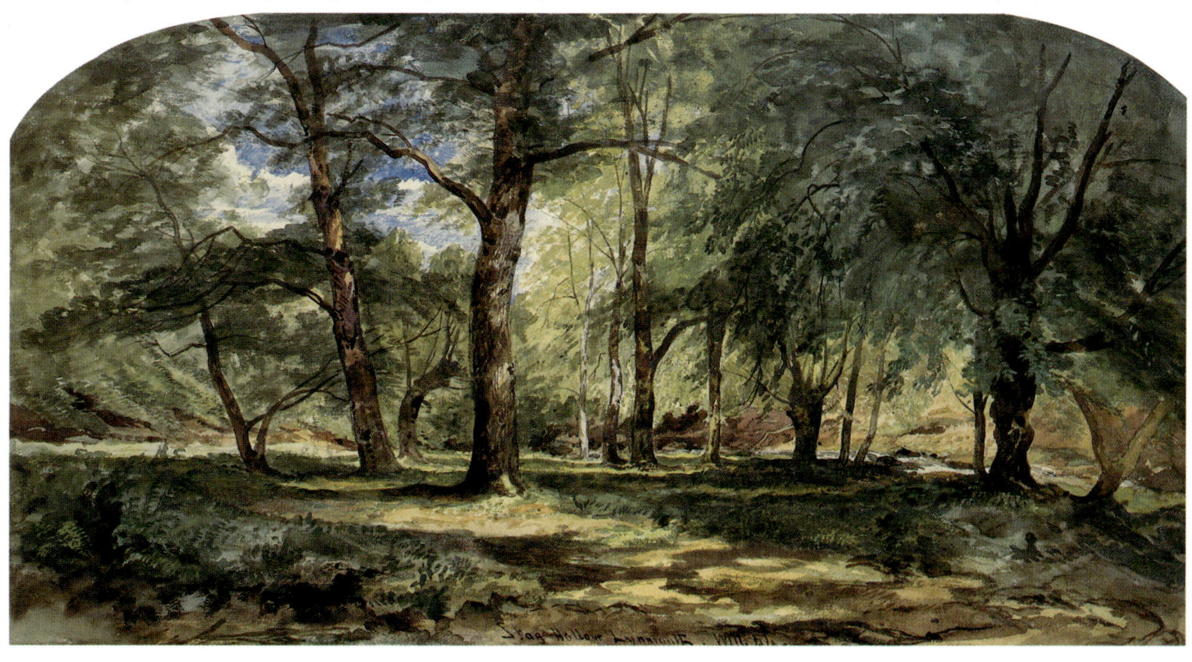

49. WILLIAM JAMES MÜLLER, *Lynmouth* (1844)

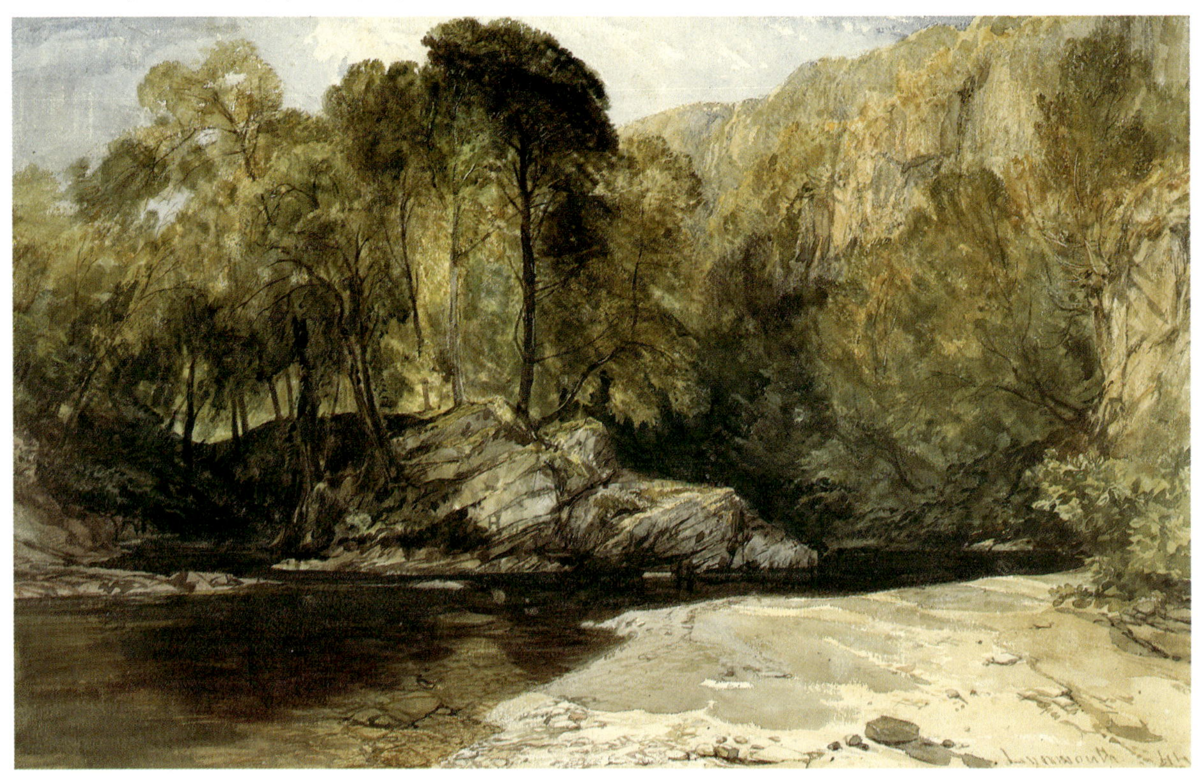

50. WILLIAM JAMES MÜLLER, *Lynton* (1844)

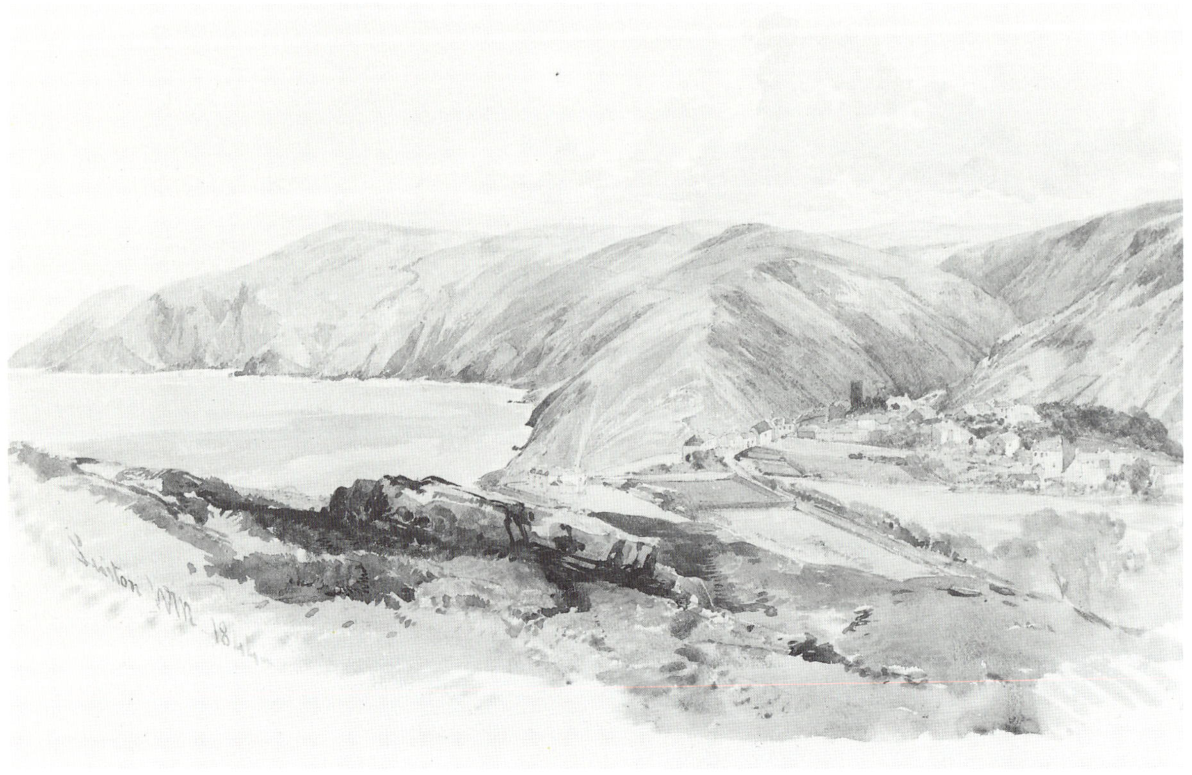

Müller notes that his stay was not exactly trouble-free. 'Here I am painting away. This week have had rain, wind, &c., so I am doing little; but, however disagreeable, I must keep to it three or four weeks longer.'[4]

47. *Rocky Stream at Lynmouth* (1844)
(Illustrated in colour on p.81)
Oil on canvas, 60.3 x 90.8 cm
Signed and dated 'Lynmouth. W. Müller.' 1844'
(lower left)
Bristol Museums and Art Gallery

Solly describes this picture, then in the collection of J.D. Weston, as follows:
'a clear stream of water falling over rocks, and sweeping round quiet, limpid pools, with overhanging trees. Neutral greys and yellows and very low-toned greens are the prevailing hues; you appear to see the stones underneath the water, and to partake of the delicious coolness of this retired glen. Although the handling is broad, there is no apparent want of finish. The painting is solid, and, like his other Lynmouth subjects, there is plenty of chiaroscuro.'[5]
It has been suggested that Müller's attention to geological detail here may have been influenced by his companion, William West, whose own work shares such concerns.[6]

48. *The Stag's Hollow, Lynmouth* (1844)
(Illustrated in colour on p.81)
Watercolour on paper, 59.1 x 80.5 cm
Signed and inscribed 'Stag Hollow WM' (lower centre)
Royal Albert Memorial Museum, Exeter

This freely-painted watercolour shows Müller responding to the particular beauties of Lynmouth's glades, perhaps finding in them similarities to the landscapes he knew around Clifton, in Bristol. Solly includes a lengthy appreciation of Müller's activities as a sketcher which is worth repeating.
'Müller knew well that a sketch ought not to be a finished work, but a vivid, true, yet generalised impression of the scene - a sort of compromise, in fact, wherein the soul or spirit of the scene was caught and rapidly made his own. In his later sketches of English country scenes... this *poetical* rendering of the subject is very striking.'[7]

This certainly seems to be true of this picture which is very free, even impetuous, in its use of what Solly refers to as 'broad washes and sweeps of his brush, supplemented by rapid markings and hatchings.'[8] Most of the sketches produced at Lynmouth were described by Solly as having 'a quiet, peaceful charm of their own - silvery, low in tone, and broad - different, in truth, from any others.'[9] Although this sketch is certainly broad, its colouring is warmer and its tone more varied than Solly suggests, while the other watercolours by Müller assembled here show that he used a variety of approaches when sketching at Lynmouth.

49. *Lynmouth* (1844)
(Illustrated in colour on p.82)
Watercolour on paper, 34.8 x 53.5 cm
Inscribed 'Lynmouth, 44. W.M.'
Trustees of the British Museum

This watercolour accentuates the drama of the site, using abrupt contrasts of light and shade to heighten the effect. In the foreground a sandy, sun-lit shore establishes a warm tone to the picture which is picked up again in the light striking the cliffs in the background. Between these two zones flows the river Lynn whose water is pellucid when it swirls over the brown stream-bed nearest to us but becomes almost black as it emerges from behind the rocky bank covered with pines and other trees. The north Devon coast was celebrated for its dramatic scenery and had great artistic potential as a sublime landscape; Müller has captured that sublimity to produce this powerful image.

50. *Lynton* (1844)
Watercolour on paper, 35.2 x 52.6 cm
Inscribed 'Lynton W.M. 1844'
Trustees of the British Museum

Lynton is an unfinished watercolour, topographical in intention and panoramic in scope and so less concerned with that close-focused attention which typifies Müller's north Devon landscapes. Rather unusually, it concentrates on the village and its relationship to the surrounding hills and headlands instead of the precipitous road leading down to Lynmouth, which was very much the mainstay of most images of the place. Müller's vantage point is above the North Walk, a popular promenade which offered spectacular views to tourists along the cliff top from Lynton to the Valley of the Rocks. (SS)

51. JOHN WILLIAM NORTH, *In An Orchard, Devon* (1864)

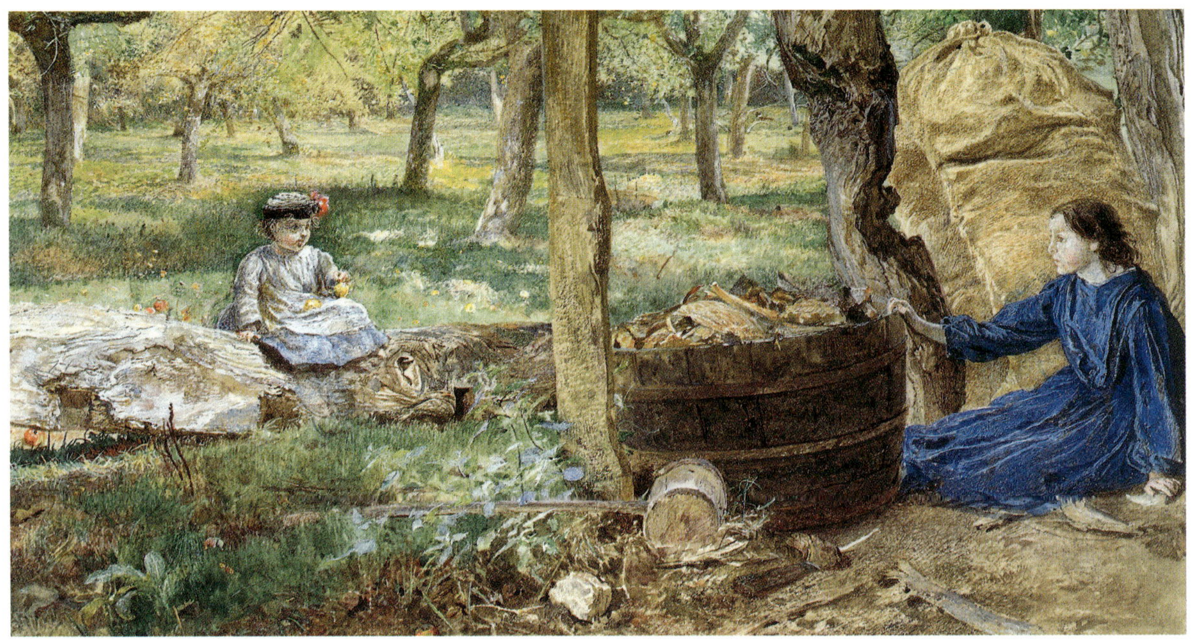

52. SAMUEL PALMER, *From the Castle Hotel, Lynton, North Devon* (1834)

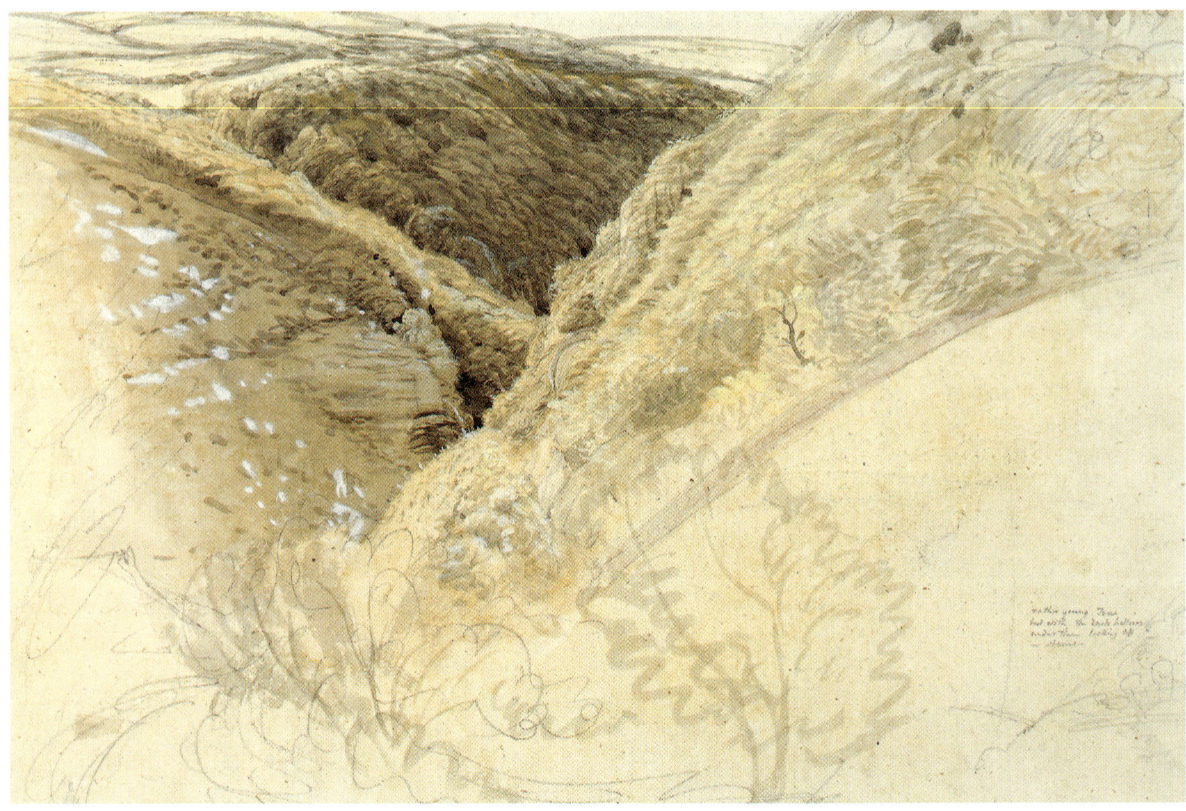

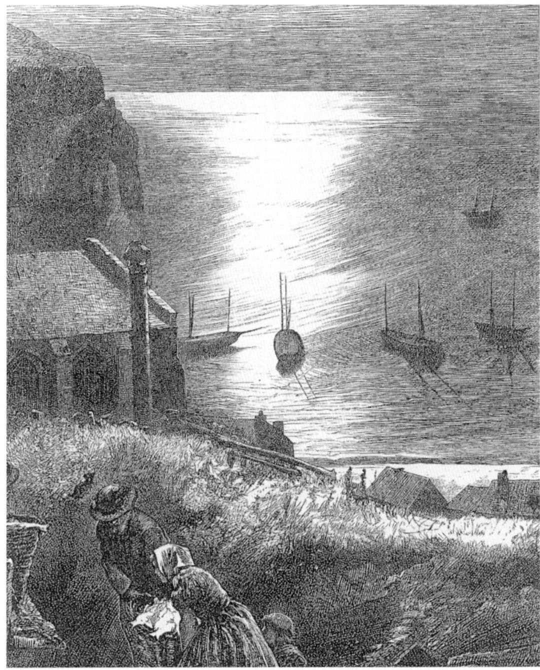

Fig.24. J.W. NORTH, engraved Dalziel, *On the Shore (Seaton)*, wood engraving, from *Wayside Posies*, 1867, p. 18.

JOHN WILLIAM NORTH (1842-1924)

51. *In An Orchard, Devon* (1864)
(Illustrated in colour on p.84)
Watercolour on paper, 11.8 x 21 cm
Dated in ink on reverse
The Board of Trustees of the
Victoria and Albert Museum, London

This exquisitely detailed watercolour is the work of a still unduly neglected artist whose landscapes were more often made in pen and ink to be engraved as black and white wood engravings. They are to be found in some of the finest illustrated books of the Victorian era. One such is *Wayside Posies* (1867) in which his own highly original compositions appear with those of his friends Fred Walker(q.v. in *Sketching from Nature*) and G.J. Pinwell. One at least of North's illustrations in *Wayside Posies* was engraved from a sketch made at Seaton in Devon to complement a poem called 'On the Shore' (fig. 24).[1] It is possible that *In An Orchard, Devon*, the watercolour here exhibited, may be connected with another of the illustrations in *Wayside Posies* engraved from an attractive watercolour, *King Pippin*, by Pinwell in the British Museum.[2] Whatever its potential connection with some literary theme it exists independently as a marvelous example of a highly finished Victorian watercolour, gem-like in its brilliant colour, dappled light, and attention to different textures such as tree bark and clothing. (MP)

SAMUEL PALMER (1805-1881)

52. *From the Castle Hotel, Lynton, North Devon* (1834)
(Illustrated in colour on p.84)
Pencil, watercolour and bodycolour on buff woven paper, 23.1 x 34.2 cm
Inscribed 'From Castle Hotel Linton D. N. Devon.' (lower left) and 'rather young Trees/ but with the dark hollows/ under them looking up/ - stems - Nightingale' (lower right)
Courtauld Institute Galleries, London
(Spooner Bequest)

Samuel Palmer was much inspired by the scenery of Devon, both in the north of the county and in the south, on the fringes of Dartmoor. Between 1834 and 1859 he made at least four trips and his letters reveal his lasting attachment to 'dear spongy Devon.'[1] Even as he worked on his invented landscapes inspired by Milton and Virgil he was 'quite haunted' by recollections of Devon, attempting to 'get its quintessence.'[2] As his son wrote: 'he idealized Devonshire, just as he idealized Italy - it enriched his imagination and influenced his choice of subject.'[3] The work exhibited here is a far cry from the imaginative invented landscapes of Palmer's later years. 'Sketches and pictures are wholly different things' as he wrote when he agreed, as late as 1864-5, to exhibit three of his Devon sketches, made years earlier, at the Water Colour Society.[4] One he called *A Study of a Middle Distance* which is also what we have here where he depicts what he well termed 'the playful heave and tumble of the lines in the hills.'[5] 'Woods and woody hills must be juicy and rich' as he wrote from Clovelly in 1849. This particular sketch has been ascribed to his first Devon visit of 1834. Palmer was a great admirer of Murray's *Hand-Book for Travellers in Devon and Cornwall*, first published in 1851. It contained, he wrote, 'a real feeling of the characteristic beauties,' 'a real savour of Devonshire perception.'[6] (MP)

WILLIAM PAYNE (1760-1830)

53. *Oakhampton Castle* (1815)
Watercolour on paper, 23.7 x 35.0 cm
Signed 'W.Payne 1815' (lower right)
Lent by the Syndics of the Fitzwilliam Museum, Cambridge

The facts of William Payne's career and even the exact dates of his birth and death have only recently been determined. This new research was incorporated in an exhibition in Exeter in 1992.[1] Payne was born in London and was not a native Devonian as had been generally believed. He worked for the Board of Ordnance in Plymouth as a draughtsman and then, in

53. WILLIAM PAYNE, *Oakhampton Castle* (1815)

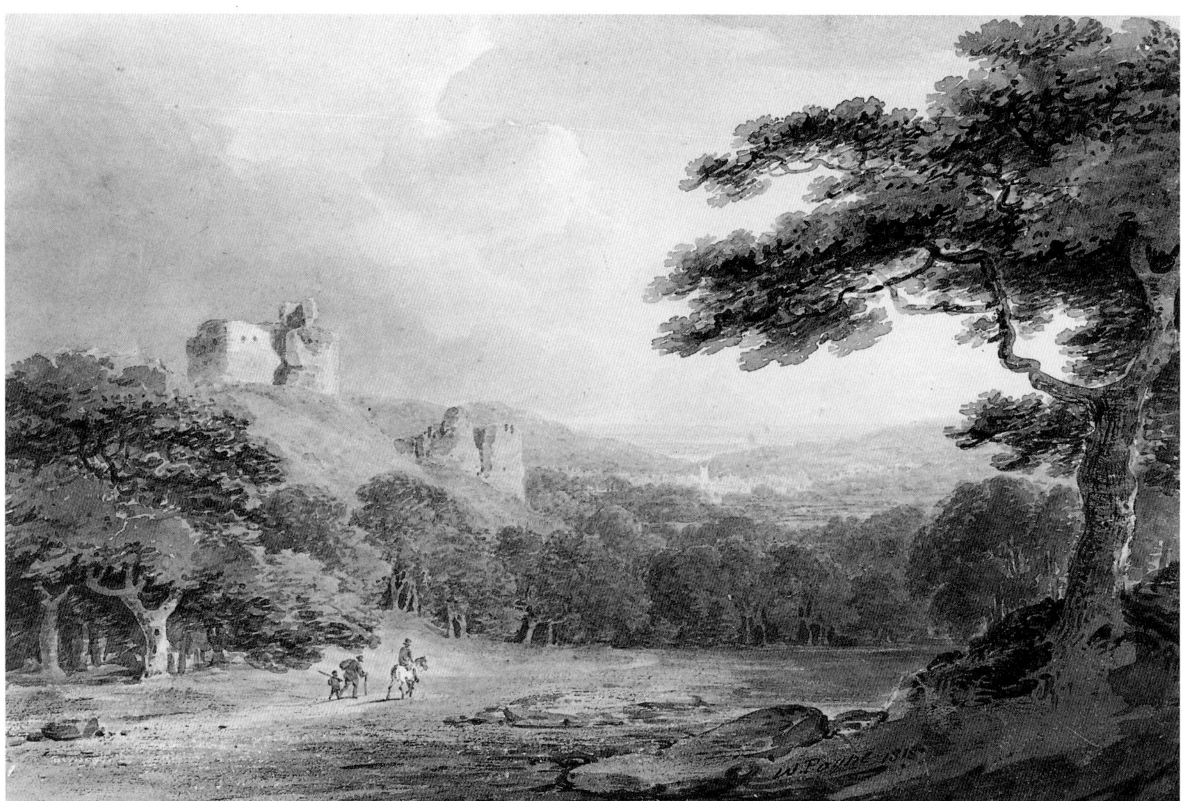

Fig.25. J.M.W. TURNER, engraved C. Turner, *Okehampton Castle on the River Okement*, mezzotint, from *Rivers of England*, 1825.

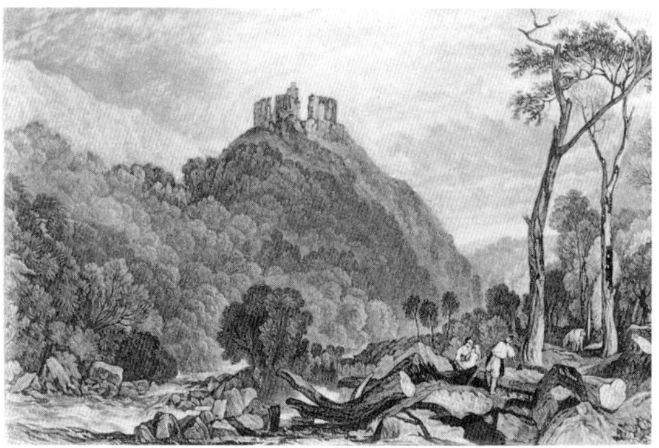

the 1790s, became a fashionable drawing master in London. He exhibited many Devon subjects there between 1786 and 1790 and then again from 1809 to 1830.[2] He made various sketching tours to the west country and one such tour, made in 1793, is very fully documented in no fewer than eighty-six small watercolours bound into two volumes.[3] These belonged to the Rev. John Swete of Oxton House, near Dawlish, who may have had lessons from Payne. He documented and illustrated his own Devon tours and was often consulted by visiting artists such as Farington (q.v.).

Okehampton Castle was often depicted and was chosen by Richard Wilson (q.v.) as a companion subject for his *Lydford Waterfall* (cat.no.86). Payne here produced a typical exercise in the Gilpinesque Picturesque, the rather obvious framing tree and generalized foreground opening up a richly wooded scene capped by the castle ruins. Okehampton is in the distance; the obligatory group of travellers gives human interest and scale.[4] Turner made two different views of Okehampton Castle (fig.25) drawing attention in each to the felling of the trees, something commented upon by T.H. Williams in 1804: 'The inhabitants... must survey with painful sensations this rapid destruction of the fine woods, which, stretched for some miles beyond the castle, afford in the summer heats an extensive shady walk, refreshingly cool, and allow the delighted eye, from the various openings, to view the different effect of the ruins from opposite positions.'[5] (MP)

AARON PENLEY (1807-1870)

54. *From Castle Hill, Devon* (1842)
Pencil and watercolour on paper, 24.8 x 27.3 cm
Inscribed 'A. Penley. from Castle Hill Devon. cornfields' (lower centre)
Lent by the Syndics of the Fitzwilliam Museum, Cambridge

54. AARON PENLEY, *From Castle Hill, Devon* (1842)

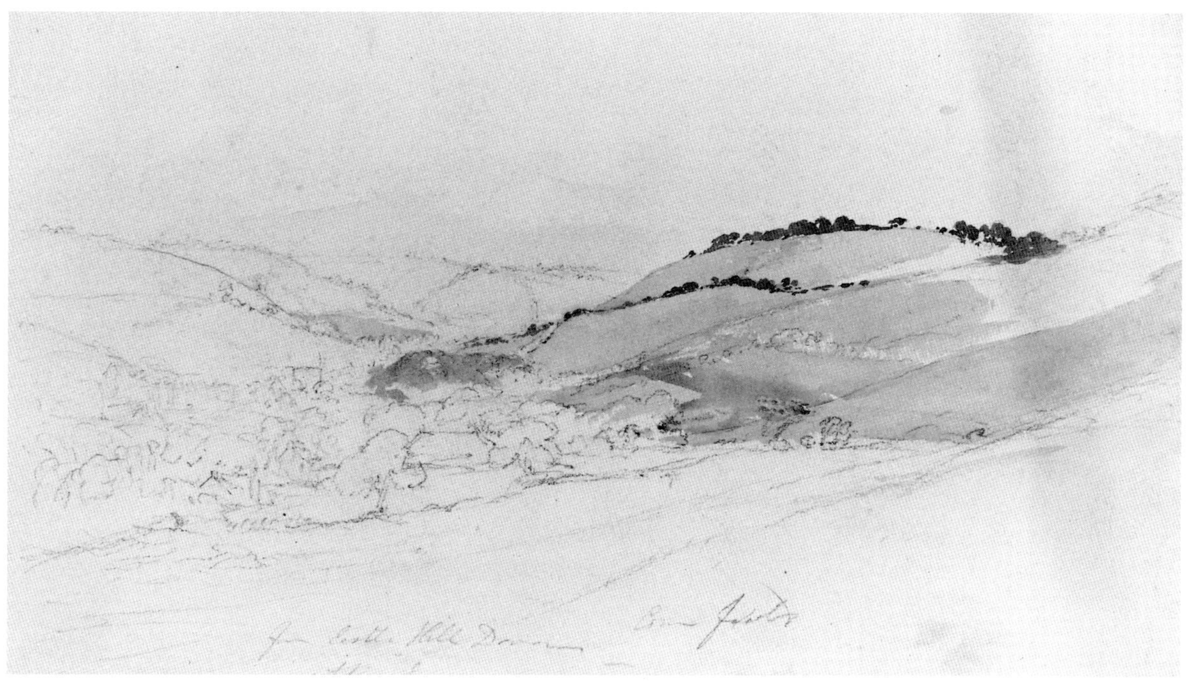

Fig.26. A. PENLEY, *Farmhouse at Ilfracombe*, chromolithograph, from *The Chromolithograph*, August 1868, p. 274.

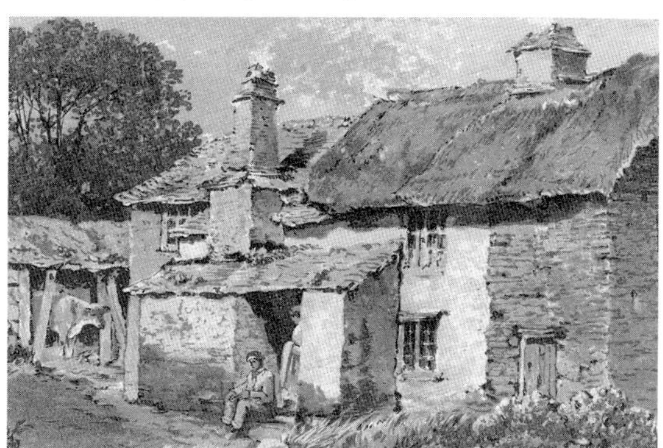

Penley is chiefly remembered as a drawing master and author of artists' manuals, who taught at Addiscombe East India College and the Military Academy at Woolwich and was appointed watercolour painter to William IV and Queen Adelaide. He probably made this drawing in the spring or summer of 1842 when he was working in Devon.[1] Earlier in the year he had placed advertisements in a Plymouth newspaper, announcing his intention to work in that town, providing 'portraits, miniatures and instruction' which included sketching outdoors.[2] He showed three pictures at Exeter and four at Plymouth in that year's autumn exhibitions and had two works chosen as three guinea prizes in the West of England Art Union.[3] Castle Hill is a mansion and park in north Devon, between Barnstaple and South Molton, belonging to

the Fortescue family. In 1842-3 the architect Edward Blore was altering this once Palladian house but the 830 acre park, with its sham village and 'ruinated' triumphal arch was left alone. It was, and is, one of the most impressive 'great houses' in Devon and was included on many tourists' itineraries. Penley's drawing is taken from the park, probably looking towards the village of Filleigh.

His *Farmhouse near Ilfracombe*, which presumably also derives from this tour, was published in *The Chromolithograph*, August 8, 1868 (fig. 26).[4] (SS)

WILLIAM PITT (fl.1849-1900)

55. *Clovelly, Devon* (c.1850s)
Pencil on paper, 43.5 x 33 cm
Inscribed 'Clovelly Devon. W.P.' (lower right)
Birmingham Museums and Art Gallery

56. *Clovelly* (c.1850s)
Pencil on paper, 39.9 x 30 cm
Inscribed 'Clovell(y)' (lower right)
Birmingham Museums and Art Gallery

Not much is known about William Pitt who lived in Birmingham and London, exhibiting widely at the Royal Academy, the British Institution and the Society of British Artists. His Devon-based subjects are a feature of the 1850s and 1860s, though most of them are of south Devon subjects.[1] Birmingham Museum and Art Gallery has a collection of over 300 pencil drawings by Pitt, chiefly of picturesque subjects in Devon and Cornwall.

Both drawings depict the same group of houses, which can still be seen today, on the street up from Clovelly quay. Sketching at Clovelly allowed artists to exploit the dramatic site for compositional purposes and here the oblique angle of view from a low vantage point is emphasised. If we compare cat.no.56 with S.H. Baker's study (cat.no.1) we can see that Pitt stresses the verticality of the scene by positioning himself lower down than Baker.

Pitt's second sketch (cat.no.55) is of the same group of houses, looking back at them from the street leading down to the harbour. Again he emphasises the vertical (it is what Clovelly was famous for, after all), bringing to mind Dickens and Wilkie Collins's description: '... the village was built sheer up the face of a steep and lofty cliff. There was no road in it, there was no wheeled vehicle in it, there was not a level yard in it. From the sea-beach to the cliff-top two irregular rows of white houses, placed opposite to one another, and twisting here and there, and there and here, rose, like the sides of a long succession of stages of crooked ladders.'[2]

Pitt's drawing style is spare and linear, drawing attention to specific features with an emphatic strengthening of line. Although he does not employ the same richness of tonal effect as Baker, he is able to indicate the play of sunlight on the houses by differentiating abruptly between darkly shadowed openings and the untouched paper next to them. (SS)

JOHN SKINNER PROUT (1806-1876)

57. *Ivybridge* (1836)
Watercolour and bodycolour with graphite on blue paper, 45.1 x 31.7 cm
Inscribed 'Ivy Bridge, Devon, July 19, 36' (lower left)
Trustees of the British Museum

John Skinner Prout was born in Plymouth and was a nephew of Samuel Prout (q.v.), but he moved away from Devon early and made his career elsewhere in England and in Australia. He passed his early adulthood in Bristol where he worked alongside members of the Bristol School, especially Müller (q.v.) with whom he toured Wales in 1833.

This study of Ivybridge is testament to its continuing popularity seventy years after Richards painted it in the 1760s (cat.no.62). Prout's position here is almost identical to Turner's (cat.no.76), which he may have known from its engraving although one suspects that this was simply the best naturally composed view to be had. In comparison with many of the finished pictures shown in this exhibition, this study from nature gives an insight into their often modest origins.

It is difficult to determine how extensive Prout's 1836 tour may have been, but the existence of engravings of *Clovelly* and *Lynmouth* published c.1837-40, suggest

56. WILLIAM PITT, *Clovelly* (c.1850s)

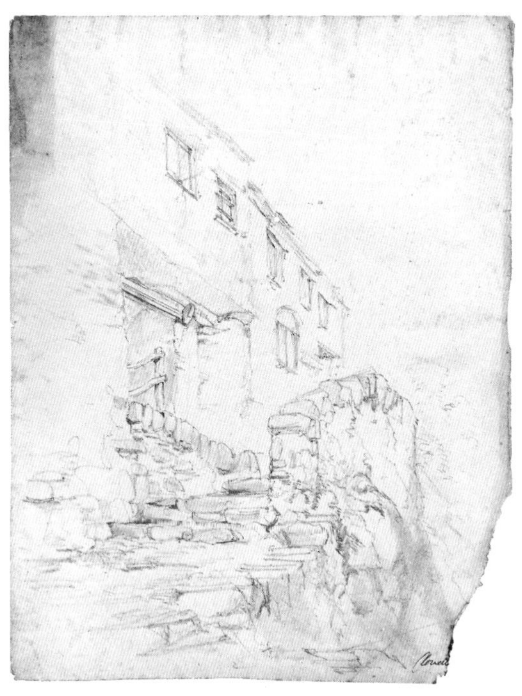

55. WILLIAM PITT, *Clovelly, Devon* (c.1850s)

that he may have visited north Devon too.[1] The British Museum owns an earlier drawing from this tour of *Sheepstor, Devon* dated July 9, 1836 so it seems likely that Prout stopped at Ivybridge on his way back from Devon. (SS)

57. JOHN SKINNER PROUT, *Ivybridge* (1836)

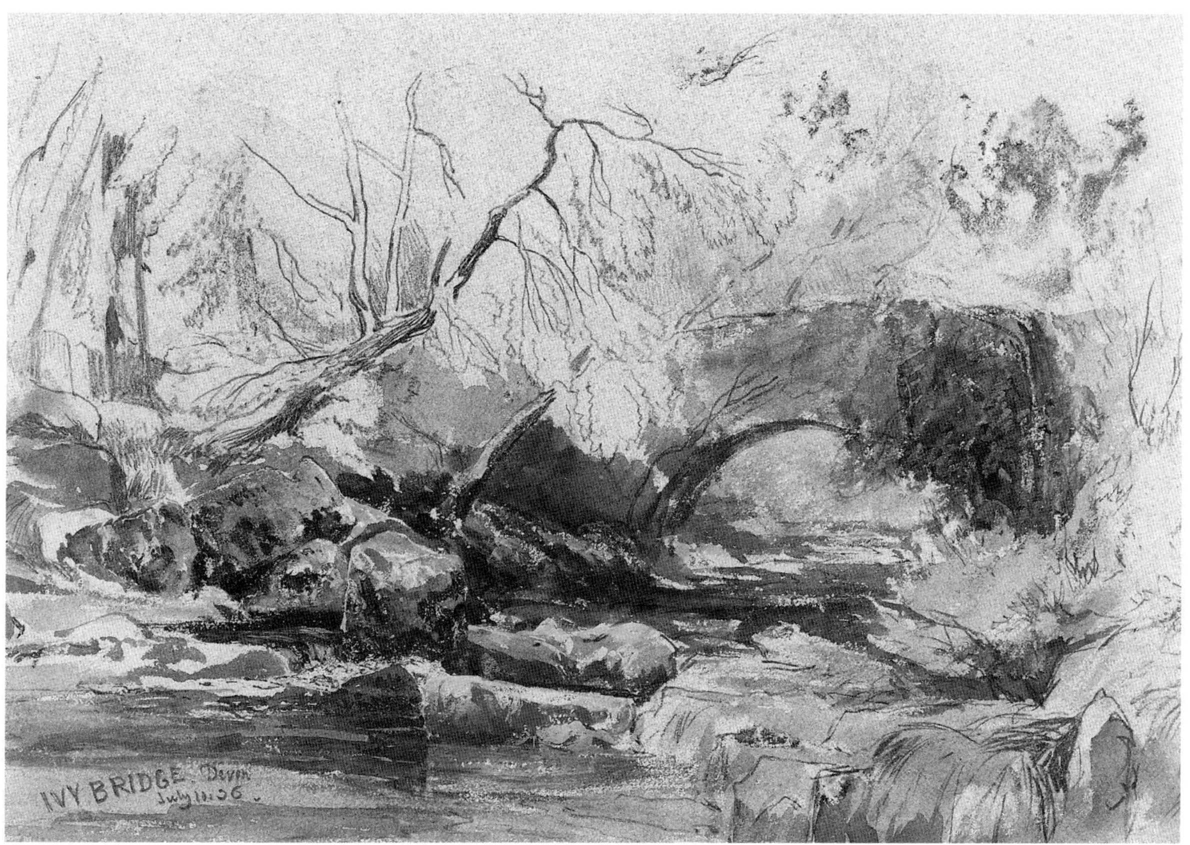

SAMUEL PROUT (1783-1852)

58. *South Zeal, Devon* (1806)
Watercolour over traces of pencil on paper,
13.9 x 19.6 cm
signed and dated 'S.Prout. 1806' (lower left centre)
Lent by the Syndics of the Fitzwilliam Museum,
Cambridge

59. *Torbrian*
Softground etching, 29.7 x 44.2 cm
Published by T. Palser, 1811

60. *At Ide*
Softground etching, 28.3 x 18.7 cm
From *A Series of Views of Rural Cottages in the West of
England Drawn and Etched in the Manner of Chalk*,
published by R. Ackermann, 1819

61. *On Dartmoor*
Softground etching, 27.4 x 19.2 cm
From *A Series of Views of Rural Cottages in the West of
England Drawn and Etched in the Manner of Chalk*,
published by R. Ackermann, 1819

Prout was born in Plymouth and received his first
instruction in art there from T.H.Williams and A.B.
Johns. His career, however, was destined to be a
metropolitan one and he moved to London in 1802.
This watercolour (cat.no.58) is a characteristic
example of Prout's early work and dates from the three
years he spent back in Plymouth from 1805 to 1808,
following a bout of ill health in London. In a letter to
his patron and employer, John Britton, dated 1805, he
speaks of Dartmoor's recuperative properties and the
origins of this picture.
'I am just returned after a months visit to the
Dartmoors. I feel much strength from the influence of
its pure air, and little Prout stands as firm as a Lion.
My object has not been so much to make sketches as
to find health. She lives on the highest torrs. I have
her blessing. The subjects in my portfolio are generally
rock-scenery, most of them coloured and highly
finished from nature... I have made sketches of the vale
at Lidford, Oakhampton and castle, the cross and
chapel at South-Zeal, Credition, the Logan-stone, &c.'[1]
As his health improved Prout resumed his former
practice of making studies of vernacular architecture.
His first exhibit at the Royal Academy in 1803 had
been *Bennet's Cottage on the Tamar, near Plymouth* [2]

58. SAMUEL PROUT, *South Zeal, Devon* (1806)

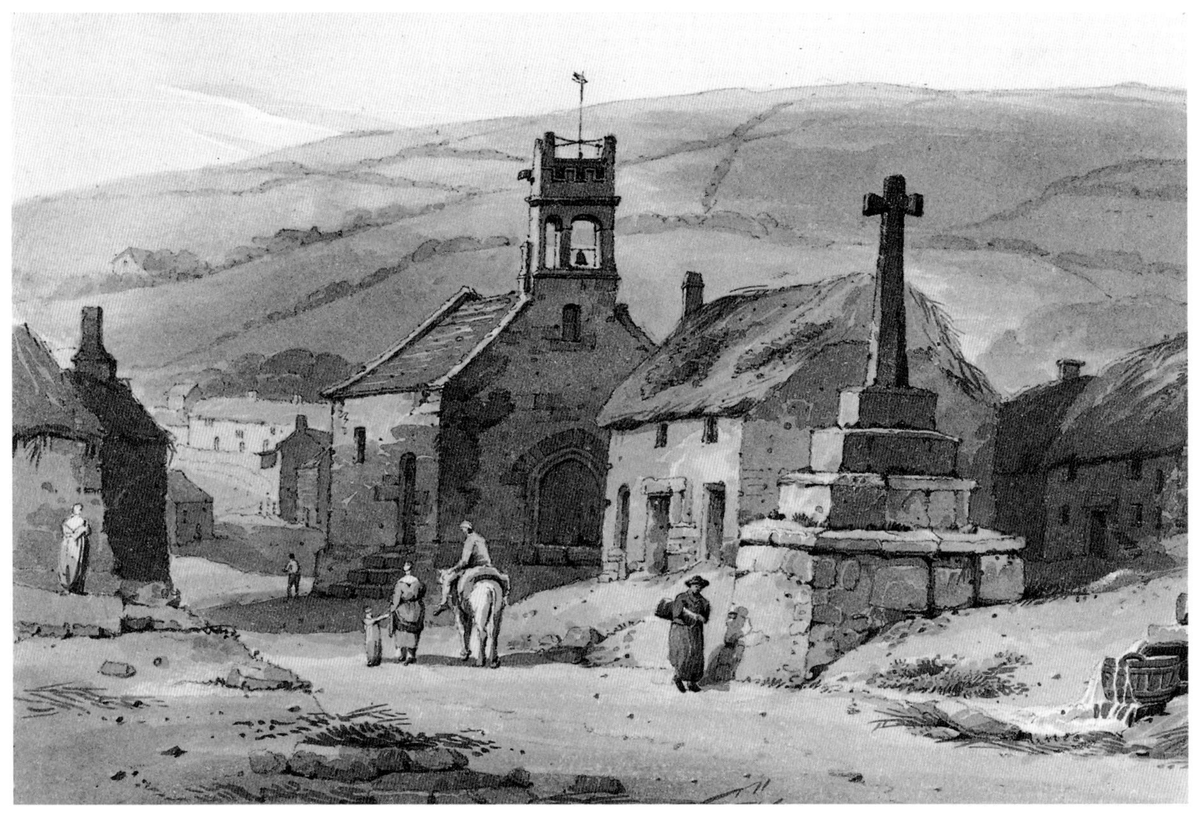

59. SAMUEL PROUT, *Torbrian* (1811)

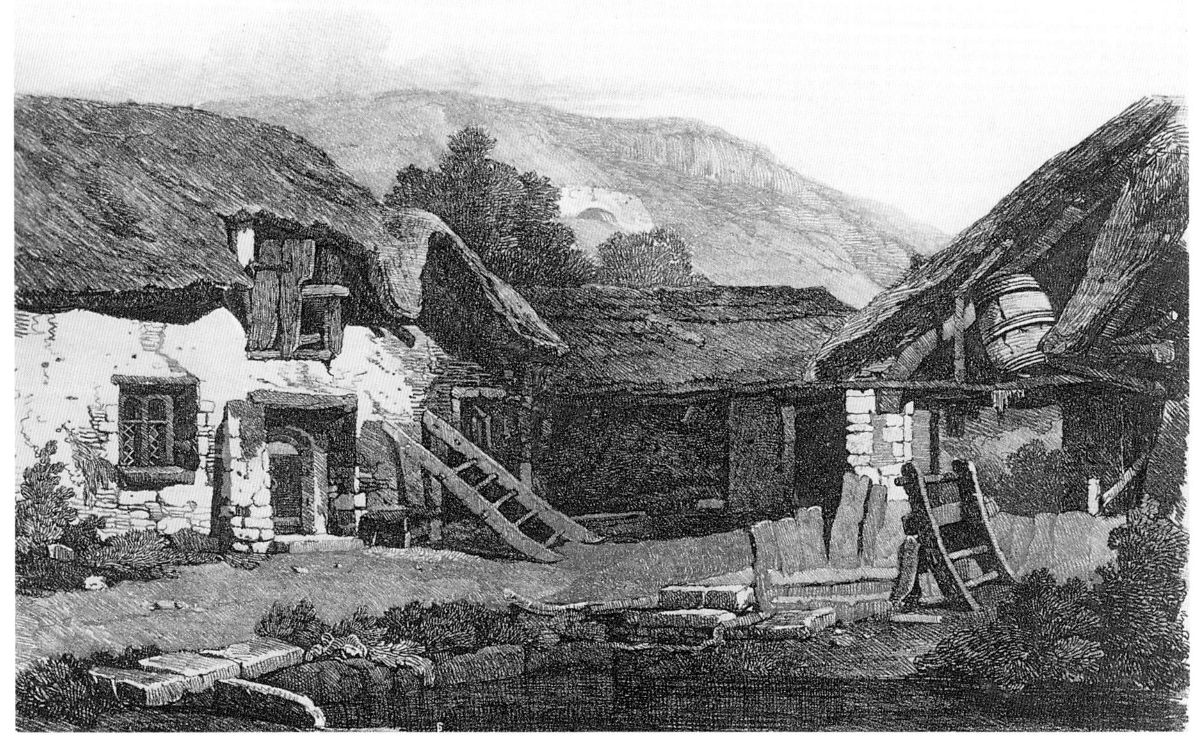

and he exhibited views of picturesque Devon at the
London exhibitions on his resumption in 1808 until
the 1820s. (A picture by Prout entitled *Zeal, Devon*
was shown at the Royal Academy in 1813). Like a lot
of his work in this period the composition of *South
Zeal, Devon* relies on a tried and tested formula of
construction. Prout establishes visual interest in the
granite cross, which anchors one end of a diagonal
moving through a pattern of light and shade to a
strongly lit feature closing the view. The simplicity of
outline and rhythmic alternation of light and shade
lend themselves to engraving which is, of course, how
most people would have encountered his work.
Prout exploited the picturesque attractions of Devon
cottages in many of his early publications although he
did not, as it were, 'invent' this genre. He had a
notable predecessor in one of his teachers, Thomas
Hewitt Williams whose *Picturesque Excursions in
Devon and Cornwall* was published in 1804,[3] but it is
Prout's name that became chiefly associated with this
sort of subject matter. Using soft-ground etching, a
sequence of publications began in 1812 with
*Picturesque Delineations in the Counties of Devon and
Cornwall* (24 plates, published by T. Palser). *Prout's
Village Scenery* followed in 1813 (11 plates also
published by Palser). *Picturesque Studies of Cottages,
Old Houses, Castles, Bridges, Ruins etc.* (16 plates,
published by Ackermann) appeared in 1816 and
*A Series of Views of Rural Cottages in the West of
England* (12 plates, also published by Ackermann)
in 1819.[4]
To these should be added the ubiquitous appearance of
West Country buildings in Prout's drawing manuals,
such as *Rudiments of Landscape in Progressive Studies*
(1813-4) and *Progressive Fragments* (1817). It is
evident that he had identified a particular approach to
this sort of material which was eminently marketable
(the fact of his 1813 publication bearing his name is
not unique in his output) and given the popularity of
such manuals in the hands of professionals and
amateurs alike it is fair to regard Prout as codifying
picturesque perceptions of Devon for many visitors in
the 1810s and afterwards. (SS)

60. SAMUEL PROUT, *At Ide* (1819)

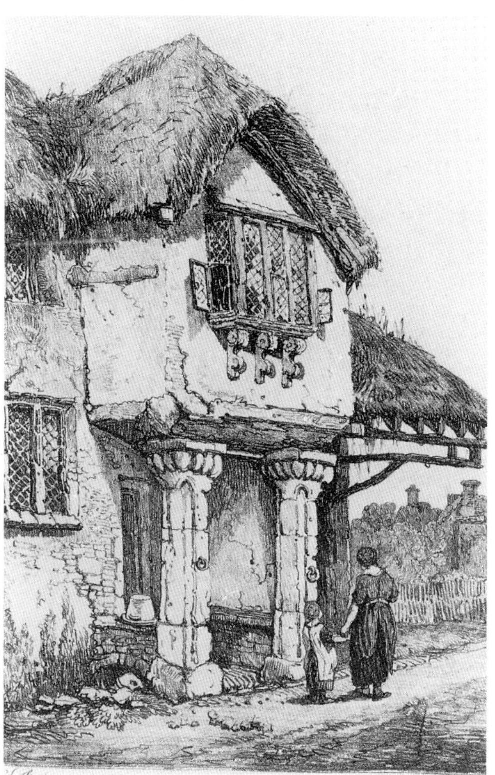

61. SAMUEL PROUT, *On Dartmoor* (1819)

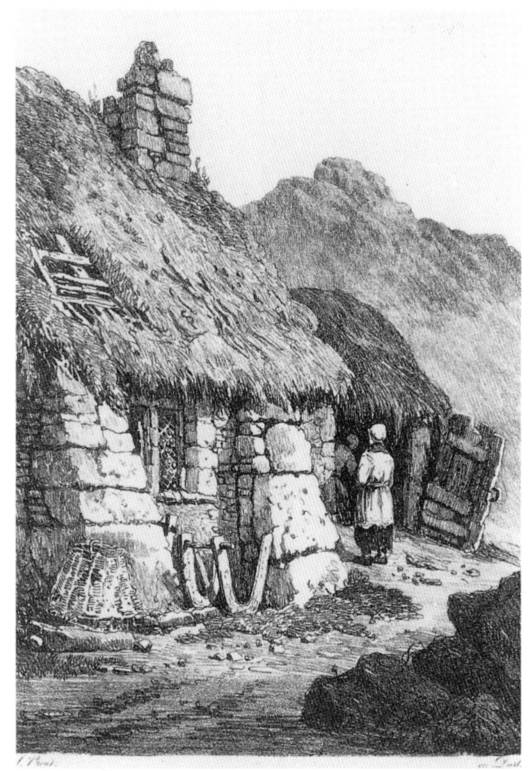

62. JOHN INIGO RICHARDS, *Ivybridge, Devon* (1768)

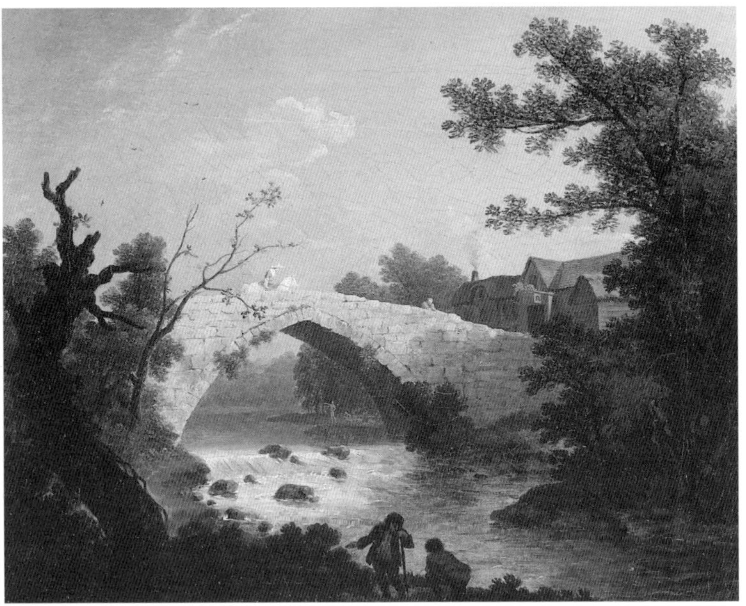

JOHN INIGO RICHARDS (1731-1810)

62. *Ivybridge, Devon* (1768)
Oil on canvas, 40.6 x 49.8 cm
Tate Gallery, London

The son of a scene-painter and Hogarth's god-son,
Richards was principal scene-painter at Covent
Garden from 1777-1803. He exhibited landscapes at
the Society of Artists, the Free Society and the Royal
Academy and was secretary to the Royal Academy
from 1788 to his death, where he frequently clashed
with Joseph Farington (q.v.).
A number of his exhibited works are of locations in
Devon and Somerset. Views of *Glastonbury*, *Halswell
House* and *Hestercombe* were shown in London
between 1763 and 1769[1] and he exhibited *A View of
Oakhampton Castle in Devonshire* at the Royal
Academy in 1770.[2] This painting must, therefore, be a
product of his search for patronage in the west
country. It is one of the earliest pictures of Ivybridge
in existence, if not the earliest,[3] for it is over a decade
before Paul Sandby produced the first printed image of
Ivybridge in his *One Hundred and Fifty Select Views in
England, Scotland and Ireland*.[4] Like Berry Pomeroy
Castle, Ivybridge elicited that enthusiasm for
picturesque motifs which remained active well into
the nineteenth century.
'It forms an object of considerable picturesque beauty,
viewed from the eastern side of the river, where its
lofty single arch, of wide span, springing from natural
abutments, embrowned with the foliage of the classic
plant,and stretching over a rude rocky bed, is seen to
the greatest advantage.'[5] (SS)

THOMAS ROWLANDSON (1756-1827)

63. *Picnic on Dartmoor* (undated)
(illustrated in colour on p.91)
Watercolour on paper, 14.6 x 22.9 cm
Inscribed 'Dartmoor' (lower left)
Leeds Museums and Galleries, City Art Gallery

64. *Honiton Devonshire* (undated)
(Illustrated in colour on p.91)
Pen, ink and watercolor on paper, 29.6 x 43.1 cm
Inscribed 'Honiton Devonshire' lower right
Royal Albert Memorial Museum, Exeter

65. *Coombe Bridge, North Devon* (undated)
Watercolour on paper, 24.0 x 38.0 cm
Courtauld Institute Galleries, London (Spooner
Bequest)

Rowlandson made frequent journeys to the West
Country to stay with his good friend Matthew
Mitchell of Hengar House near Bodmin. During a
period of more than twenty years he made many
lyrical watercolours of Cornish and Devon scenes.[1]
These sometimes have a very generalised appearance
and their inscriptions, where they exist, cannot always
be believed as correctly identifying the locality. It is
clear, however, that he did visit and paint views of
Exeter, Honiton, Plymouth and north Devon.[2]
The three examples here illustrate in different ways
his native wit and extraordinary talent for comic
characterization. *Honiton* (cat.no.64) is as near as he
gets to topography, to depicting with accuracy a
particular place, but it is really the figures which give

63. THOMAS ROWLANDSON, *Picnic on Dartmoor*

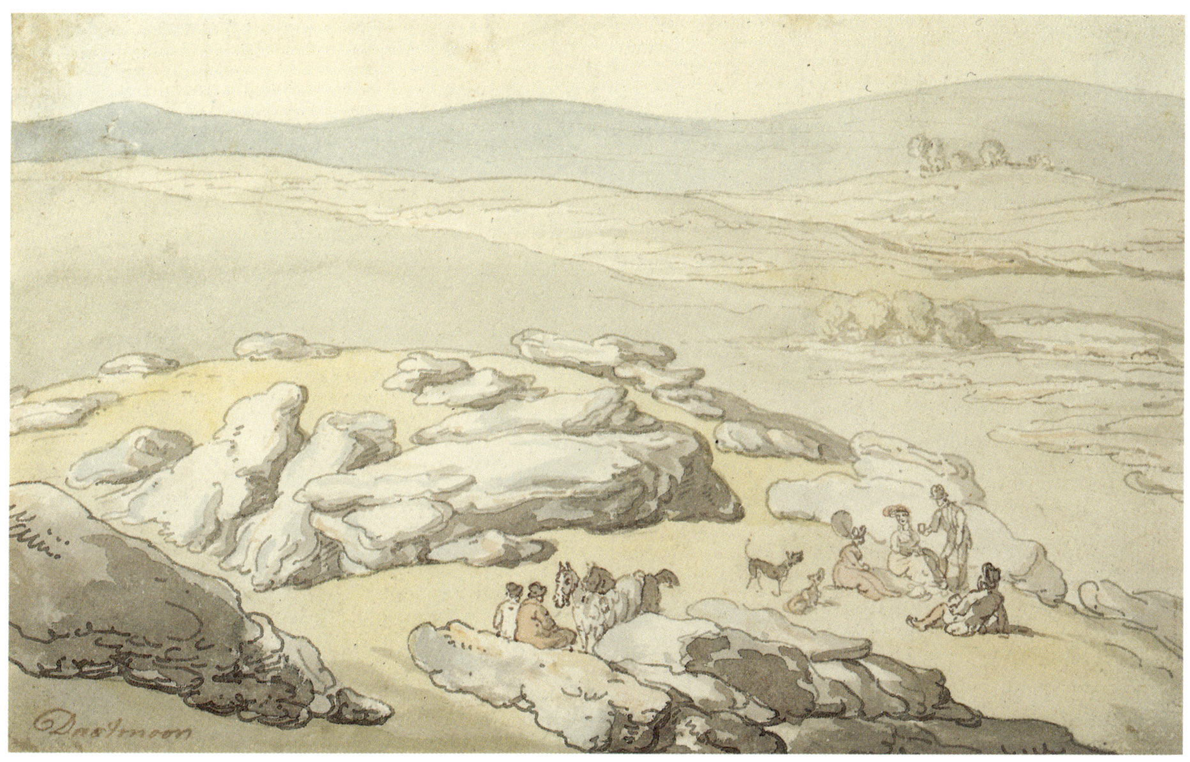

64. THOMAS ROWLANDSON, *Honiton, Devonshire*

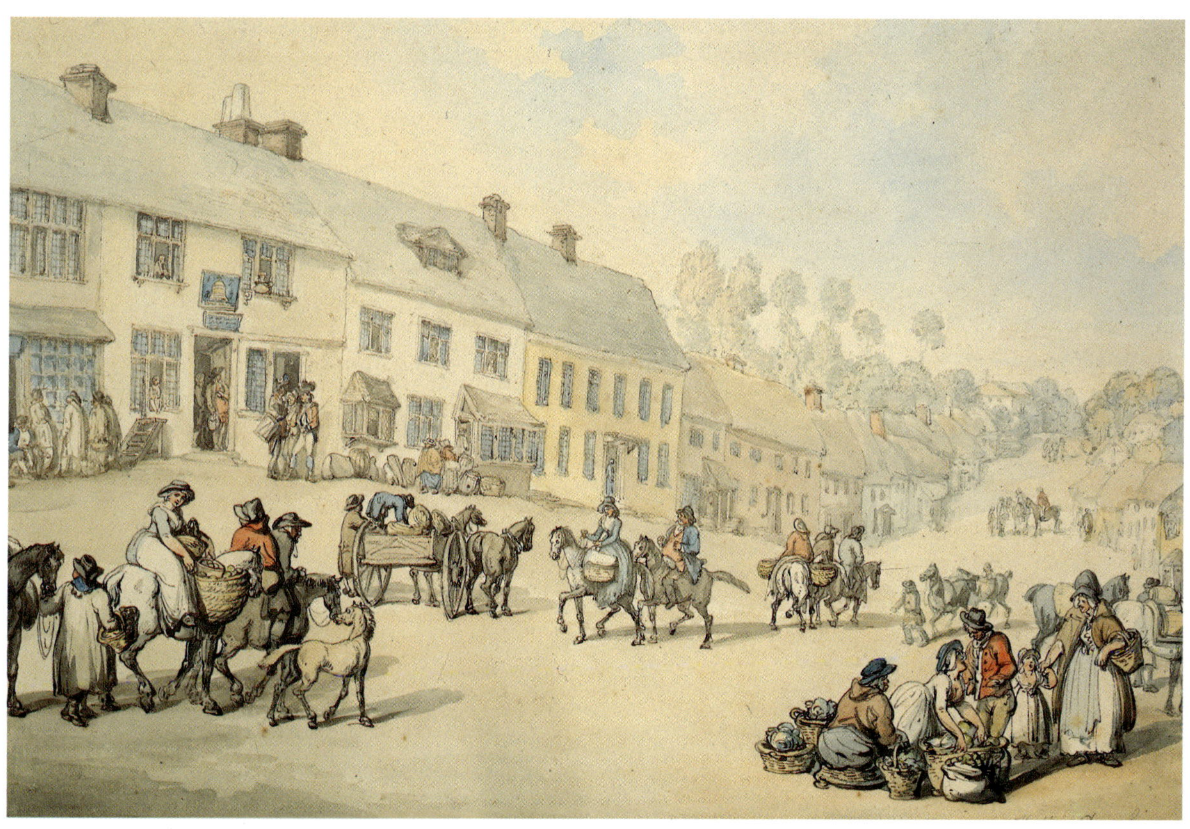

65. THOMAS ROWLANDSON, *Coombe Bridge, North Devon*

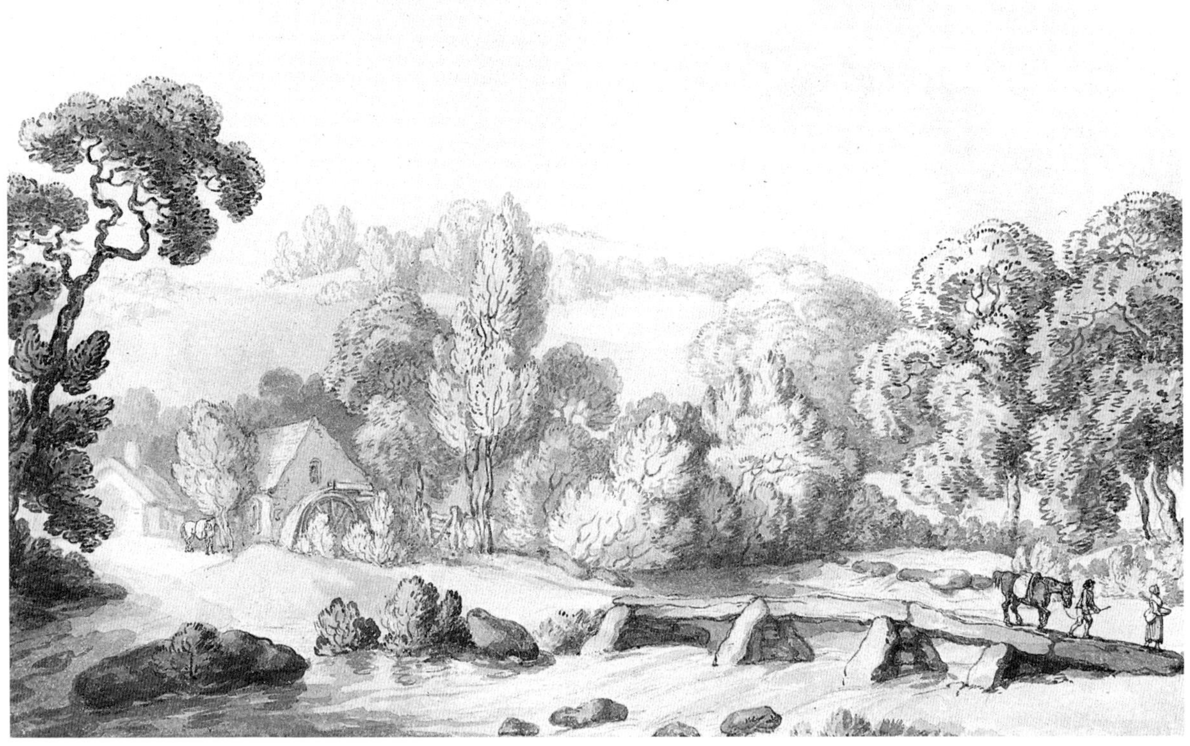

life and interest to this scene. The street is alive with
people on their way to market, with others gossiping
at the Bell Inn. The group in the right foreground
easily attracts our attention with Rowlandson, as so
often, hinting at suggestive goings-on. The red-coated
male gazes admiringly at the cleavage of the crouching
buxom market girl while the old woman looks on
disapprovingly. It was such powers of observation that
caused a local guide book to recommend Rowlandson
as the artist to depict the seine fishermen at
Teignmouth.[3]

Coombe Bridge (cat.no.65) is in every sense a typical
Rowlandson landscape; elegant, frothy rococo trees
seem to communicate with each other as much as his
figures do. The overshot mill, fast flowing river, and
clapper bridge together signal 'Devon'. In *Picnic on
Dartmoor* (cat.no.63) four tourists have stopped to
picnic on a bleak plateau of large boulders. Their
horses and attendants wait at a distance. No one
seems remotely interested in the 'grand' scenery.
Rowlandson brilliantly caricatured the fad for
picturesque sketching in his illustrations of
Dr. Syntax, who, on his horse Grizzle, rides out in
search of scenic wonders such as these.[4] Two other
versions of this scene are known, one being called
View on Exmoor.[5] (MP)

66. BRADFORD RUDGE, *On the West Lynn* (?1830s)

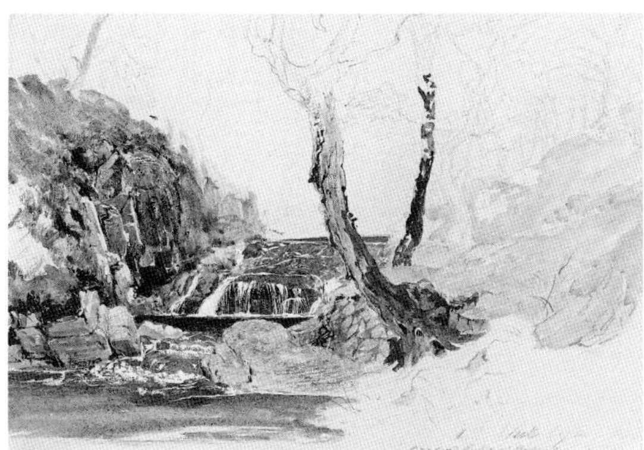

67. HENRY COURTNEY SELOUS, *Exeter Quay* (1831)

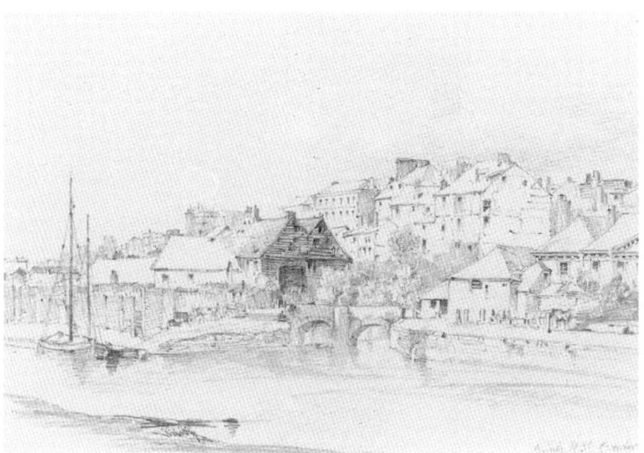

BRADFORD RUDGE (1805-1885)

66. *On the West Lynn* (?1830s)
Pencil, watercolour and bodycolour on grey paper,
22.8 x 32.5 cm
Inscribed 'On the West Lynn. Bradford Rudge of
Bedford' (lower right)
Stephen Wildman

Bradford Rudge is a little known artist who worked in
Bedford as a landscape painter, drawing master and
lithographer. He exhibited landscapes at the London
exhibitions from the 1840s to the 1880s. Rudge must
have visited Devon in the 1830s as he produced two
lithographs of Blundell's School c.1840.
This striking watercolour is an excellent example of
an unfinished study from nature and witnesses Rudge's
considerable abilities as a sketcher. In concentrating
attention on the waterfall he seems to be in tune with
Eagles (q.v.), who recommended the West Lynn as a
sketching ground where 'there is nowhere to be found
so much beauty of painter's detail, of water, foliage,
stones and banks, within so small a space.'[1] One
particular descriptive passage might almost describe
Rudge's study.
'Here it was almost placid, running off into
meandering rivulets - here shooting with rapidity over
large smooth masses, bearing on its rich transparent
bosom white bubbles, like fairy-barks in a race - here
pouring over the narrow passages of congregrated
fragments... and here in a collected body rushing
down, glistening in the power and dignity of a
cascade. All this is seen under the green light of
overhanging foliage, waving only to give entrance to
the partial sunbeams...'[2]
Rudge's father had sketched here in the 1820s and
presumably recommended Lynmouth as a sketching
ground to his son.[3] (SS)

HENRY COURTNEY SELOUS (1811-1890)

67. *Exeter Quay* (1831)
Pencil on paper, 18.8 x 27.7 cm
Inscribed '9 July 1831 Exeter'
Royal Albert Memorial Museum, Exeter

68. *Engine Bridge, Exeter* (1831)
Pencil on paper, 18.9 x 27.8 cm
Royal Albert Memorial Museum, Exeter

69. *Tavistock* (1831)
Pencil on paper, 27.5 x 37.7 cm
Royal Albert Memorial Museum, Exeter

Selous (or Slous as he was known until the late 1830s)
is best known as a Victorian book illustrator. He was
also a history painter and occasional landscape painter
as well as being involved in the production of
panoramas from 1829 until at least 1861.[1] In this
connection it is possible that he came to Devon in
1831 to accompany P. Daguire and Co.'s *Panorama of
the French Revolution of 1830* which was exhibited in
Exeter in the Great Room of the Swan Tavern from
July 14, 1831 until early October.[2]
These three pencil sketches are part of a group of
thirteen in the museum's collection which show
Selous to have sketched widely in south Devon from
Exmouth to Plymouth. Despite recent civic
improvements which altered the look of the
picturesque city sketched by Farington (q.v.), Selous
found numerous subjects for his pencil in Exeter.
Exeter Quay (cat.no.67) shows warehouses on the left,
the old Elizabethan bridge, the Customs House on the
right and to its left and above the bridge the same
group of houses on Cricklepit Street which are at the
centre of Farington's sketch (cat.no.20), though much
of the right hand side of the latter's drawing had now

70. FRANCIS STEVENS, *Lustleigh Cleave* (1820)

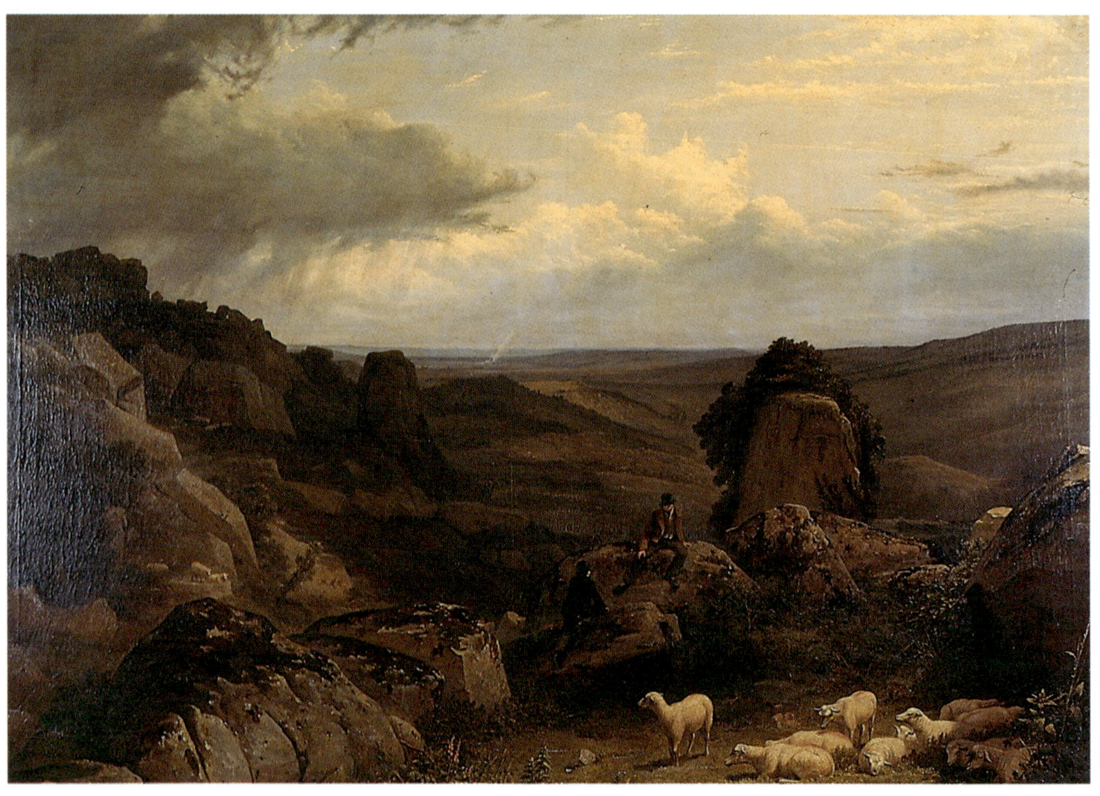

72. J.M.W. TURNER, *The Plym Estuary from Boringdon Park* (1813)

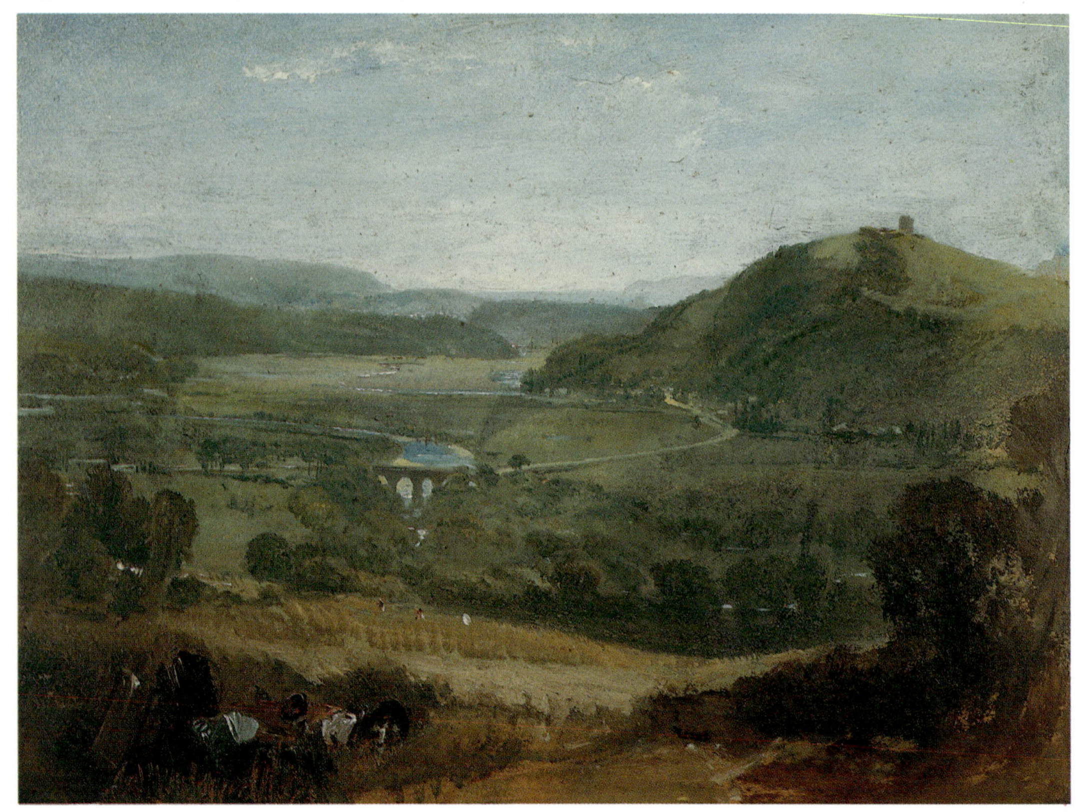

68. HENRY COURTNEY SELOUS, *Engine Bridge, Exeter* (1831)

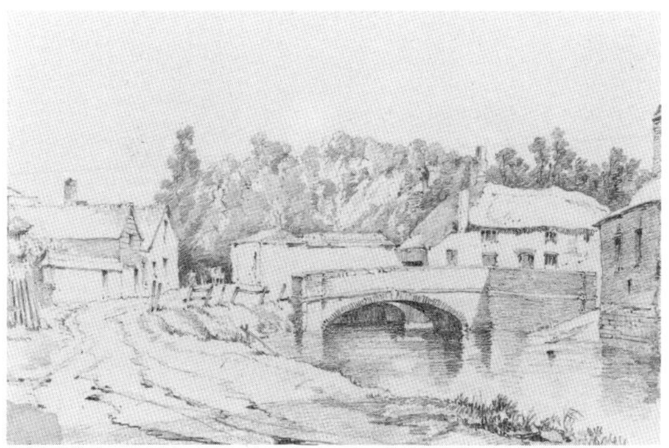

69. HENRY COURTNEY SELOUS, *Tavistock* (1831)

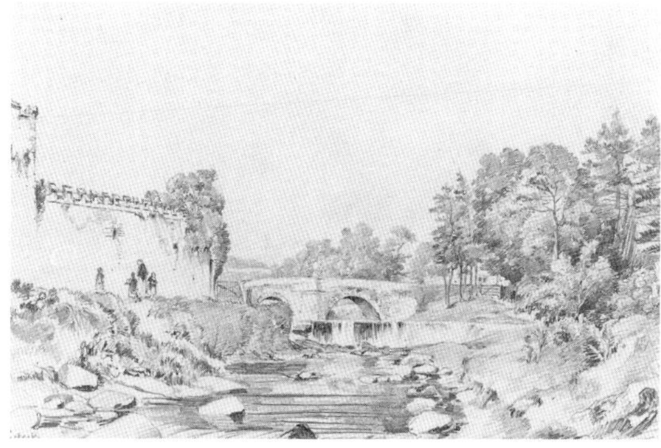

been demolished. Cat.no.68 shows the point where
the Longbrook joins the Exe at the bottom of Exe
Lane: part of the Head Weir Mill is on the left and the
little bridge with houses beyond is the site of the
pumping engine which supplied the town with water.
Selous seems to have been particularly interested in
the Exe, with its quayside, weirs and factories, a taste
which links these studies to developments in
naturalism associated with the circle of John Linnell
in the 1810s. His other Devon sketches are more
conventionally picturesque as seen here in his view of
Tavistock (cat.no.69). Selous returned to Devon at
the end of his life, dying in Beaworthy. (SS)

FRANCIS STEVENS (1781-1823)

70. *Lustleigh Cleave* (1820)
(Illustrated in colour on p.96)
Oil on canvas, 120 x 190 cm
Signed and dated lower left
The Devon and Exeter Institution

Stevens is today a shadowy figure. He was probably
born in Exeter but only settled there as a drawing
master in 1817 having previously exhibited in London
and Norwich, but never very prolifically. He was,
however, well connected in the formal and informal
societies established by the watercolourists in London
in the early nineteenth century. Many of Stevens's
fellow artists had their works etched by him for a
publication dealing with picturesque buildings
published in 1815.[1] It included a humble Devon
farmhouse at Seaton etched from a drawing by George
Samuel (fig.27). Such subjects long remained popular
with sketchers. Stevens presented a copy of his book
to the newly founded Devon and Exeter Institution,
established in 1813. They also received in 1820 a large
oil painting of Lustleigh Cleave (cat.no.70). It is an
early example of the kind of scene captured in words,
and later in pictures, by many admirers of Dartmoor
and its fringes and borders. The lichen-covered rocks
and vegetation are well observed and there is a real

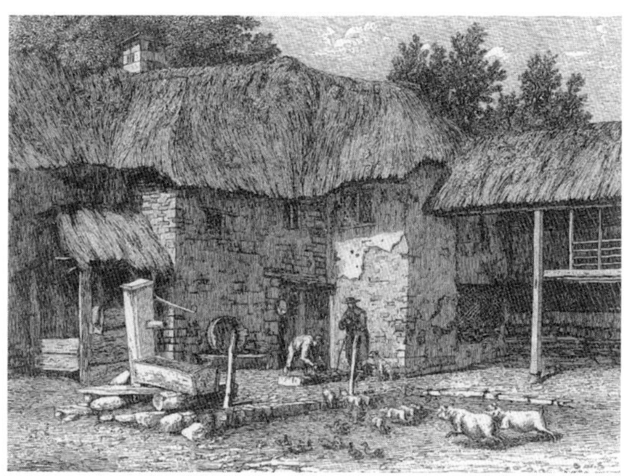

Fig.27. G. SAMUEL, engraved F. Stevens, *Seaton, Devonshire,*
etching, from *Cottages and Farmhouses in England and Wales,* 1815.

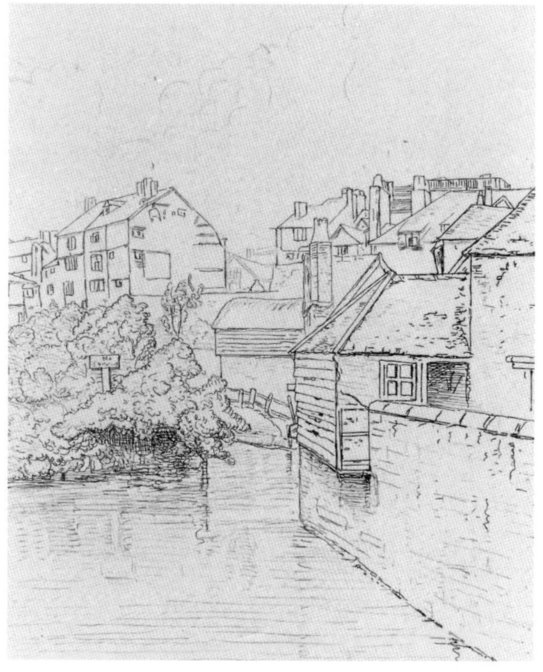

Fig.28. F. STEVENS, engraved F.C. Lewis *Exeter from the Quay Bridge,*
etching, from *The Scenery of the River Exe,* 1827

71. WILLIAM TOMKINS, *View of Plymouth Sound, taken from the Rope House, Plymouth Dock* (1769)

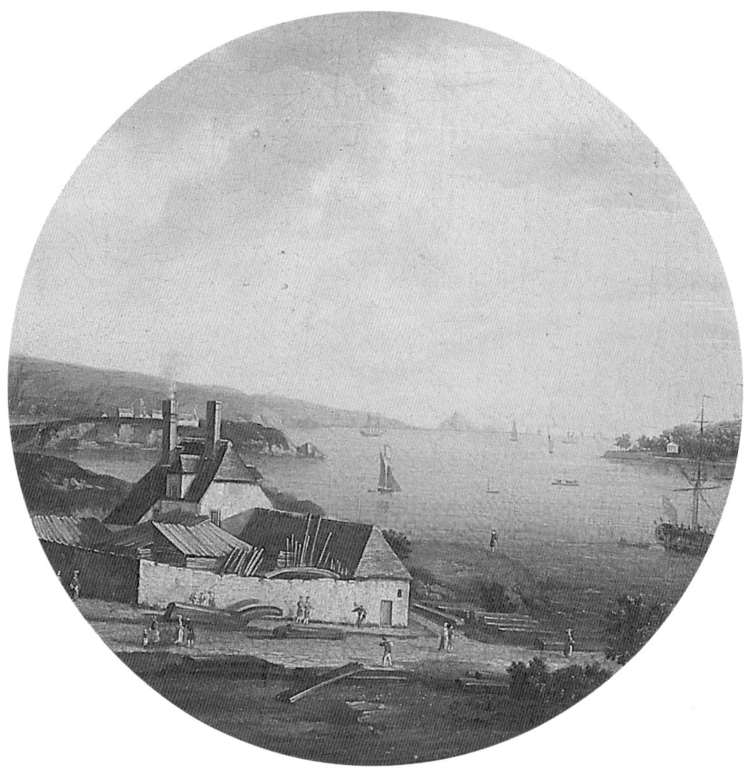

sense of light and space in the middle distance.
The rising plume of white smoke creates a resting
point for the eye. The two male figures scrambling up
on to the rocks look as if they might soon get a
soaking as rain is already falling from the approaching
dark clouds.

At the Royal Academy in 1819 Stevens had exhibited
Evening View on the Teign, Devonshire, and his last
exhibits of Devon scenes appeared at the Watercolour
Society in 1823. In that year his career was ended by
his untimely death leaving unfinished and unpublished
a planned work 'illustrative of Exeter and its vicinity'.[2]
F.C. Lewis (q.v.), who must have received useful hints
from Stevens in searching for his own Devon subjects,[3]
etched six small outline drawings by Stevens (fig.28) as
well as his view of Exeter under a rainbow for his own
series of Exe etchings (1827). (MP)

WILLIAM TOMKINS (c.1732-1792)

71. *View of Plymouth Sound, taken from the
Rope House, Plymouth Dock* (1769)
Oil on canvas, 46 x 46 cm
Signed and dated lower left
Plymouth City Museums and Art Gallery
(Mount Edgcumbe House Collection)

Tomkins is known as a painter of the estates of the
aristocracy and landed gentry in that easy eighteenth-
century style which is associated with the work of
George Lambert. This view, together with its
companion picture, *View of Mount Edgecumbe, taken
from the west end of the new rope-house, Plymouth Dock*,
was exhibited at the Royal Academy in 1770 and it
inaugurates a series of West Country subjects by
Tomkins shown there over the next fifteen years. Like
John Inigo Richards (q.v.), but apparently with more
success, Tomkins was evidently moving around Devon's
great houses and securing commissions, for he produced
pictures associated with Ugbrooke, Saltram, Mamhead,
Tapley and Maristow as well as Mount Edgcumbe.[1]
Plymouth Sound lies open before us with Drake's
Island visible on the left, the Mew Stone on the
horizon and the shore of Mount Edgcumbe on the
right. The foreground is dominated by baulks of
timber, masts and spars whose solidity contrasts with
the social rituals carried on beside them. This
seemingly undisturbed world is qualified by Tomkins'
title and circular format which draws attention to the
fact that we are looking at this prospect from the attic
window of the Rope House, one of the new naval
facilities erected between 1763-72 during the
expansion of the Dockyard.[2]
This view and its companion were engraved in
etching and aquatint and published by his son,
Charles Tomkins in 1790. (SS)

73. J.M.W. TURNER, *A Bridge with a Cottage and Trees beyond* (1813)

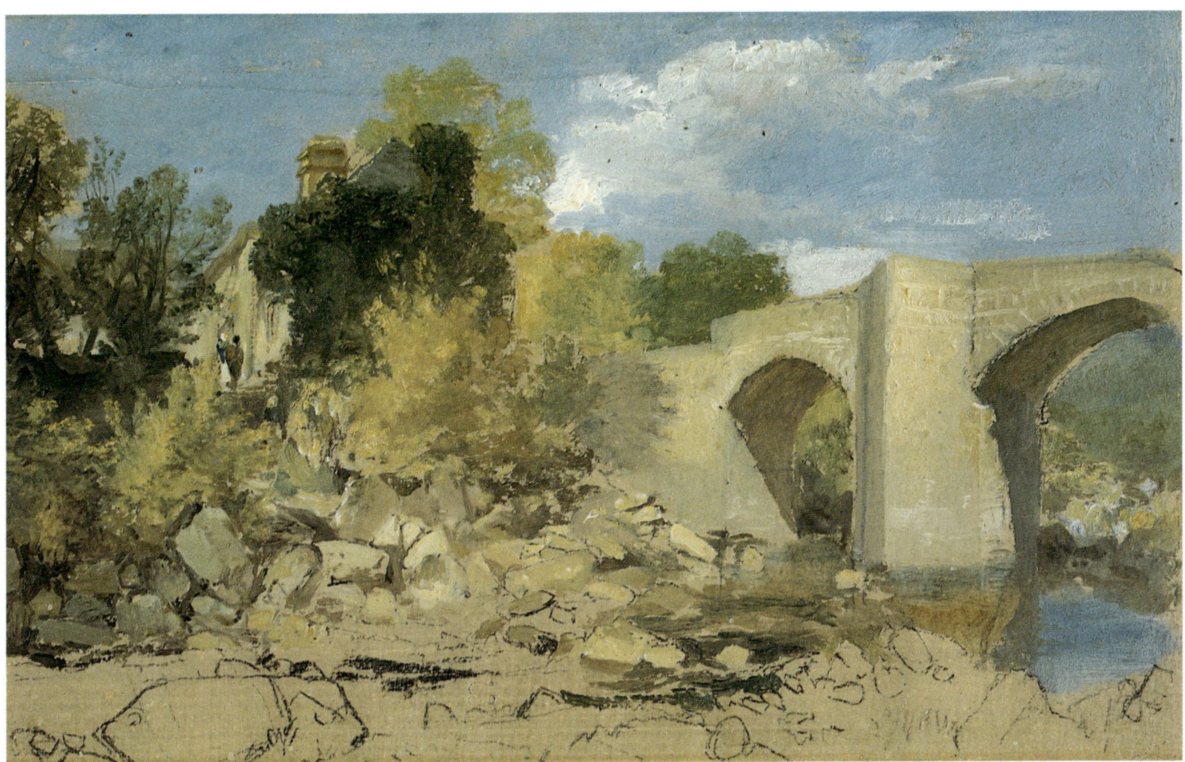

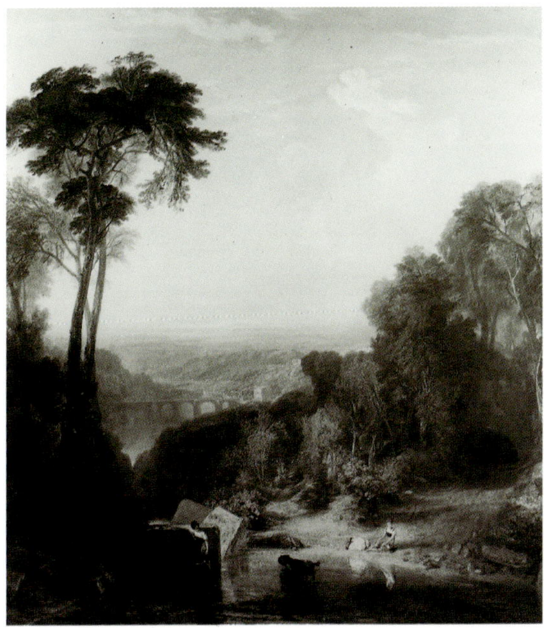

Fig.29. J.M.W. TURNER, *Crossing the Brook*, 1815, oil on canvas, 193.0 x 165.1 cm , The Tate Gallery, London.

J.M.W. TURNER (1775-1851)

Turner made three trips to Devon in the 1810s. The first of them took place in the summer of 1811 when he was working on commission for W.B. Cooke's

Picturesque Views on the Southern Coast of England, a work of topography illustrating the English coast from Cornwall in the west to the Nore in the east. Cooke's publication exemplifies the increasingly ambitious illustrated topography which began to appear in the early nineteenth century; from 1800 to the mid 1820s about 60 such publications appeared incorporating Devon subjects and Cooke's *Southern Coast* itself, which was published from 1814 to 1826, is arguably the most impressive of all of them.[1]

There is evidence to suggest that Turner had been thinking of touring Devon from at least 1798, so his acceptance of Cooke's commission would have been mutually satisfactory to both parties.[2] It is likely that Devon had an additional personal attraction for Turner; his father had been born in South Molton and he called on his uncles in Exeter and Barnstaple on the 1811 tour.[3] In about eight weeks, from mid-July to mid-September, he travelled along the south coast of the county then on into Cornwall and back along the north coast making pencil sketches of motifs that would be later worked up into watercolours in London. His work for Cooke was an important part of the venture's success and he was eventually to contribute 40 of the 80 plates in the *Southern Coast*. Ten of these were of Devon subjects.[4]

Two years later, in the summer of 1813, Turner returned to Devon. This second trip was designed to

74. J.M.W. TURNER, *A Quarry* (1813)

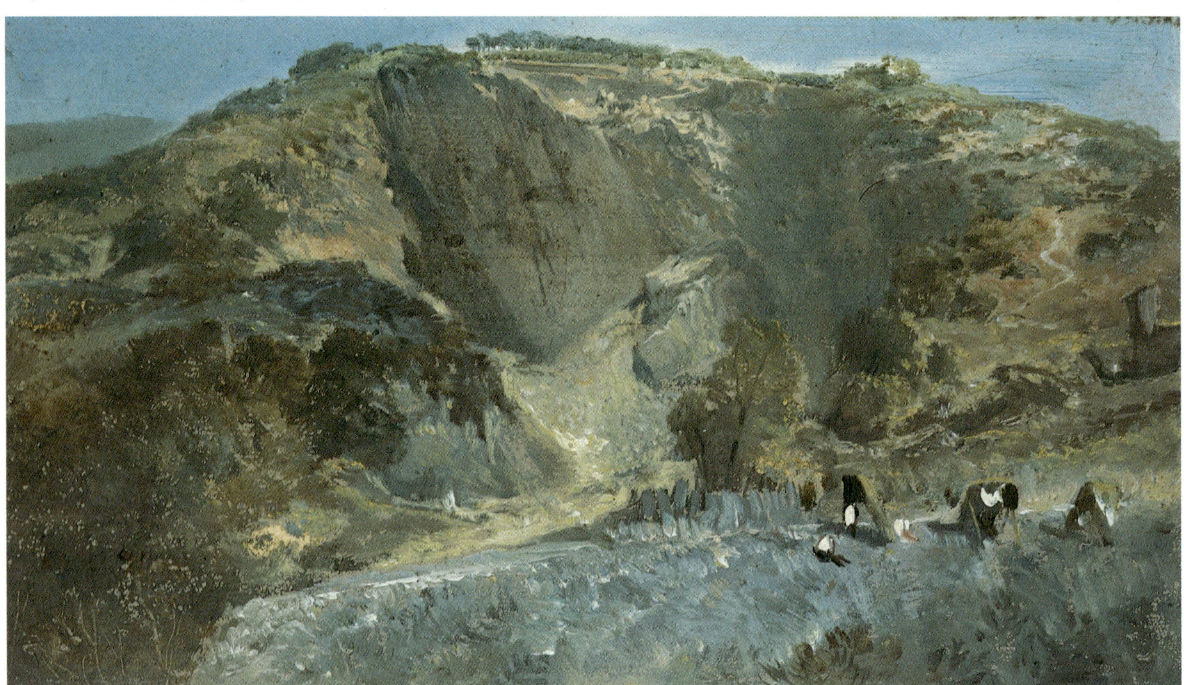

explore at leisure what he had only seen briefly in 1811, and it is evident that he intended to commit himself to this landscape for more than one visit, if a local witness can be trusted.

'Dined at Wm. Eastlake's met a pleasant party, amongst them Mr. Turner the Artist whose works I have so much admired he is brought hither by the beautifull scenery of our neighbourhood, there is a chance of his occasionally residing amongst us, I heartily wish this may take place...'[5]

Turner's enthusiasm for Devon as a sketching ground may be explained by its having one immediate and obvious resource for him, its Italianate appearance. Just as the resorts might be touted as climactically similar to Montpellier or Nice, so visitors and residents were disposed to describe the scenery, the light and the colour of south Devon in Mediterranean terms. In the early 1810s Turner needed a landscape which would reconcile his admiration for Claude's Italianate landscapes on the one hand with his own naturalist *credo* as a painter on the other. Turner faced critical opposition in these years from Sir George Beaumont, whose admiration for Claude was as deep as was his dislike for Turner, and he needed to make a response. Near Plymouth lay scenery whose light and landscape was widely considered to be Claudian; it was probably this revelation that brought Turner back to Devon. Italy itself, which he had yet to visit, was difficult to reach because of the war and Devon was pressed into service as the closest approximation to the poetic landscape of Turner's great predecessor.

Certainly it seems more than a coincidence that a group of his most Claudian-looking pictures was produced immediately after his work here in the early 1810s.[6] Cyrus Redding, a local journalist who was with Turner for some of the 1813 visit, has recorded Turner's admiration for this landscape.

'Turner said that he had never seen so many natural beauties in so limited an extent of country as he saw in the vicinity of Plymouth. Some of the scenes hardly appeared to belong to this island.'[7]

And, in a later memoir, Redding recalls even more emphatically Turner's idealistic reactions to the hinterland of Plymouth: 'He observed that some of the scenery was worthy of Italy.'[8]

The most immediate result of the 1813 sketching campaign is his early masterpiece *Crossing the Brook* (1815) (fig.29) which seems to insist on a point by point comparison with Beaumont's favourite possession, Claude's *Hagar and the Angel* (National Gallery, London). Based on studies made in and around the Tamar valley, *Crossing the Brook* takes Gunnislake Bridge and aspects of the industrial life of the Tamar (chiefly copper mining) only to subject them to an exercise in light, colour and composition which belongs to ideal landscape. Topography is here subservient to what Turner refers to as 'Elevated landscape', by which he means the artist's need to blend observation with imagination.[9]

We are fortunate that three eye-witnesses have left evidence of Turner's visit to Plymouth in 1813.[10] From their accounts we can tell that Turner was shown the

75. J.M.W. TURNER, *Shaugh Bridge, near Plymouth* (1813)

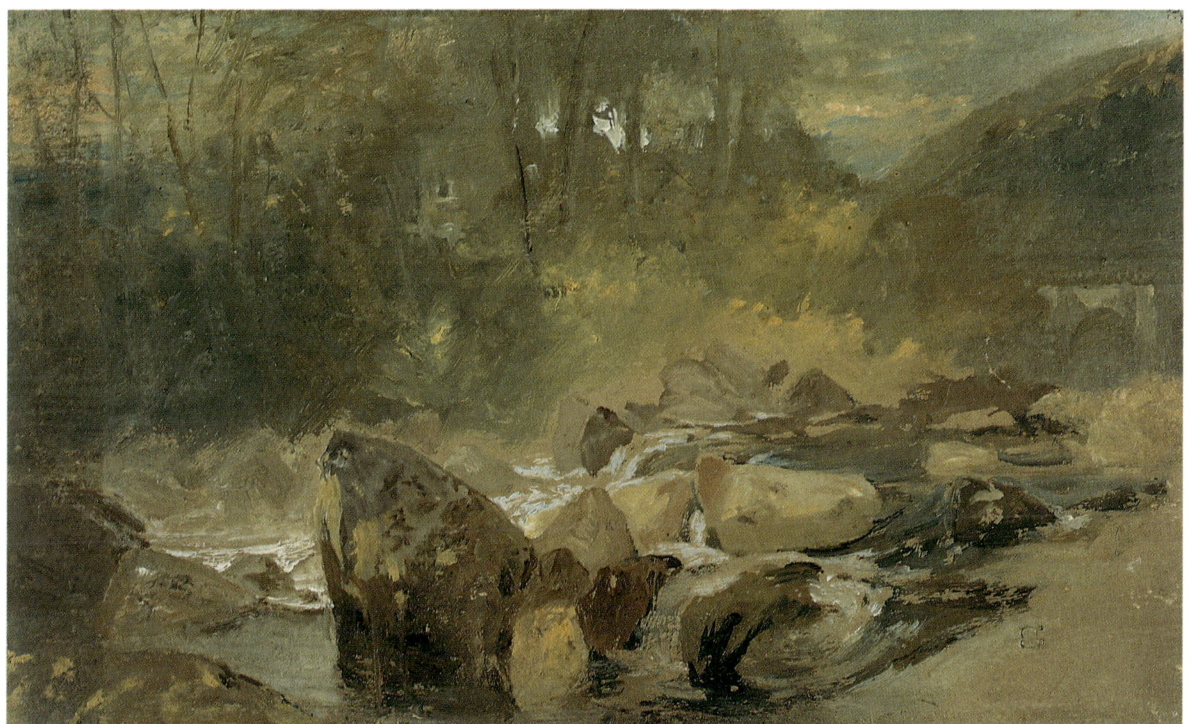

sights by an eager group of artists and amateurs and that he reciprocated their generosity. He kept close to Plymouth on this trip making excursions on foot, by boat or in a carriage. As with the 1811 trip to Devon, most of his sketches were in pencil but a group of oil studies was also produced (cat.no.72-75) and these give the 1813 trip a special prominence. Turner was not in the habit of sketching from nature; he had produced a series of distinctive oil sketches on the Thames in the previous decade but in general he found the method too slow and cumbersome. Charles Lock Eastlake was in Plymouth, painting portraits, when Turner visited and his account reveals that Turner's scruples about oil sketching were overcome with the assistance of the local landscape painter A.B. Johns, who had fitted out a portable painting-box containing all that was necessary.

'When Turner halted at a scene and seemed inclined to sketch it, Johns produced the inviting box, and the great artist, finding everything ready to his hand, immediately began to work. As he sometimes wanted assistance in the use of the box, the presence of Johns was indispensable, and after a few days he made his oil sketches freely in our presence.... Turner seemed pleased when the rapidity with which those sketches were done was talked of... he himself remarked that one of the sketches (and perhaps the best) was done in less than half an hour.'[11]

Turner's third and final visit to Devon occurred in 1814.[12] One of his companions in 1813, Henry Woollcombe, a Plymouth solicitor and founder of the Plymouth Institution, met him in London earlier that year and reported to his sister that Turner 'is a warm admirer of the scenery of Devonshire and proposes another visit in the present year.'[13] On this last trip he made further sketches around Plymouth and took a boat trip down the river Dart from Totnes to Dartmouth, which he mentioned in a letter to A.B. Johns that autumn.

'Give my respects to Mrs. Johns. be so good as to thank her for me "say that I got rid of my cold by catching a greater one, at Dartmouth being obliged to land from the boat half drownded with the spray as the gale compeled the boatmen to give up half way down the *Dart* from Totnes.'[14]

His relations with those he had met at Plymouth remained cordial; he contributed two paintings to the inaugural exhibition of the Plymouth Institution in October, 1815[15] and kept in contact with Johns and others for the next decade. Inevitably, however, Turner's ambitions altered as his art developed; the work of his maturity proved increasingly incomprehensible to his friends at Plymouth and Turner, for his part, evidently saw no reason to return to Devon. The work he produced here in the 1810s should be seen, therefore, as a highly specific encounter between a particular landscape and Turner's projection on to it of his own needs.

76. J.M.W. TURNER, *Ivybridge* (c.1814)

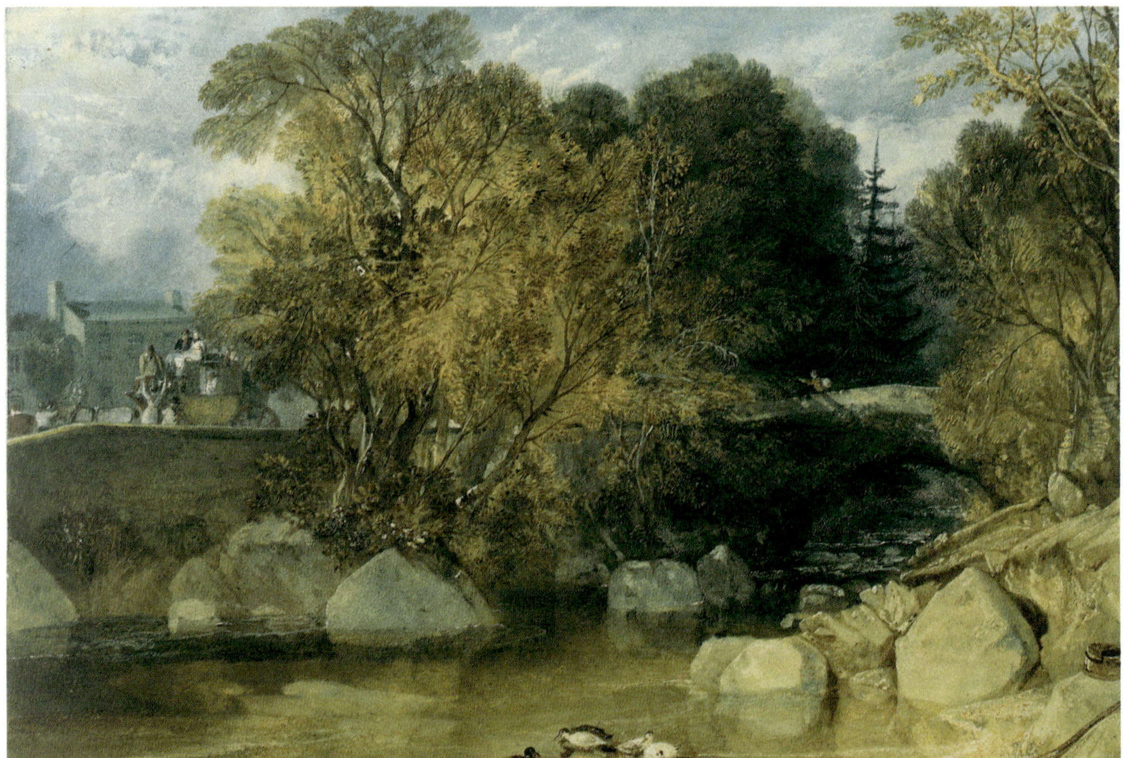

Nevertheless, whatever his original motives, Turner's involvement with Devon is probably more extensive than any of the artist visitors in this period, both in terms of the sheer quantity of work and also in its variety, exploring all aspects of the county's maritime and inland scenery. As well as the work for the *Southern Coast* Turner produced other Devon watercolours for further series such as *The Rivers of Devon*, *The Rivers of England*, *Picturesque Views in England and Wales* and *The Ports of England*. If to these we add watercolours which were not engraved, Turner produced in all about 30 finished watercolours of Devon subjects. He also painted at least five large oils, *Ivybridge Mill*,[16] *Teignmouth*[17] and three of the landscapes around Plymouth: *Hulks on the Tamar*,[18] *Saltash with the Water Ferry*[19] and *Crossing the Brook*.[20] In terms of preliminary material from his Devon tours, the Turner Bequest includes numerous pencil sketches and some watercolour studies and at least fifteen oil sketches are extant in various collections.

72. *The Plym Estuary from Boringdon Park* (1813)
(Illustrated in colour on p.96)
Oil on prepared paper, 23.5 x 29.8 cm
The Turner Collection, Tate Gallery, London

In this oil sketch Turner is looking down on the Long Bridge over the river Plym and its estuary, the Laira,

beyond. The angle of the sun and the fact that the Plym's mud-banks are visible indicate that he made this sketch one afternoon in the last week of August or the first week in September. A corn-field is being harvested in the foreground and one of the reapers lies asleep in the shade closest to us. The view out towards the sound is seen through a heat-haze and the blue of the sky is reflected with greater intensity in the Plym and the sea beyond.

73. *A Bridge with a Cottage and Trees beyond* (1813)
(Illustrated in colour on p.99)
Oil over black chalk on prepared paper, 15 x 23.5 cm
The Turner Collection, Tate Gallery, London

The subject of this sketch may be the river Walkham, near Tavistock, but its precise identification still remains to be discovered. Turner's viewpoint allows him to emphasise again the intense blue of the sky and to contrast it with a range of warm tones from the stone-work of the bridge to the yellow foliage of the bushes and trees on the farther bank. As with a number of the Devon oil sketches, this may represent a deliberate attempt to capture the 'Italianate' light and colour of this landscape and it is significant that some of the work exhibited immediately after the Devon tours was criticised precisely for its use of intense blues and yellows.[21]

77. J.M.W. TURNER, *Totnes* (c.1824)

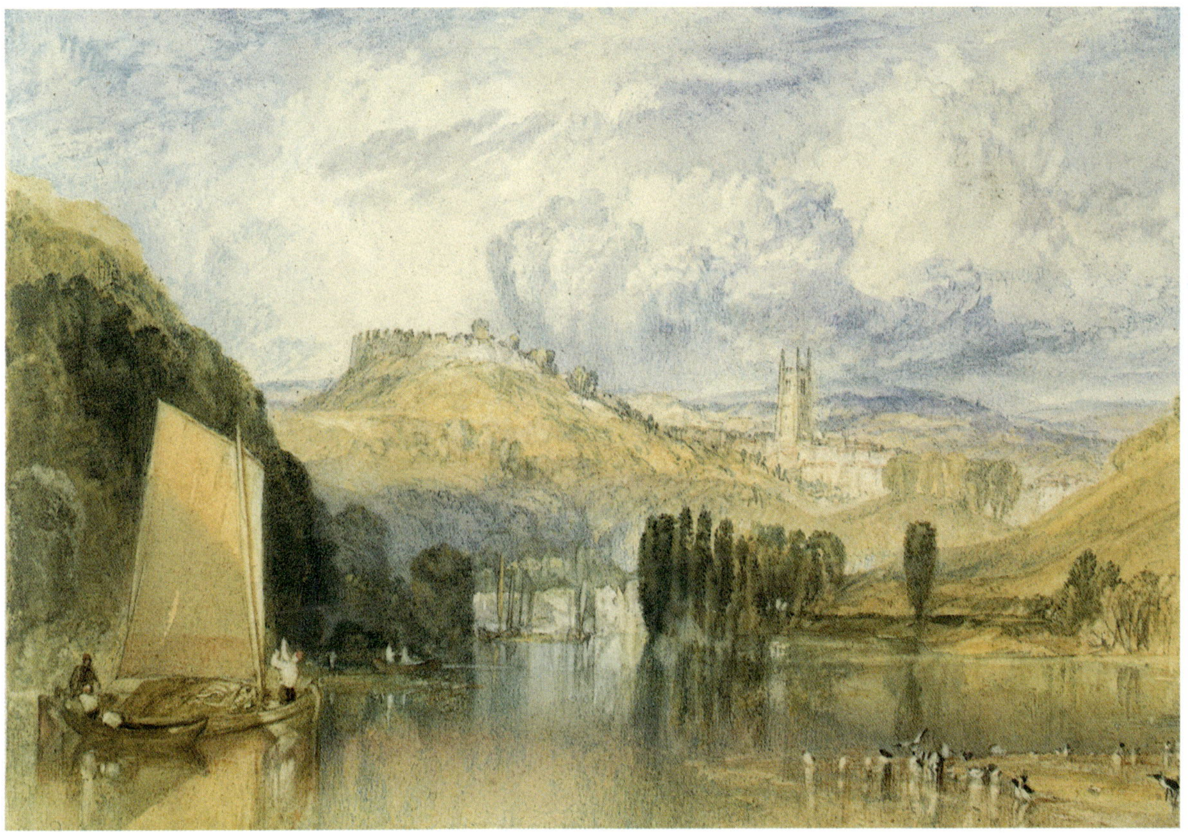

74. *A Quarry* (1813)
(Illustrated in colour on p.100)
Oil on prepared paper, 13.5 x 23.5 cm
The Turner Collection, Tate Gallery, London

The heaps of stone seen in the foreground suggest that
this is a slate quarry in the vicinity of Plymouth. It
may be Crabtree Quarry or Cann Quarry on the Plym,
both of which were recognised sketching grounds for
local Plymouth artists. The intensity of the sunlight
and the warmth of colour are again significant features
of this sketch.

75. *Shaugh Bridge, near Plymouth* (1813)
(Illustrated in colour on p101)
Oil on prepared paper, 15.9 x 26.7 cm
The Turner Collection, Tate Gallery, London

Shaugh Bridge lies six miles north of Plymouth at the
confluence of two Dartmoor streams, the Plym and
the Meavy. It was already established as a popular
beauty spot and sketching ground at the time of
Turner's visit. Cyrus Redding records that he and
Turner 'had a pic-nic on the romantic banks of the
Plym, and visited the crags and precipes of Sheep's Tor
together' towards the end of his stay.[22] The hill rising

in the background to the right leads to another
favourite beauty spot, Dewerstone Rock, the subject of
Inchbold's painting of 1854 (cat.no.33).

76. *Ivybridge* (c.1814)
(Illustrated in colour on p.102)
Watercolour on paper, 28 x 40.9 cm
The Turner Collection, Tate Gallery, London

One of the reasons that Ivybridge occurs so often as a
subject for artists is that it was possible to sketch the
most picturesque aspects of the locality without
moving away from the main coach route. C.R. Leslie's
experience there in the autumn of 1818 must have
been typical.
'I left Totness on one of the coaches that passes
through, and about half-past three o'clock arrived at
Ivy-bridge, a pleasant village situated on a picturesque
stream, which dashes over a bed of rocks in a
continual series of waterfalls with a constant roar. It is
crossed by a high picturesque bridge of one arch,
clothed with ivy, from which the village takes its
name. I dined at this beautiful place and strolled about
till dark. The next coach came past at seven, and on
that I proceeded to Plymouth, where I arrived
between nine and ten o'clock.'[23]

78. J.M.W. TURNER, *Dartmouth* (1822)

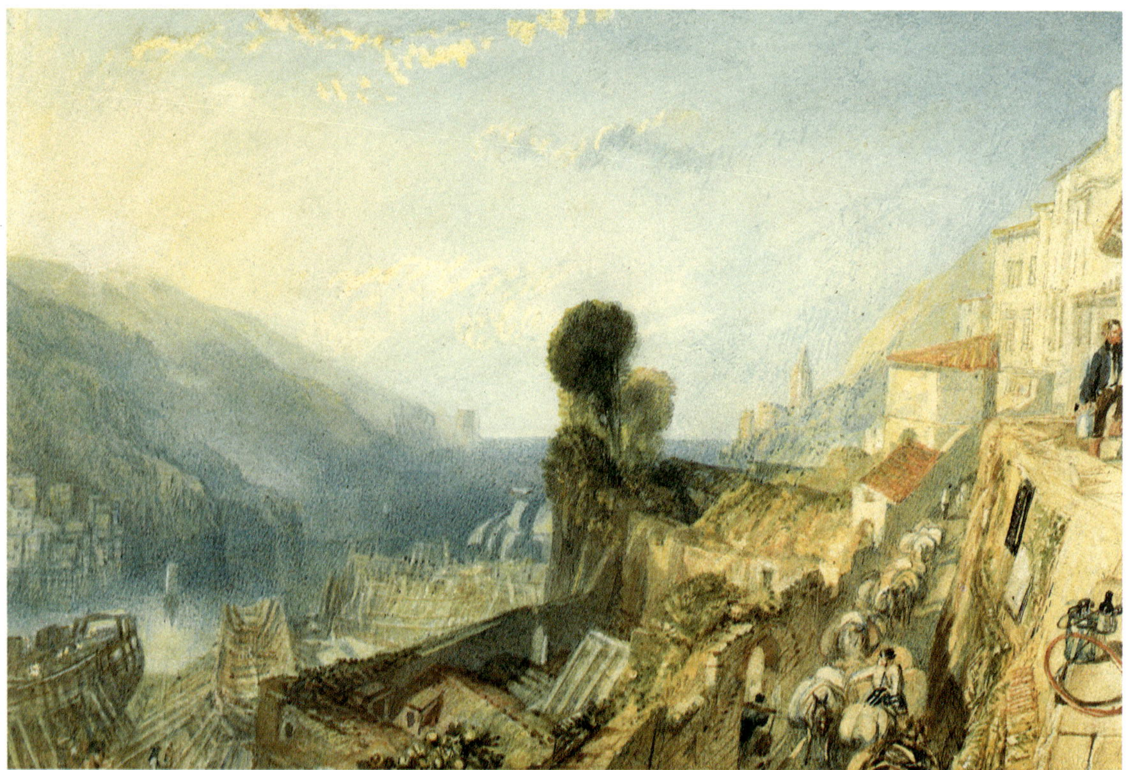

Turner first sketched here in 1811, making a drawing that would be used as the basis for his oil painting of *Ivy Bridge Mill,* exhibited in 1812.[24] This exhibit was commissioned by W.B. Cooke for a projected but unrealised publication, *The Rivers of Devon.*[25] It is at least partly based on a sketch made in 1814, on Turner's third trip to Devon, when he again passed through the place.[26] The figure running across the bridge to catch the afternoon coach might well stand for the artist who lingered too long sketching this well-known beauty spot, but the discarded objects in the foreground and the figure on the extreme right of the composition are indications that Ivybridge has another, slower rhythm to set beside the coaching timetable. Turner's handling of different varieties of tree is an object lesson in observation and his technique is at its most refined in his ability to capture the limpidity of the river Erme, so that we see both the reflections on its surface and glimpses of the stream-bed beneath. In the foreground he employs a characteristic device, placing the extremes of the picture's tonal range in close and contrasted proximity in the group of ducks at the water's edge.

77. *Totnes* (c.1824)
(Illustrated in colour on p.103)
Watercolour on paper, 16.2 x 23 cm
The Turner Collection, Tate Gallery, London

There are pencil sketches of Totnes from the 1811 tour but this particular composition seems to owe more to a sketch made in 1814.[27] Turner shows the town with a storm passing off, the river Dart glassy still and the returning sun already beginning to brighten the foreground. The Norman castle and parish church of St. Mary have yet to receive this warmer light and offer a cooler, paler contrast to the yellow sail and iridescent reflections in the foreground. The sense of recent rain is aided by his treatment of the trees in the middle distance, their forms blurred by the moisture in the air, whose blotted outlines show them to have been literally formed from water. The surface of the river is beyond imitation; no one but Turner could conjure up such reflections as if by breathing on a polished mirror.
The watercolour was engraved by Charles Turner for W.B. Cooke's *Rivers of England* series in 1827 but the plate was cancelled.

78. *Dartmouth* (1822)
Watercolour on paper, 15.7 x 22.7 cm
The Turner Collection, Tate Gallery, London

There are drawings of Dartmouth from the 1811 and 1814 tours[28] and this image may well be a composite worked up from a number of studies and memories. Turner depicts the activities of early morning.

79. J.M.W. TURNER, *Buckfastleigh* (c.1826)

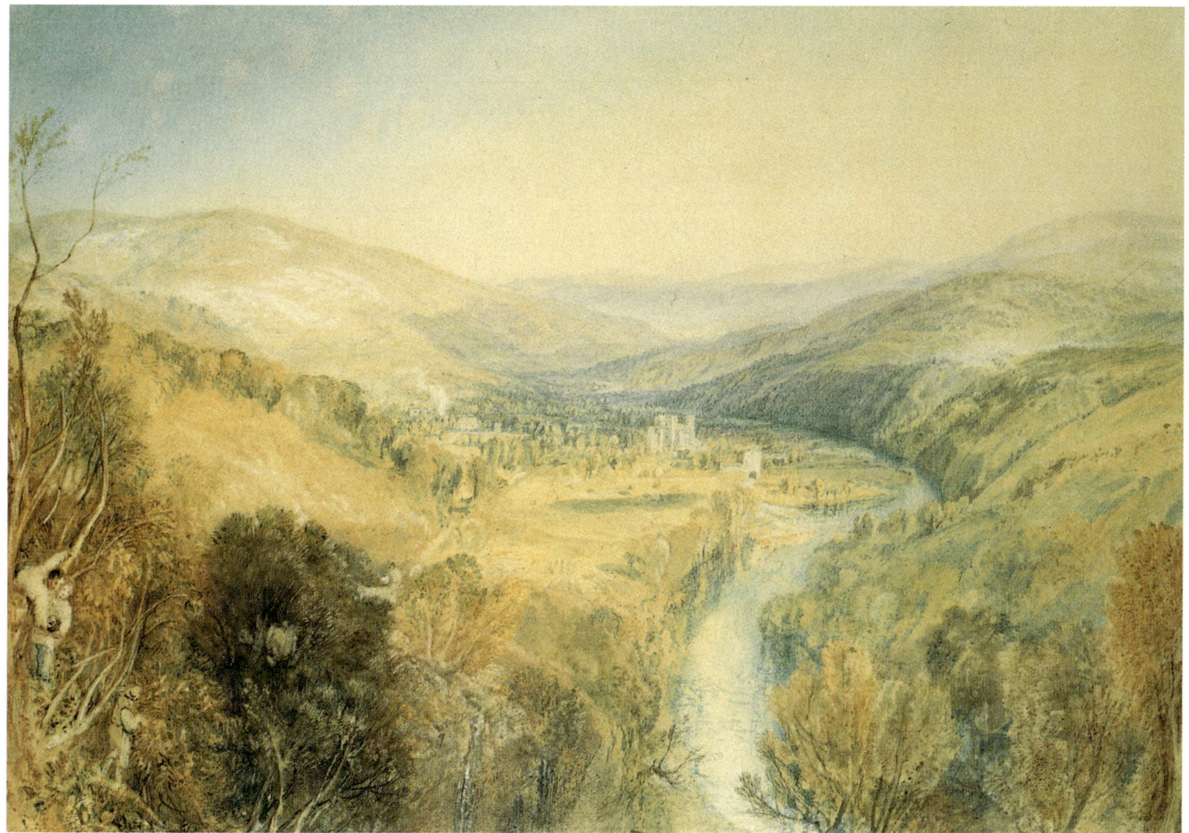

A milkman's pail and a discarded child's hoop lie in
the foreground of the composition while the milkman
himself knocks at a door on the right. In the road
below him a train of pack-horses[29] descends towards
the market, and below them our eye is led over
Dartmouth's ship-yards, the river Dart and the village
of Kingswear on the farther shore. Looking out to sea,
the blockhouse of Kingswear Castle on the left is
almost dissolved by light while Dartmouth Castle,
with the tower of St. Petrock's church closes the
distance on the right. The sun rising behind
Kingswear eats into the contour of the hill and the
brilliance of its light is enhanced by Turner's use of
tiny stippling brushstrokes on the left of the
composition which seem to capture the dazzle caused
by our looking into the sun. The combination of
warm sunlight, white stuccoed facades and red roofing
tiles produce the closest approximation to a
Mediterranean apearance.
The watercolour was engraved by S.W.Reynolds in
1825 for W.B.Cooke's *Rivers of England* series.

79. *Buckfastleigh* (c.1826)
Watercolour on paper, 27.4 x 39.4 cm
Royal Albert Memorial Museum, Exeter

We are positioned on the eminence on which stands
Buckfastleigh church, looking up the river Dart
towards Holne Chase and Dartmoor. Turner shows
mist rising from the valley and drifting across the hills
in the background as the early morning sun begins to
strengthen. Buckfast Abbey, a diminutive feature in
the middle distance, was remodelled about 1806 by its
owner Samuel Berry who left only the tower and
gateways of the original mediaeval monastery intact
when he built a house and woollen mill on the site.
The three boys on the left are birdnesting and behind
them a shepherd is driving some sheep up the road
towards us. Knowing Turner's penchant for symbolic
allusions it is tempting to link the boys' robbery and
the shorn flock leaving the valley with the predatory
dissolution of Buckfast Abbey in 1539 by Henry VIII.
The watercolour was engraved by R. Wallis in 1828
for Charles Heath's *Picturesque views in England
and Wales*.

80. J.M.W. TURNER, *Exeter* (c.1827)

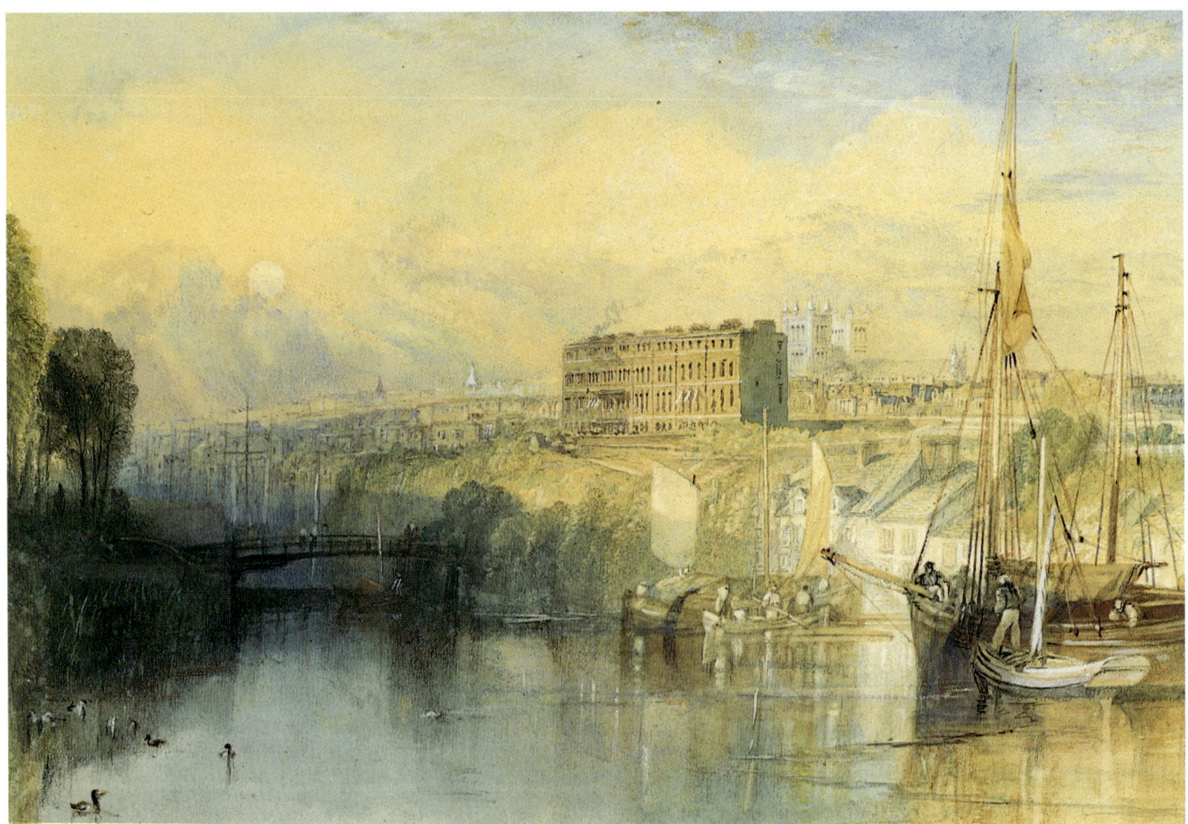

80. *Exeter* (c.1827)
Watercolour with some bodycolour on paper,
30 x 42.8 cm
Manchester City Art Galleries

Turner shows the river Exe and the port of Exeter from a point close to the King's Arms sluice, the floodgate at the entrance to the Exeter Canal. Beyond the swing-bridge to the left (which seems, for once, to be artistic licence occasioned by a faulty memory) a cluster of masts hints at the busy quayside of the city's port. The centre of the composition is dominated not by the Cathedral but by the newly erected Colleton Crescent designed by Matthew Nosworthy. As has often been pointed out, Turner's treatment of the houses on the far bank is curious for they seem to lie below the water level of the river, but this might be explained by his viewpoint and the way the bright reflection in the water obscures the riverside. The v-shaped ripple in the water is perhaps intended to signal the division of the river to our right from the canal behind us. It is typical of Turner's attitudes to topography that although he was on commission for picturesque views he should concentrate on commerce and new building developments rather than the venerable mediaeval city which so delighted artists and tourists alike.

The watercolour was engraved by T. Jeavons in 1829 as part of Charles Heath's *Picturesque Views in England and Wales*. (SS)

81. CORNELIUS VARLEY, *John Heathcoat's Lace Factory at Tiverton* (1824)

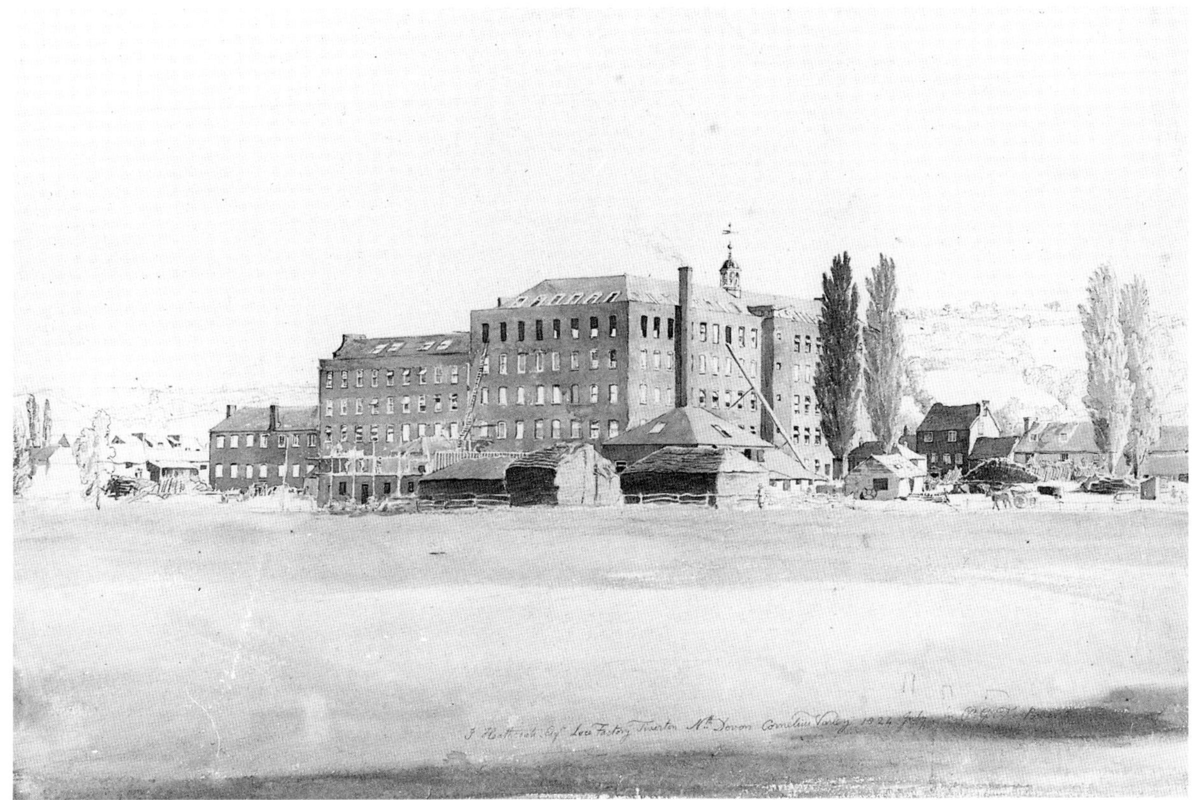

82. CORNELIUS VARLEY,
John Heathcoat's Lace Factory at Tiverton (1824)

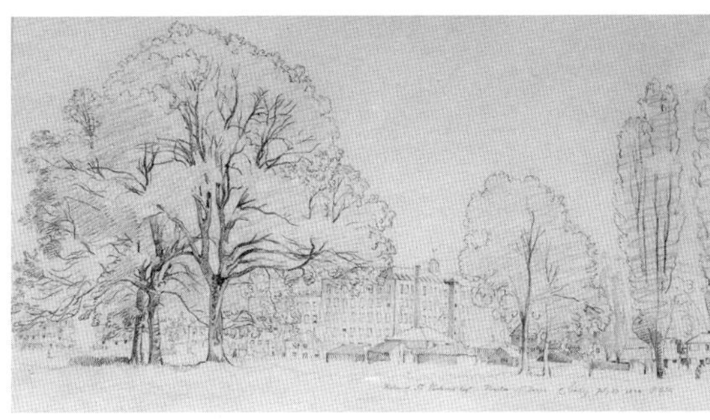

CORNELIUS VARLEY (1781-1873)

81. *John Heathcoat's Lace Factory at Tiverton* (1824)
Watercolour on paper, 38.0 x 55.2 cm
Signed and dated 'July 1824'; inscribed 'J. Heathcoate
(sic) Esq Lace Factory Tiverton Nth Devon in
P.G.T. Power 2'
Sir Ian Amory, Bt.

82. *John Heathcoat's Lace Factory at Tiverton* (1824)
Pencil on paper, 32 x 53.5 cm.
Signed and dated 'July 13, 1824'; inscribed 'Factory of
Jn. Heathcoat Esq, Tiverton, N. Devon. P.G.T.'
The National Trust (Heathcoat-Amory Collection)

Cornelius Varley came to Devon in the summer of
1824, not with the usual picturesque sketching tour in
mind, but to visit John Heathcoat of Tiverton.
Heathcoat was a very large employer of local labour in
his massive lace factory which was an extremely
important part of the local economy. Varley was almost
as much of a scientist as he was an artist, and as well as
making drawings for Heathcoat he worked as a consult-
ing engineer, assisting with iron castings in the new
foundry which began operating on April 6, 1824.[1]
Heathcoat had moved from Loughborough in 1816 'in
consequence of the Luddite disturbances' and set up his
machinery for making bobbin net at Tiverton in what
had originally been a cotton mill. He introduced
improvements including a gasworks, the foundry and,
in 1826, one of the largest water wheels in England. His
factory mostly used silk, and was something of a
landmark:
'The ingenious and beautiful machinery and process
employed in this manufactory induces most strangers
to pay it a visit. The proprietor, with great liberality,
seldom or ever refuses, if the parties are known, or are
introduced by respectable inhabitants of the town.'[2]
All Cornelius Varley's Devon drawings are of the
Tiverton area and most if not all were drawn with his
own patented invention, the Graphic Telescope
(hence 'PGT' inscribed on his sketches).

83. WILLIAM FLEETWOOD VARLEY, *Exeter seen from Alphinton (sic) Fields* (1796)

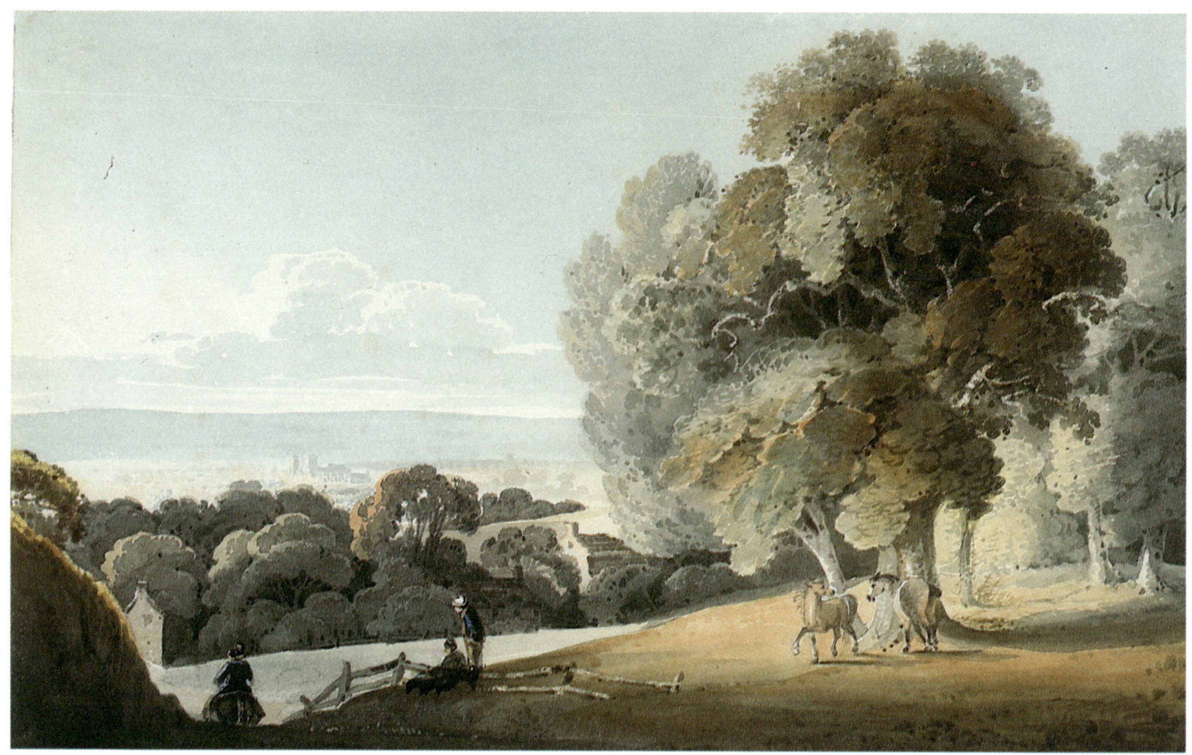

84. JOHN RAWSON WALKER, *View of Torquay* (c.1850)

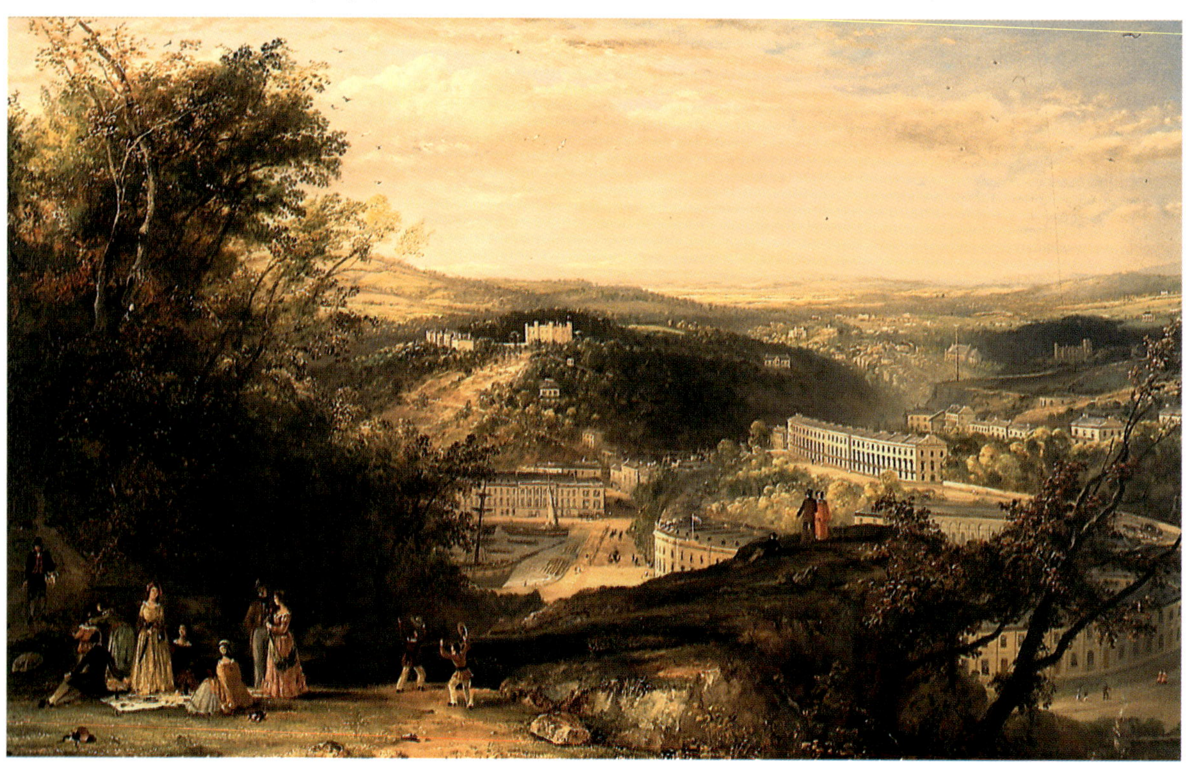

85. FRANCIS WHEATLEY, *View near Ilfracombe* (1778)

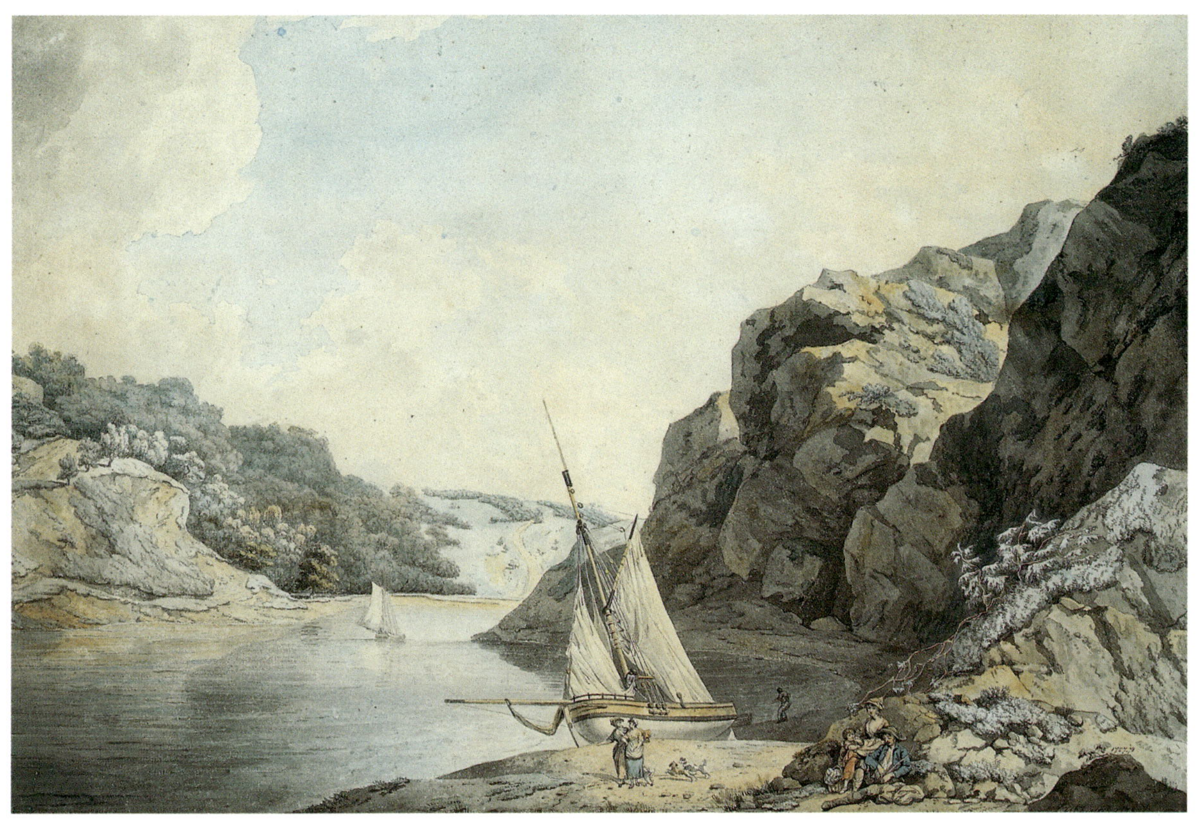

86. RICHARD WILSON, *Lydford Waterfall* (c.1771-2)

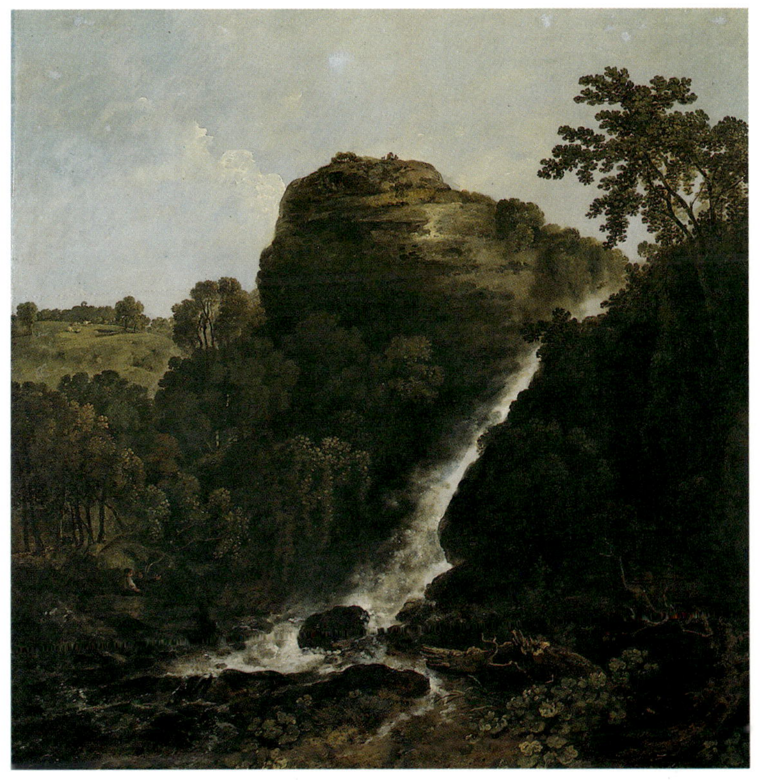

This apparatus enabled quite distant views and buildings to be drawn with greater accuracy.[3] Other visiting artists used various kinds of drawing aids, including Farington, Stevens and Palmer (see *Sketching from Nature*). (MP)

WILLIAM FLEETWOOD VARLEY
(1785-1856)

83. *Exeter seen from Alphinton (sic) Fields* (1796)
(Illustrated in colour on p.108)
Watercolour on paper, 18.7 x 29.9 cm
The Board of Trustees of the
Victoria and Albert Museum, London

William Fleetwood Varley was the youngest, and remains the least recognised, of the well-known Varley family. The very specific title and date for this watercolour both sound appropriate, but in 1796 William was only eleven; which would make him very precocious. William is supposed to have practised as a drawing master in Cornwall c.1810, which time suggests a more appropriate date for this exhibit if the attribution to W.F. Varley is correct.[1] It has attractive, somewhat artificial colours of the kind often seen in hand-coloured aquatints of the late eighteenth and early nineteenth century. The scene has been carefully composed and treated very decoratively.
Like his brothers, William was a drawing master. Although he wrote down his *Principles of Art* these were not published.[2] His brother John, on the other hand, *did* publish his ideas on composition as
A Treatise on the Principles of Landscape Design in 1816-18. One of its plates is of Totnes with its component parts re-arranged for the purposes of making a picturesque art work.[3] John visited Devon in 1810 and made some watercolours of local views for Lord Clifford of Ugbrooke park. These were referred to in local guidebooks and are still there today.[4] Farington (q.v.) and John Varley were both in Devon in the autumn of 1810 and the former records in his diary (October 15) that John Varley was on a visit to Lord Clifford's agent whose main hobby was oil painting. (MP)

JOHN RAWSON WALKER (1794-1873)

84. *View of Torquay* (c.1850)
(Illustrated in colour on p.108)
Oil on canvas, 76.5 x 122 cm.
Borough of Torbay, Torre Abbey Collection

Walker was one of the more notable Nottingham landscape painters who rose to some prominence in the middle of the nineteenth century. He exhibited classically-inspired paintings at the Royal Academy and elsewhere and has been credited with providing an inspirational example for local Nottingham artists.[1]

Walker first visited Torquay in 1829 on his honeymoon and later settled there for a few years from about 1845 to the early 1850s.[2] He developed a method of 'Carbonic Drawing' which was analagous to mezzotint in its procedure, rubbing the paper all over with charcoal and then using special tools to remove it wholly or partially to introduce the highlights. The drawing was then fixed, using a method invented by Walker which could be used out of doors.[3] A drawing in this style, *Old Kiln, near Kerswell, Devonshire*, is in the collection of the British Museum.
In this painting Torquay is depicted in all its early splendour, with fashionable streets such as The Strand, The Terrace and Vaughan Parade prominently displayed. The two red-cloaked figures at the bottom right are probably meant to depict two eccentric sisters, the Misses Durnford, known as 'The Alphington Ponies,' who dressed in identical and outlandish clothes and promenaded in the town every afternoon.[4] (SS)

FRANCIS WHEATLEY (1747-1801)

85. *View near Ilfracombe* (1778)
(Illustrated in colour on p.109)
Watercolour on paper, 46.7 x 65.1 cm
Signed and dated 'F. Wheatley 1778' (lower right)
The Board of Trustees of the
Victoria and Albert Museum, London

This large watercolour is a typical example of Wheatley's finished style of working, with clear, wiry pen outlines and light tints of colour using greys, grey-blues, ochres and pale orange and with only slightly more prominent colours on the foreground figures. It is a self-consciously attractive work with picturesque scenery and figures. The two groups, one comprising two women and three dogs, the other a man, woman and child, are not so much active participants engaged in some discernible occupation as incidental staffage. They have their backs to the pleasant scene which is depicted for *our* enjoyment. They are not appreciative spectators of nature's charms. In 1778, when this watercolour was painted, Wheatley exhibited *View near Ivy Bridge, Devonshire* at the Royal Academy. The same subject was included in his own sale of 'beautiful high-finished' watercolours held in May 1784 when it was paired with a picture of *A Salmon Leap at Leixlip, in Ireland*. This sale also had a *View of a Part of Plymouth opposite Mount Edgecombe* paired with *Conway Castle*.[1] Such linked scenes denoted the growing taste for high quality, elegant, decorative scenes, tasteful adornments for the homes of well-to-do cultured tourists who, like Wheatley himself, were in the habit of making summer tours in search of the picturesque, whether in Devon, Wales or Ireland. (MP)

Fig.30. RICHARD WILSON, *Okehampton Castle,*(c.1771-72) oil on canvas, 169.4 x 165 cm.
Manchester City Art Galleries

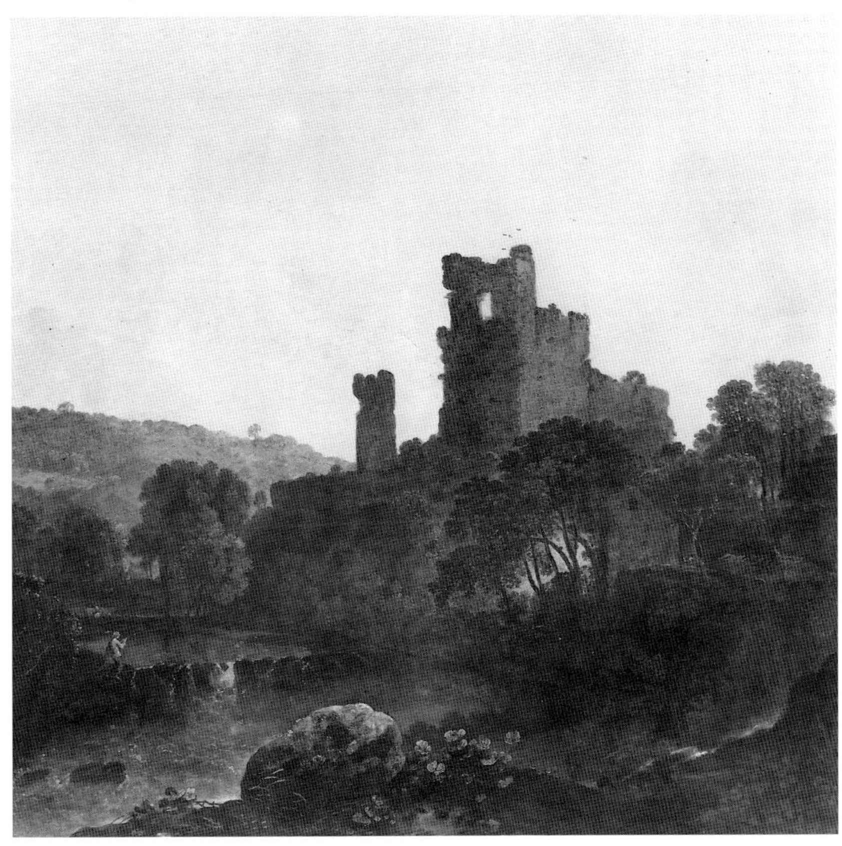

RICHARD WILSON (1713?-1782)

86. *Lydford Waterfall,* (c.1771-2)
(Illustrated in colour on p.109)
Oil on canvas, 169.4 x 165 cm
National Museum of Wales, Cardiff

Wilson painted two companion pictures for Lord
Courtenay in the early 1770s: *Lydford Waterfall*
(National Museum of Wales) and *Oakhampton Castle*
(City of Manchester Art Galleries). They are very
significant examples by a major artist of Devon's grand
and romantic scenes.[1] The unusual, nearly square
format suggests that they were made for a specific
setting at Powderham Castle. After the dispersal of its
'celebrated' picture collection at Christie's in 1816
Powderham was said to have little interest for the
visitor, its 'former splendour' replaced by 'neglect and
delapidation.'[2]
It is surprising that Farington (q.v.), a former pupil of
Wilson and a great admirer of his landscapes, did not
make the short trip to Powderham to see these
pictures during his extended stays in Exeter in 1809
and 1810. They are referred to in a guide book of
1809: 'Two pictures; one of Oakhampton castle; the

other, of a waterfall in this county; Wilson.'[3]
Farington did, however, get a first-hand report of both
these landmark sites from another visiting artist, the
portrait painter J.J. Masquerier. He told him that the
formerly rich wooded scenery around Okehampton
Castle had been much reduced and that Lydford
waterfall was like a 'white ribbon', good for 'Ladies to
visit in fine weather,' but not magnificent or very
interesting: 'no rocks, no grandeur, a scene not to be
spoken of by those who have been in Wales.'[4] Local
guidebooks, not surprisingly, took a different view: the
waterfall was 'one of the grandest and most sublime
scenes, of which this part of England can boast.'[5]
A vignette of Lydford Cascade appears on the title
page of the most important illustrated account of
Devon, with claims that it was 'calculated to inspire
feelings of deep and chastened pleasure.'[6]
Wilson probably came to Devon in 1771. He
exhibited a large view of Okehampton Castle at the
Royal Academy in 1774 (now in City of Birmingham
Art Gallery). His memorandum book contains notes
on expenses incurred on his trip via Honiton,
including £1-16-0d. for the coach journey and 8/6d.
for the post-chaise from Exeter to Powderham.[7] (MP)

NOTES

Artists, Tourism and the Discovery of Devon

1. Henry James 'North Devon' from *English Hours* (1905),
Oxford University Press, 1981, p.53.

2. There was even some early interest in industrial sites, especially
mining.

3. As in 1872, so now there are many people who do indeed envisage
'broad England' as the rural picturesque. One has only to think
of the Prime Minister's recent evocation of what a community at
ease with itself is like (although John Major's vision conjures up
a later, Edwardian idyll) to understand the strength of that
appeal.

4. From Chapter One of W.H. Mallock's *An Immortal Soul* (1908);
quoted in Gilbert Sheldon 'Devonshire Scenery as depicted in
English Prose Literature', *Transactions of the Devonshire Association*,
vol. LXIII, 1931, p.289.

5. See John F. Travis *The Rise of the Devon Seaside Resorts, 1750-1900*,
University of Exeter Press, 1993, pp.7-9, 24. I am indebted to this
indispensable study for most of my information on the
development of resorts and road improvements.

6. Cf. Robert Fraser's belief that Devon was a better place for invalids
to winter than Lisbon and 'may be justly denominated the
Montpellier of England.' In Robert Fraser *General View of the
Agriculture of Devon with Observations on the means of its
Improvement*, London, 1794, p.9.

7. Travis, *op.cit.*, pp.26-47.

8. Stebbing Shaw recommends a tour of the dockyards in his
A Tour to the West of England in 1788, London, 1789, pp.366-7, as
does Richard Warner in *A Tour through Cornwall in the Autumn of
1808*, Bath, 1809, pp.62-6. The American artist Leslie noted that
only British tourists were allowed to tour the naval facilities, for
security reasons. See Tom Taylor (ed), *Autobiographical
recollections by Charles Robert Leslie, R.A.*, London, 1860, p.72.

9. Travis, *op.cit.*, pp.13, 31. Not all coaches travelled at maximum
velocity, however. Leslie's journey from London to Exeter, for
example, still took 24 hours in 1818. See Taylor, *op.cit.*, p.65.

10. Margaret Baker *Discovering the Exeter Road*, Shire Publications,
Tring, 1968, p.5.

11. 'C. Dibdin's Account of Travelling in North Devon in 1801,'
Devon and Cornwall Notes and Queries, vol. 22, 1942-46, p.124.

12. Travis, *op.cit.*, pp.49-50, 76-81.

13. David Elliston Allen plausibly suggests that this enthusiasm can
be explained by a new readership for more popular natural history
and the removal of excise duties on glass in 1845. See *The
Naturalist in Britain - A Social History*, Penguin, Harmondsworth,
1978, pp.136-138.

14. Travis, *op.cit.* pp.168-172, has a useful discussion of the impact of
these enthusiasms.

15. See, for example, Walter White *A Londoner's Walk to the Land's
End and a Trip to the Scilly Isles*, London, 1855.

16. Wilkie Collins and Charles Dickens' *A Message from the Sea*
(published as the Christmas number of *All the Year Round*, 1860)
also helped to establish Clovelly's reputation.

17. See for example Robert Fraser *General View of the Agriculture of
Devon with Observations on the Means of its Improvement*, London,
1794, William Marshall *The Rural Economy of the West of England*,
London, 1796, Charles Vancouver *General View of the Agriculture
of the County of Devon*, London, 1808.

18. Fraser, *op.cit.*, p.9. C.R. Leslie noted the same politeness in 1818.
See Tom Taylor (ed) *Autobiographical Recollections by Charles
Robert Leslie, R.A.*, London, 1860, p.69.

19. Vancouver, *op.cit.*, p.359. Richard Warner shared these sentiments
but only with respect to 'the peasantry of north Devon' in his
A Walk through some of the Western Counties of England, Bath,
1800, pp.120-1, 181-2.

20. Vancouver, *op.cit.*, pp.446 and 464-70.

21. For an examination of rural poverty see Francis Heath
The "Romance" of Peasant Life in the West of England, London,
1872. Although mainly concerned with the situation in Somerset,
Heath discusses Girdlestone's work to alleviate suffering in Devon.

22. James, *op.cit.*, p.53.

23. Turner's work would have to be excused from this statement.
Examination of his West Country pictures reveals a continual
investigation of the social as well as the natural. For an
examination of one such investigation of Cornish industry see
S.A. Smiles 'Picture Notes: *St Mawes at the Pilchard Season,
St Mawes Cornwall, Falmouth, St Mawes Cornwall' Turner Studies*,
vol. 8, no.1, Summer 1988, pp.53-57.

24. The only significant exception to this generalisation among artists
is the work of J.C. Hook in the 1850s and 1860s, who painted
aspects of the fishing industry in Devon. (See *Sketching from
Nature* note 31 and *Hemy* note 5 below). Among writers, Stephen
Reynolds' book *A Poor Man's House*, London, 1909, details the
lives and occupations of a fisherman's family in Sidmouth.

25. T. H. Williams, *Picturesque excursions*, pp.75-6.

26. In 1831 Devon was the fouth most populous county in England.
By 1861 it had dropped to seventh place as Britain's industrial
and manufacturing economy altered the pattern of population. By
this date Exeter's population of 41,749 was of middling size, while
Plymouth and Devonport's 113,039 was exceeded only by
Birmingham, Bristol, Leeds, Liverpool, London, Manchester and
Sheffield.

27. For information on local art production see S.A. Smiles
'Plymouth and Exeter as Centres of Art, 1820-1865,' unpublished
Ph.D dissertation, University Of Cambridge, 1982, especially
pp.38-153.

28. See Felicity Owen *John Gendall (1789-1865) 'Exeter's Forgotten
Artist,'* Royal Albert Memorial Museum, 1979.

29. See S.A. Smiles 'Turner in Devon: some additional information
concerning his visits in the 1810s,' *Turner Studies*, vol. 7, no.1,
Summer 1987, pp.11-14.

30. In three of his letters to Jackson Gainsborough speaks variously of
a visit to Exeter and his intentions to visit Exmouth and
Teignmouth. One of these is undated, one is dated June 9, 1770
and the third is dated July 8, 1779. In this last letter he proposes
sketching alongside Jackson and asks him to show the landscape
painter Edmund Garvey around: '...get him a sight of whatever is
worth his seeing in Exeter.' See Mary Woodall (ed.) *The Letters of
Thomas Gainsborough*, London, 1963, pp.111 and 123.

31. The annotated sketchbook used on this tour is now in The Devon
and Exeter Institution. The Turner in question is probably
T. Turner who exhibited Devon landscapes in London in the
1820s and 1830s.

32. K. Garlick, A. Macintyre and K. Cave (eds) *The Diary of Joseph
Farington*, Yale University Press, 1978-84, 23 September 1809;
10 November - 6 December 1810, *passim*. Patch had a good
collection of pictures by Turner and others, according to Southey
who saw it in 1799. Farington maintained these contacts until his
death.

33. *The Diary of Henry Woollcombe*, West Devon Record Office
710/392, 393, 394, 396. Although they were visiting the county
Downman, Prout and Haydon had, of course, been born in
Devon. As Woollcombe's diary attests, William Eastlake's house
was often the venue for these meetings.

34. Farington, *op.cit.*, October 8 and 12, 1809. Wilkie Collins,
Memoirs of the Life of William Collins, R.A., London, 1848,

vol. I, p.157, 183.

35. There is a Girtin drawing of Sharpham, on the Dart, inscribed 'Bastard Esq'. *cit.* Thomas Girtin and David Loshak *The Art of Thomas Girtin*, London, 1954, no.205. E.P. Bastard bought Collins' *Buckland, on the River Dart* (Royal Academy, 1824) and *Kitley, Devon* (Royal Academy, 1825). Wilkie Collins, *op.cit.*, vol. I, pp.233-4.

36. For Hoppner see Farington, *op.cit.*, October 2, 1803. for Turner see Cyrus Redding, 'The Late J.M.W. Turner', *Fraser's Magazine*, XLV, 1852, p.153.

37. Farington knew Champernowne from at least 1797. See his diary, *op.cit.*, March 2, 1797. For De Wint and F.C. Lewis see relevant essay and catalogue entries below.

38. See the relevant essay and catalogue entries below.

39. Examples of their work is still to be found in all of these houses.

40. Collins, letter dated 26 August, 1819, in Wilkie Collins, *op.cit.*, vol. I, p.157.

41. Murray's *Handbook* (third edition, 1856) referred to pictures by Collins (p.44), Turner (p.48) and Creswick (p.68) to aid tourists' understandings.

42. See Peter Howard *Landscapes: The Artists' Vision*, Routledge, London, 1991, pp.4, 87. Although this finding is significant it should be treated with caution as it may merely reflect a peculiarity of Royal Academy exhibits. Examination of titles of landscapes exhibited at the Society of British Artists and the Society of Painters in Water-Colours does not seem to offer such unequivocal results.

43. William Howitt *The Rural Life of England*, London, 1838, vol. II, pp.378-9.

44. Dartmoor, for example, was avoided by Gilpin and its appreciation was slow to develop. The Royal Society for Literature offered a premium for the best poem on the subject in 1821 which was won by Felicia Hemans, but the poem which was widely considered the best was by the local writer N.T. Carrington, published in 1826. See S.A. Smiles *Plymouth and Exeter as Centres of Art*, pp.19-24 and cat.no.33 below.

45. *Letters of the late Thomas Rundle, L.L.D. to Mrs. Barbara Sandys*, Gloucester, 1749, vol. I, p.CLIV. Letter to Rev. Dean Clarke dated 9 September, 1740.

46. As, for example, Thomas West's *A Guide to the Lakes, in Cumberland, Westmorland, and Lancashire* (1778) whose second edition of 1780 included Thomas Gray's account of the Lakes written in 1769.

47. (Robert Southey) *Letters from England: by Don Manuel Alvarez Espriella. Translated from the Spanish*, London, 1807, reprinted Gloucester, 1984, pp.165-6.

48. Gilpin's Wye tour, made in 1770, was the first of his tours to be published, appearing in 1783. His views had, however, already had an impact, for his manuscripts were widely circulated in the 1770s.

49. William Gilpin *Observations on the Western Parts of England*, London, 1798 pp.186, 245 and 259

50. *Ibid.*, p.173.

51. *Ibid.*, p.217

52. *Ibid.*, pp.230-237.

53. *Ibid.*, pp.243-44. Southey, too, failed to respond to Devon's charms, describing south Devon in 1799 as 'a country which has been so over-praised as completely to disappoint me. Some particular spots were striking, but the character of the whole is bald high hills, with hedges and no trees, and broad views that contained no object on which the eye could fix'. J.W.Warter (ed) *Selections from the Letters of Robert Southey*, 1856, vol. I, p.84.

54. 'E' 'Lines written in the West of England', *The Gentleman's Magazine*, May 1790, p.452.

55. Fraser, *op.cit.*, p.20.

56. W.B. Pope (ed) *The Diary of B.R. Haydon*, Cambridge, Mass., 1960-63, vol. III, p.396.

57. Maurice Exwood & H.L. Lehmann (eds) *The Journal of William Schellinks' Travels in England, 1661-1663*, Camden Fifth Series, Offices of the Royal Historical Society, London, 1993, p.111. Drawings from this tour survive in the British Museum and in the famous Van der Hem *Atlas*, now in the National Library, Vienna, which contains three prospects of Exeter and two of Dartmouth.

58. Place's drawings of Plymouth and its surroundings are now in the collections of Leeds and Plymouth City Art Galleries. See Richard Tyler *Francis Place, 1647-1728*, York Art Gallery, 1971, cat.no.23, p.52.

59. These 1676 etchings are untitled but show Plymouth Fort and the Sound, the Sound with Drake's Island and the Catwater. Place knew and admired Hollar so it is conceivable that he made use of Hollar's knowledge of Plymouth in 1678.

60. Martin Hardie (ed.) Edward Norgate *Miniatura or the Art of Limning*, (1648-50), Oxford, 1919, p.42.

61. *Buckland-Priory, Buckfastre-Abby, Berry Pomery Castle, Dartmouth-Castle, Dartington-Temple, Frithelstoke-Priory, Ford-Abby, Okehampton-Castle, Ottery-Priory, Powderham Castle* (two views), *Tavistock-Abby, Tiverton-Castle* were published in 1734; *Exeter* (two prospects) and *Plymouth* (two prospects) were published in 1736.

62. J. Mason and Canot after S. (G?) Lambert, S. Scott & C.W. Bampfylde, published J. Boydell et al., London, 1755.

63. The comprehensive study is J.V. Somers Cocks *Devon Topographical Prints, 1660-1870 - A Catalogue and Guide*, Devon Library Services, Exeter, 1977.

Sketching from Nature

1. *Art Union*, November 1846, p.310. Ford was reviewing the second annual exhibition of the Devon and Exeter Society for the Encouragement of Art which had opened in September at their Southernhay premises.

2. *Punch*, June 26, 1852, '"Our Critic" among the Pictures', p.7.

3. *Athenaeum*, June 12, 1852, p.657. Lee's contibution to the depiction of Devon is deserving of appraisal and critical attention.

4. *Fun*, January 24, 1863, p.181. 'The Rising Generation. Art "in Articulis".'

5. Rev. R. Warner *A Walk through some of the Western Counties of England*, Bath, 1800, p.128.

6. N.T. Carrington et al. *The Teignmouth, Dawlish, and Torquay Guide...*, Teignmouth, (1830), p.7. T.H. Williams put down William Gilpin's lack of enthusiasm for Devon scenery to 'a continuance of bad weather, which represses curiosity, and confines the tourist to an inn'. *Picturesque Excursions in Devonshire and Cornwall*, 1804, p.98.

7. D. and S. Lysons *Magna Britannia*, vol.VI, 1822, *Devon*, pp.CCLI-CCLIII: 'Surface and Scenery.'

8. Warner, *op.cit.*, p.177.

9. *Picturesque Views on the River Exe*, Tiverton, 1819, p.15.

10. F. Stevens *Views of Cottages and Farm-houses in England and Wales*, R. Ackermann, London, 1815, introduction, p.III. See also Peter Bicknell and Jane Munro *Gilpin to Ruskin. Drawing Masters and their Manuals, 1800-1860*, Fitzwilliam Musuem, Cambridge, 1988.

11. Stevens, *op.cit.*, p.2.

12. *Athenaeum*, June 5, 1847, p.599. The studies noted in Collins's sale at Christies were of *Hartland Quay* (cat.no.8), *Dartmouth Castle, Lanacombe* and *Near Buckland* 'all fine as delineations of Devonshire scenery.'

13. Stevens, *op.cit.*, p.27.

14. *Ibid.*, p.29.

15. W. Collingwood, 'Reminiscences of J.D. Harding', *Magazine of Art*, December 1897, p.82. Harding's paper was unbleached, with the 'rough side having a pleasant tooth.' 'This must not be judged', wrote Collingwood, 'by the rubbish afterwards turned out with his initials upon it, which is a libel on his reputation.' Other artists liked special paper. Aaron Penley's original sketch, illustrated here as a chromolithograph (fig.26, p.87), was on paper 'known as *whitey-brown*, and, in this instance, was sent from the grocer's as a paper bag containing starch.' A. Penley, 'On Landscape Painting in Water Colours', *The Chromolithograph*, August 8, 1868, p.269. The subject is a farmer's house near Ilfracombe.

16. Tom Taylor (ed) *Autobiographical Recollections by Charles Robert Leslie, R.A.*, London, 1860, p.67.

17. A.H. Palmer *The Life and Letters of Samuel Palmer*, London, 1892, p.106.

18. A.H. Palmer 'The Story of an Imaginative Painter', *The Portfolio*, 1884, pp.148-9.

19. See Leslie Parris et al. *Landscape in Britain c.1750-1850*, Tate Gallery, 1973, pp.124-54: 'Optical Instruments', for illustrations of all these aids, and commentaries.

20. Isaac Taylor *Personal Recollections. VI - The Summer of the Comet of 1811. Devonshire and Dartmoor*, in *Good Words*, 1864, p.519.

21. See below, *Francis Danby*, note 15.

22. Taylor, *op.cit.*, p.516.

23. *Ibid.*, p.521.

24. R. Lister, *Palmer Catalogue Raisonné*, No. 574. The comet was Donati's comet, which was also depicted by William Turner of Oxford and William Dyce.

25. Arthur H.D. Acland (ed) *Memoir and Letters of the Right Honourable Sir Thomas Dyke Acland*, 1902 (privately printed), p.248. T.D. Acland's father (of the same name) was also a notable sketcher and patron of the arts, to whom a good many prints were dedicated. The four-day Dartmoor sketching trip is described by Acland's fellow sketcher, D.R. Fearon, pp.247-52. Two years later P.H. Gosse sketched on Dartmoor during a two week stay. He had been inspired by his second wife (née Eliza Brightwen), who had had drawing lessons from J.S. Cotman. 'These landscapes, if they were not very artistic, were often marked by his keenness of observation and originality of aspect.' He always selected view points 'from which nothing which suggested human life was visible.' Edmund Gosse *The Naturalist by the Sea Shore. The Life of Philip Henry Gosse*, London, 1896, pp.349, 362.

26. Warner, *op.cit.*, p.110.

27. Rev. J. Eagles *The Sketcher*, London, 1856, p.10.

28. 'Land-slip near Linton, North Devon. Remarkable Escape.' (From an unidentified source, probably the *Illustrated London News*).

29. *Athenaeum*, March 20, 1858, p.375. The painting, at the Portland Gallery, was by J. Morten. The varied reactions of the onlookers made it 'a full and humorous picture, ...full of real fun, not the worse for being a trifle caricatured.'

30. *Athenaeum*, May 7, 1859. Royal Academy review.

31. A.J. Hook *Life of James Clarke Hook, R.A.* (3 vols., privately printed, 1929-32), vol. I, p.90.

32. J.G. Marks *Life and Letters of Frederick Walker, A. R.A.*, London, 1896, pp.272-5. Preliminary sketches for *The Unknown Land* are illustrated on pp.259, 263, 292.

33. It was soon represented in prints which were on sale locally. Fifteen are listed in J.V. Somers Cocks *Devon Topographical Prints, 1660-1870 - a Catalogue and Guide*, Exeter, 1977.

34. C.G. Carus *The King of Saxony's Journey through England and Scotland in the year 1844*, translated S.C. Davidsen, London, 1846, pp.196, 201.

35. *Ibid.*, p.205.

36. Hablot K. Browne (Phiz) *Sketches of the Seaside and the Country*, The Graphotyping Company, London (1860s). John Leech, 'Sketching the Castle' from *Once a Week*, July 16, 1859. P.H. Gosse was reminded of Leech's caricatures of female beachcombers while he was out hunting for specimens.

37. Arthur Wragg *Jesus Wept. A Commentary in black and white on ourselves and the world today*, London, n.d. (1930s).

Frederick Christian Lewis and the Rivers of Devon

1. Twenty eight at the Royal Academy and British Institution, and Dart scenes at the Watercolour Society in 1818 and 1820. He also exhibited Devon scenes in Exeter between 1845-47.

2. *Scenery of the River Dart, being a Series of Thirty-five Views, Representing the most interesting features in its course...*(1821); *The Scenery of the Rivers Tamar, and Tavy, in Forty Seven Subjects, Exhibiting the Most Interesting Views on their Banks...*(1823); *The Scenery of the River Exe* (1827).

3. *Scenery on the Devonshire Rivers* (1843). Twenty eight further Devon scenes are included in Lewis's *Scenery of the Rivers of England and Wales* (1845-8): nineteen in part one; two in part two; and seven in part three. Some of them are his earlier plates, further reworked.

4. Anna Bray, *Borders of the Tamar and Tavy*, vol. III, p.264.

5. *Athenaeum*, July 17, 1847. 'Fine Arts Exhibition at Westminster Hall.' Pl.38 in *Rivers of England and Wales*, part two, is entitled *Study for the Picture Exhibited at Westminster Hall*, and on that basis one can entirely sympathise with the reviewer.

6. Anna Bray, *op.cit.*, p.286. She mentions this in connection with a recent trip paid by Lewis to Tavistock in 1835.

7. *Ibid.*, pp.282-3

8. *Scene on the Dartmoor, Devon, from Ben She Tor*, Royal Academy, 1820.

9. G. Grigson, 'Meanings of Landscape' in *Places of the Mind*, 1949, p.113.

10. *Scenery of the River Dart*, title page.

11. S. D. Kitson *The Life of John Sell Cotman*, 1937, pp.321-2. fig.138 illustrates one of Cotman's 'masterly chalk drawings.' This same scene from Lewis's *Benshe Tor*, pl.6 of his *Dart* series, is also illustrated (with the source also unrecognised) in A. Holcomb, *John Sell Cotman*, (British Museum Prints and Drawings Series), 1978, pl.84.

12. *Western Luminary*, August 12, 1823.

13. *Ibid.*, April 10, 1827.

14. *Ibid.*.

15. April 13, 1836. The *Athenaeum*, March 11, 1848, p.274 recorded a meeting at which 'Mr. F.C. Lewis's Book of English Scenery and Studies in Devonshire was on the tables and looked at with renewed pleasure.'

16. M. Lewis, *John Frederick Lewis, R.A.*, 1978, p.14. F.C. and J.F. Lewis were at Dartington in 1829 and F.C. again probably in 1842 (undated letter with watermark 1842 in Fitzwilliam Museum).

17. *Athenaeum*, June 24, 1843, p.596. 'Fine Arts. New Publications.'

18. All the Lewis quotations, written in the third person, are from his 'Introductory Remarks.'

Notes to the Catalogue

SAMUEL HENRY BAKER

1. See Stephen Wildman *The Birmingham School*, Birmingham City Museum and Art Gallery, 1990, pp.46-47.

JAMES BOURNE

1. He exhibited *Sidmouth* (no.91) and *Coast Scene, Sidmouth* (no.115) at the first exhibition of the Royal Manchester Institution in 1827. See M.J.H. Liversidge 'James Bourne - an assessment of his life and work', *The Connoisseur*, vol. 163, Sept.-Dec. 1966, pp.161-165. The Usher Art Gallery's *Cottage at Buckland* and *Chudleigh Rocks at Ugbrooke House* suggest that Bourne's Devon work was extensive.

2. For example, Alexander Cozens *A New method of Assisting the Invention in Drawing Original Compositions of Landscape* (1785).

3. Liversidge, *op.cit.* p.162, suggests that Bourne may have toured Wales with Beaumont in 1800.

4. E. Butcher *An Excursion from Sidmouth to Chester in the Summer of 1803*, 1805, p.452. Cited in Travis, *op.cit.*, p.38.

GEORGE PRICE BOYCE

1. *Athenaeum*, December 7, 1862, p.850. 'The Water-Colour Painters' Lancashire Relief Fund Exhibition.'

2. For an account of Boyce's work see C. Newall and J. Egerton, *George Price Boyce*, Tate Gallery, 1987, and V. Surtees (ed.) *The Diaries of George Price Boyce*, 1980. Boyce made other watercolours of Devon and spent some months in north Devon in the latter half of 1858. *The Diaries*, *op.cit.*, p.76 deals with the very favourable reviews of a picture of Anstey's Cove (now lost) which must have been made in 1853 and seems to have shared the same kind of careful observation as found in *Babbacombe Bay*.

3. *A Guide to the Watering places, on the Coast, Between the Exe and the Dart...1817*, p.47.

4. *Voyage Round Great Britain*, vol. VIII, 1825, p.14.

5. Somers Cocks, *op.cit.*, Nos.3027-3067 with dates between 1825
and c.1875.
6. Palmer to Julia Richmond, September 1866. In R. Lister (ed.)
The Letters of Samuel Palmer, Oxford, 1974, vol. II, p.746.
7. E. Gosse *The Naturalist of the Sea Shore. The Life of Philip Henry
Gosse*, London, 1896, p.237.
8. *Ibid.*, p.237.
9. Thirteen different reviews are quoted from in an advertisement for
A Naturalist's Rambles, in P.H. Gosse, *The Aquarium: An Unveiling
of the Wonders of the Deep Sea*, London, 1854.
10. 'H.J.', 'Sea-Side Life', *Once a Week*, August 2, 1862, p.150.
Gosse is referred to in Rev. W. Houghton, *Sea-side Walks of a
Naturalist with his Children*, 1860s, p.31.
11. E. Gosse, *op cit.*, p.237.
12. *A Guide to the Watering Places, on the Coast, Between the Exe and
the Dart*, 1821, seventeen page section at the end of the volume.
13. Rev. J.G. Wood, *The Common Objects of the Sea Shore*, 1861, p.19.
See also J.G. Francis, *Beach-Rambles in search of Sea-Side Pebbles
and Crystals*, 1859.
14. E. Gosse, *op cit.*, p.237.

HENRY BRIGHT
1. *Art Union*, June 1, 1844, p.75. See M. Allthorpe-Guyton,
Henry Bright 1810-1873, Norfolk Museums Service, 1986,
cat.no.38, p.67.
2. See Allthorpe-Guyton, cat. no. 37, p.67. This is called *Beach Scene
with Figures* but on the basis of a preparatory sketch for it
(unrecognised as such), cat.no.39, it should be titled *Rocky
Coast, Polperro*, a version of which he exhibited at the British
Institution in 1844.
3. Allthorpe-Guyton, pp. 41-3 for Bright's exhibited works.
4. *Athenaeum*, May 6, 1843, p.443.
5. *Fraser's Magazine*, June 1844, cit. G. Saintsbury (ed.) *The Paris
Sketch Book and Art Criticisms* by William Makepeace Thackeray,
vol. 2 of the Oxford Thackeray, n.d., pp.635-6.

FRANCIS CHANTREY
1. See Alex Potts, *Sir Francis Chantrey*, National Portrait Gallery,
1980.
2. *Portfolio*, 1886, p. 44. *Peak Scenery; or, Excursions in Derbyshire*,
1822.
3. *Plymouth and Plymouth Dock Weekly Journal*, September 20, 1821.
4. In addition to this statue, St Andrew's, Plymouth, contains a
monument by Chantrey to Mrs. Risdew (died 1818) and St.
Margaret's, Topsham, contains monuments to Admiral Sir John
Duckworth (died 1817) and Lt. Col. G.H. Duckworth (died 1811).
Later commissions in Devon include monuments to Jane Barker
(dated 1829), also in St. Andrews, and Richard Rosdew (died 1837)
in St. Mary's, Plympton.

WILLIAM COLLINS
1. Letters to Francis Collins, August 10, 1829 and to David Wilkie,
September 8, 1836 in Wilkie Collins *Memoirs of the Life of
William Collins, R.A.*, London, 1848, vol. I, p. 68, vol.II, p.70.
2. *Ibid.* vol. I, pp.157-8.
3. A watercolour of Dartmouth was at Colnaghi's, August 1964,
lot no. 64 (illustrated).
4. Engraved E. Finden and published 1824. Collins also contributed
Sidmouth, Devon, and *Hall Sands* (both engraved W.B. Cooke and
published 1821) and *Linmouth, or Lynemouth* (engraved W.B.
Cooke and published 1824) to this series. The latter print derives
from work done on his 1821 tour.
5. *The Diary of Henry Woollcombe*, West Devon Record Office
710/396. Entry for September 3, 1821; Constable to John Fisher,
November 3, 1821, in Beckett, *Constable's Correspondence:
VI – The Fishers*, Suffolk Records Society, Vol.XII, 1968, p.81.
6. Wilkie Collins, *op.cit.*, pp.182-184. From sketches made on this
tour Collins exhibited *Woodcutters - Buckland in the Moor* and
Clovelly, North Devon at the Royal Academy in 1822. The latter,
'the sea-piece of the year' was based on a sketch made after the
storm, with the sea still rough and clouds flying above the village.
Wilkie Collins, *op.cit.*, vol. I, p.190.
7. This sketch was included in P.H. Delamotte *The Art of Sketching

from Nature, (London, 1871), second edition, London, 1888,
p.41, figure 3. Delamotte describes Collins as 'one of the most
faithful sketchers of English coast scenery' and calls cat.no.8
'a vigorous sketch from nature, with more power and force than
Collins's works generally possess... there is no striking point of
attractive interest in the whole line of scarcely varying coast and
hills all the way from the foreground to the far headland in the
distance. It is only the influence of light on this very simple
subject that gives it interest and attractiveness. A gleam of
sunshine brightens up the rain-laden clouds, which drift sea-ward
before a fresh wind; it pours an almost unbroken breadth on the
calm sea, gilding the line of the horizon against the mass of
distant and deep grey clouds behind it; it plays around the shadow
and the cloud on the edge of the water in every inlet, wandering
amid the dark rocks and dank seaweed, darkened still further by
the effect of contrast. As a study of light and shade, a more
favourable or instructive example could scarcely be given: as a
lesson in composition, it is excellent - the forms are happily
balanced, and the lines are varied and agreeable. The original
drawing is a very freshly-painted, unaffected study of nature.'
Ibid., pp.65-6.
8. Wilkie Collins, *op.cit.* vol. II, pp.275-81, 297-8. *Hall Sands* is now in
the collection of the Victoria and Albert Museum.

DAVID COX
1. See N. Neal Solly *Memoir of the Life of David Cox*, London, 1873,
p.42.
2. *Torquay*, engraved J.Rogers, published I.T.Hinton, London, 1830;
The Tor, Devonshire, engraved J.C.Allen, published I.T.Hinton,
London, 1830, both for Hinton's *Watering Places of Great Britain*,
1831; *Off Teignmouth*, engraved A. Willmore, published by the
Art Union of London, 1870.
3. Solly, *op.cit.*, p.42.
4. Solly, *op.cit.*, pp.319, 331. A possible third trip is suggested by the
existence of a gouache entitled *The Pier at Lynmouth, Devon, with
the Hills of Wales seen across the Bristol Channel*, 12.1 x 18.1 cm,
inscribed and dated on the back in Cox's hand 'Lynmouth Pier
taken from the Linton Ro[ad]/ 1822.' Also inscribed on the back is
'D. Cox's best respects / to J.R. Walker' which suggests that Cox,
working out of Birmingham, knew John Rawson Walker
(cat.no.84), working out of Nottingham. See *David Cox,
1783-1859*, Anthony Reed, London, 1983, cat.no.10.
5. Solly, *op.cit.*, p.46. Cox exhibited watercolours entitled *Lymouth
Pier* (sic) at the Society of Painters in Water Colours exhibitions
of 1824 (no. 250), 1826 (no.193) and 1828 (no.209); *Ibid.*,
pp.319-320.
6. David Cox *A Treatise on Landscape Painting and Effect in Water
Colours*, 1813, reprinted as a special number of *The Studio*, 1922,
pp.16-17
7. *Ibid.*, p.17.

FRANCIS DANBY
1. F. Greenacre *Francis Danby*, Tate Gallery and City of Bristol
Museum and Art Gallery, 1988, cat.no.105, p.144; p.168 notes a
pencil drawing 'The River Dart One Mile below Totnes',
19.4 x 34.3 cm, private collection.
2. *Ibid.*, p.168 lists 'View of Star Cross from Exmouth', watercolour,
36.5 x 67.9 cm, Sun Life Assurance, Bristol.
3. William Daniell, *A Voyage Round Great Britain*, vol. VIII, 1825,
p.11.
4. R.W. Prothero *The Letters of Richard Ford, 1797-1858*, London,
1905. Letter dated April 30, 1845.
5. *Athenaeum*, February 21, 1852, p.230. 'Fine Arts. British
Institution.'
6. *Art Journal*, February 1857, p.41. 'Visits to Private Galleries of the
British School. The Collection of Thomas Miller, Esq. of Preston.'
7. Geoffrey Grigson, *The Harp of Aeolus and other Essays on Art,
Literature and Nature*, London, 1948. 'Some Notes on Francis
Danby, A.R.A.', p.66.
8. *Ibid.*, p.75.
9. See Charles Hadfield, *Atmospheric Railways. A Victorian Venture in
Silent Speed*, David and Charles, 1967. Pl. xv depicts a

contemporary watercolour of the Starcross engine house in use. Pl. xvi shows the interior after its conversion for use as a chapel. Chapters 9 and 10, pp.143-176, are devoted to the South Devon line. Public services on the atmospheric line ran between Exeter and Teignmouth from 13 September 1847 to 5 September 1848.

10. N.T. Carrington and others, *The Teignmouth, Dawlish and Torquay Guide; with an account of the surrounding Neighbourhood*, Teignmouth, n.d. (early 1840s), pp.223-4.

11. Noticed in the *Art Union*, 1847, p.196.

12. F. Danby to J. Gibbons, November 22, 1848, in Greenacre, *op.cit.*, p.35.

13. F. Danby to J. Gibbons, August 24, 1851, *cit.*, Adams, *Francis Danby: Varieties of Poetic Landscape*, Paul Mellon Centre for Studies in British Art, New Haven and London, 1973, p.112.

14. F. Danby to H. Mogford, February 13, 1853. Yale Center for British Art, Henry Bicknell album. Danby's daughter Frances married the Devon painter John Mogford.

15. *The Western Luminary*, April 7, 1857, p.5.

16. *Art Journal*, March 1855, p.80. 'British Artists - Their Style and Character.'

WILLIAM DANIELL

1. K. Garlick et al. *The Diary of Joseph Farington*, March 3, 1811.

2. *Babicome, Devon* was published in 1825 in vol. VIII.

ANTHONY DEVIS

1. See *Anthony Devis (1729-1816) a 'picturesque traveller,'* Harris Museum and Art Gallery, Preston, 1993; Sydney H. Pavière *The Devis Family of Painters*, Leigh-on-Sea, 1950, pp.73-98.

2. Harris Museum and Art Gallery, Preston. The Harris collection also contains a view on the river Dart.; Pavière, *op.cit.*, pp.84-5.

3. Newport Museum and Art Gallery; Pavière, *op.cit.*, p.83

4. H.L. Bradfer-Lawrence collection; Pavière, *op.cit.*, p.90

5. B.A. Dunk collection; Pavière, *op.cit.*, p.79. Devis sometimes sketched with his nephew Robert Marris whose exhibits at the Royal Academy in the early 1780s also include views of Barnstaple and Ilfracombe (1780), Torrington, Linton and the Valley of Stones (1781) and Clovelly (1783).

6. W. G. Maton *Observations*, pp.83-4. It included an aquatint *The Valley of Stones* by S. Alken after Revd. T. Rackett.

PETER DE WINT

1. Cit. Hammond Smith, *Peter DeWint*, London, 1982, p.125. At the Water Colour Society in 1842 De Wint exhibited *Falls of the West Lynn, at Lynmouth, North Devon* (no. 11), and in 1844 *A Salmon Leap at Lynmouth, North Devon* (no.3). One of these may be the watercolour of the West Lynn now in the collection of Birmingham Museum and Art Gallery.

2. *Athenaeum*, May 12, 1849, p.496.

3. Hammond Smith, *op.cit.*, p.125.

4. David Scrase, *Drawings and Watercolours by Peter De Wint*, Fitzwilliam Museum, Cambridge, 1979 , pp.50-52. Another study of Dart scenery was sold at Christie's, 6 November 1973 (215), called *Cattle watering in a Pool on the Dart* (photo. Witt Library).

5. *Rivers of Devon*, Introduction, p.4.

REVEREND JOHN EAGLES

1. See Francis Greenacre *The Bristol School of Artists - Francis Danby and Painting in Bristol 1810-1840*, Bristol 1973, cat. nos. 300 and 301, p.247. An oil painting of Lynmouth c.1835 is listed as cat.no.293, p.244.

2. John Eagles, *The Sketcher*, London, 1856, p.76.

3. *Ibid.*, p.208.

4. *Ibid.*, pp. 158-60, 192-3, 211, 220.

HENRY EDRIDGE

1. K. Garlick et al., *The Diary of Joseph Farington*, April 9, 1818. Other artists and amateurs profitted from Farington's knowlege of Devon. Among at least half a dozen enquirers Farington gave Callcott such advice on July 29, 1812.

2. See J.V. Somers Cocks, *Devon Topographical Prints*, nos. 127 and 129.

3. Further views include (*Sid*)*mouth*, August 22, 1818 , Oppé

Collection; *Branscombe*, August 25, Jupp Catalogue, Royal Academy, vol. IV; *Exeter Cathedral*, sold at Sotheby's, March 16, 1978, lot 58.

JOSEPH FARINGTON

1. K. Garlick et al. *The Diary of Joseph Farington*.

2. The Devon volume of *Magna Britannia* was published in 1822 and contained four Exeter subjects by Farington as well as views at Clovelly, Ilfracombe, Lynmouth, Dawlish, Sidmouth, Berry Pomeroy and Plymouth.

3. *Diary*, September 21, 1809.

4. *Ibid.*, November 23, 1810.

5. *Ibid.*, November 24, 1810.

6. *Ibid.*, October 27, 1810.

MYLES BIRKET FOSTER

1. Tom Taylor preface to *Birket Foster's Pictures of English Landscape*, 1863, (preface dated July 1862).

2. Watercolour, 10.2 x 14 cm, sold Christie's, March 4, 1975, lot 91, illus. pl.20.

3. *Illustrated London News*, August 24, 1850 and January 11, 1851.

HENRY GASTINEAU

1. A drawing of Dartington Hall is in the Whitworth Art Gallery, Manchester.

2. No. 214. Information kindly supplied by Stephen Wildman.

3. James, 'North Devon' pp.56-7.

THOMAS GIRTIN

1. Private collection. Another version was at Sotheby's, July 14, 1994, lot 116. The four watercolours exhibited at the Royal Academy in 1798 were: *Coast of Dorsetshire* (342), *Berry Pomeroy Castle* (343), *Inside of Exeter Cathedral* (538) and *A Mill in Devonshire* (677).

2. Leeds City Art Gallery

3. National Gallery of Victoria, Melbourne, and Yale Center for British Art, New Haven.

4. Both British Museum.

5. Yale Center for British Art.

6. Both in private collections.

7. Moore's *A List of the Principal Castles and Monastries in Great Britain* was published in 1798. Turner certainly made use of this book, copying out the names of Devon sites, among others, which Moore had starred as particularly worthy of attention in the flyleaf of his 'Dinevor Castle' sketchbook (1798), TB XL. Could Girtin have recommended Moore to him?

8. Mrs Calvert exhibited *Appledore* (no.91) and an unnamed *View* (no.102) by J. (*sic*) Girtin at the sixth annual exhibition of pictures at the Plymouth Institution, 1821.

9. The version in the Sir Hickman Bacon collection has 'Mr. Ambrose Johns/Plymouth' inscribed on the back of the mount. In this connection it is worth noting that an Exeter artist, James Leakey, owned a sketch purportedly by Girtin for a projected picture of Exeter Cathedral which was never executed. It was bequeathed to the Dean and Chapter of Exeter Cathedral by Leakey's executors. See *Exeter Flying Post*, October 18, 1865. The authenticity of this sketch has, however, been doubted.

10. Thomas Girtin and David Loshak *The Art of Thomas Girtin*, London, 1954, p.66 where it is incorrectly described as a view of Exmouth. The correct identification was first published in Francis Hawcroft's *Watercolours by Thomas Girtin*, Whitworth Art Gallery and Victoria and Albert Museum, 1975, pp.38-39.

11. *A View on the River Taw looking from Braunton Marsh towards Instow and Appledore* (1800: private collection) and *The Estuary of the River Taw* (1801: Yale Center for British Art).

12. Whitworth Art Gallery, pencil inscription on page 48 verso. Further corroboration from the *Shepherd Sketchbook* may lie in its containing a drawing inscribed 'Battersea Reach' which would become *The White House, Chelsea*, one version of which is connected to A.B. Johns (see note 9 above). If Girtin used that sketchbook in 1800 at Plymouth he might have showed it to Johns, who requested a version of the Battersea Reach composition and was later offered the replica which has his name on it.

13. In the Ashmolean Museum and the National Gallery of
New Zealand respectively.

14. Sold Sotheby's 11 July, 1990 lot 92. See Susan Morris
'Two Girtin Discoveries,' *Sotheby's Art at Auction*, 1989-90,
pp.56-59.

15. See Susan Morris *Thomas Girtin, 1775-1802*, Yale Center for
British Art, New Haven, 1986, pp.16-18, 21-23.

16. *Copper Plate Magazine*, pl.CLXI, October 1, 1798; pl.CLXXI,
March 1, 1799; pl.CCXXXVII December 2, 1801.

17. J.Walker *The Itinerant: A Select Collection of interesting and
Picturesque Views, in Great Britain and Ireland*, London,1799-1801,
containing six line engravings after Girtin, James Moore, Rowe
and Miss Rolle.

JOHN GLOVER

1. T.H. Williams, *Picturesque Excursions in Devonshire and Cornwall*,
1804, p.99.

2. *Ibid.*, p.106.

3. Bradley Mill subjects were exhibited in 1812, 1816 and 1829.
For Glover's exhibited works see Basil Long, *John Glover*,
Walker's Quarterly, No. 15, April 1924, pp.33-51.

4. Farington's *Diary*, November 11, 1810.

JAMES DUFFIELD HARDING

1. British Institution 1827, nos. 268, 280, 282. Lithographs of
Appledore (c.1830) and *Clovelly* (1833) must be derived from the
same tour.

2. Drawings inscribed 'The Ness, Shaldon Devo(n), Sept. 20, 1858,'
Victoria and Albert Museum; 'South Brent, Devon 1858,' Trustees
of the Royal Society of Painters in Water-Colours; 'South Brent
Sep. 15, 1858,' Tate Gallery.

3. Mrs. Bray *The Borders of the Tamar and Tavy*, 1836, vol. III, p.264.

4. Mrs Bray, *op.cit.*, pp.282-3.

5. *Endsleigh, Devon* Sept. 1827; *Chudleigh Rocks Devon* Sept. 1835;
Shipley Bridge, Devon, dated 1859; *Old Bridge at Brent, Devon*,
dated 1860. A chromolithograph after Harding of *Lydia Bridge on
the Brent* was published in 1861, size 18" x 22" and priced at 12/-.

6. *The Ports, Harbours, Watering-Places, and Coast Scenery of Great
Britain.*, 2 vols., G.Virtue, 1842. Of the seven Devon scenes in
volume one, six are after Harding: *Sidmouth, Exmouth, Budleigh,
Ladram, Plymouth* (2 views). The seventh, of *Brixham*, is after
Edward Duncan.

CHARLES NAPIER HEMY

1. See *Charles Napier Hemy R.A.*, Laing Art Gallery, Newcastle, 1984.
Catalogue by Andrew Greg.

2. *Ibid.*, p.21. the catalogue also draws attention to the work of the
little known J.G. Naish.

3. *Athenaeum*, February 12, 1859, p. 226. In the same exhibition
(The British Institution) Moore's *The Coast of North Devon -
Squally Weather* was described as 'so minute and hard that to tell
the real truth, it looks rather like a slice of bad cake'! York Art
Gallery possesses two of Moore's Devon pictures, both
representing Holne bridge on the river Dart. (York Art Gallery,
Catalogue of Paintings, vol. III, Nos. 137, 249).

4. These extracts from reviews of Gosse's *A Naturalist's Rambles on the
Devonshire Coast* (1853) come from an advertisement in Gosse's
The Aquarium (1854). William Morris had criticized Hemy for his
over-attention to a close study of nature ('what Ruskin calls a
picture'). *Hemy, op.cit.*, p.25.

5. *Athenaeum*, May 7, 1859, p.618.

6. *Ibid.*, March 20, 1858, p.376. In 1864 *The Times* commented:
'seashore pictures abound, and Cornwall and North Devon are
favourite "pitches" for this kind of subject.' (*Cit.*, *Landscape in
Britain 1850-1950*, Hayward Gallery, 1983, p.75).

7. For Hook see A.H. Palmer, *The Portfolio*, 1888, a series of five
essays, and A.J. Hook, *Life of James Clarke Hook*, 3 vols, privately
printed, 1929-32.

8. *Hemy, op.cit.*, pp.24-5.

HOPKINS HORSLEY HOBDAY HORSLEY

1. Stephen Wildman, *The Birmingham School*, p.46.

2. *Ibid.*, pp.8-9.

3. Sketches inscribed 'Dawlish June 1847' and 'East Ogwell Mill
nr. Newton July 1847' are in the collection of Birmingham City
Museum and Art Gallery.

4. He must have returned to Devon on at least one further occasion,
as the Birmingham collection has a drawing of Sidford dated
September 1865.

5. Coincidentally Prout had, in fact, exhibited *Cottages at Bishop's
Teignton, Devon* (no.82) at the Associated Artists in Water-
Colours exhibition of 1810.

JOHN WILLIAM INCHBOLD

1. Christopher Newall *John William Inchbold, Pre-Raphaelite Landscape
Artist*, Leeds City Art Galleries, 1993, pp.50-1. N.T. Carrington's
Dartmoor- a Descriptive Poem was published in London in 1826,
with 12 etchings by the Plymouth artist P.H. Rogers. It quickly
established itself as the descriptive standard for Dartmoor,
eclipsing Felicia Hemans' poem of 1821. A memorial to
Carrington was placed at the top of the Dewerstone.

2. Allen Staley *The Pre-Raphaelite Landscape*, Oxford, 1973, p.116.

3. Newall, *op.cit.*, p.50.

4. *Ibid.*, pp.53-54.

5. Henry Carrington *The Plymouth and Devonport Guide*, 1828, p.255.

6. Published in Plymouth with 11 lithographs after the local artist
C.F. Williams. For changing attitudes to Dartmoor see S.A.
Smiles 'Plymouth and Exeter as Centres of Art, 1820-1865,'
pp.19-24.

7. Newall, *op.cit.*, pp.54-5.

SAMUEL PHILLIPS JACKSON

1. See Jack Kingston 'The History of the Torpoint Ferry'
Old Cornwall, vol. VII, no.5, 1969, pp.198-206. Rendel's ferry was
operational from 1834.

2. William White *History, Gazetteer, and Directory of Devonshire*,
Sheffield, 1850, p.713.

FREDERICK CHRISTIAN LEWIS

1. *Guide in a Tour to the Watering Places, and their Environs on the
South-East Coast of Devon*, (1802), p.99.

2. J.V. Somers Cocks, *Devon Topographical Prints*, no.s 114-161.

3. *Scenery of the Rivers of England*, pl.17 dated 1845, and pl.44.

4. *A Guide to the Watering Places, on the Coast, Between the Exe and the
Dart...*, 1817, pp.48-9. The volume contains a view of Berry
Pomeroy Castle engraved by Havell after W.B. Noble.

GEORGE ROBERT LEWIS

1. 1853: two paintings of *Chapel Island, Ilfracombe*
(nos. 619 and 1011); 1855: *Ilfracombe* (no.1154).

2. Lindsay Stainton, however, suggests that cat.no.41 probably dates
from the 1820s or 1830s, though noting that its handling seems to
anticipate the Pre-Raphaelites. See *British Landscape Watercolours,
1600-1860*, British Museum, 1985, p.62, no.135.

3. A water-colour by Lewis in the British Museum entitled
Water-Break Ilfracombe and probably of the same date further
explores the geology of the coast by concentrating on a natural
rock arch.

JOHN FREDERICK LEWIS

1. A watercolour *The Valley of the Lynn, Devon*, was in the Witt
Collection; sold Sotheby's, 19 February 1987, lot 155 (illustrated
in colour). 1830 exhibits were *Waterfall, near Linton (sic)*,
Devonshire (350), *Water Mill in the North of Devon* (60).
Two drawings of Lynmouth are known, one in the Courtauld
Institute (Witt Collection) and one in Birmingham City Art
Gallery.

2. *The Glen*, Henry E. Huntington Library and Art Gallery, California
(photo. Witt Library).

3. *On the Terrace, Lyneham, near Plymouth* (illustrated in *Apollo*,
April 1972).

4. Mrs. Bray, *op.cit.*, vol. III, p.283. The Lewis watercolour is in
Blackburn Corporation Art Gallery. It is illustrated as Pl.5 in
John Frederick Lewis R.A., Laing Art Gallery, Newcastle upon
Tyne, 1971, catalogue by Richard Green.

5. Another drawing in the Fogg Art Museum, Harvard, is inscribed

'Peter Tavy' (photo. Witt Library). It is of similar size to
cats.nos. 42, 43 and 44 and like them is worked in pencil
heightened with white bodycolour.

PHILIPPE JACQUES DE LOUTHERBOURG
1. See *Philippe Jacques de Loutherbourg, R.A., 1740-1812*, London,
   1973, n.p. catalogue by Rüdiger Joppien.
2. An undated drawing by De Loutherbourg of Teignmouth is in the
   Turner Bequest, Tate Gallery.
3. Maton, *Observations...*, pp.126-7. The volume contains an aquatint
   of Dartmouth Castle by T. Rackett, engraved by S. Alken, which
   is comparable to de Loutherbourg's view.

JOHN MIDDLETON
1. *Illustrated London News*, May 23, 1846, p.338.
2. Another view made at Ivy Bridge (which Middleton also etched)
   is in the Norwich Castle Museum collection. An oil version of
   the present exhibited watercolour is also at Norwich and is dated
   1854. Views at Lynmouth are in Norwich and in the Huntington
   collection. A watercolour of *Woolfardisworthy, Devon* was sold at
   Sotheby's, March 12, 1987 (lot 120, illus.).

WILLIAM JAMES MÜLLER
1. Letter to J. Gooden, Paris, April 30, 1844, quoted in N. Neal Solly
   Memoir of the Life of William James Müller, London, 1875, p.219.
2. West exhibited a number of pictures of the north Devon coast
   from 1845. There is an imposing oil painting of *Cheyne Beach,
   Ilfracombe* (c.1845) in the collection of Bristol City Art Gallery.
3. *Ibid.*, p.220. Solly lists the following paintings of Lynmouth
   subjects.
   Oils:
   (1) *Limekiln, Lynmouth, above the meet of the waters*
   (priced at £32-11-0d. on the third day of Christie and Manson's
   sale of Müller's works, April 1-3, 1846, no.451), (p.344);
   (2) *Rocky Stream at Lynmouth*: oval (cat.no.47), J.D.Weston
   collection, now in Bristol Museum and Art Gallery,
   (pp.220, 346);
   (3) *Rocky Stream, Lynmouth*, John Henderson collection, (p.346).
   Henderson also owned the two watercolours, cat.no. 49 and 50
   in this exhibition;
   (4) Upright landscape of *Lynmouth*, William Kenrick collection,
   (p.220) (see note 5 below).
   Watercolours:
   (1) *Lynmouth*, (p.267);
   (2) *Rocky Valley, Lynmouth*, (p.268);
   (3) *Study of Rocks at Lynmouth*, (p.270) all in Thomas Wood
   collection.
   In addition to those shown in this exhibition, there are two
   watercolours of Lynmouth in the Tate Gallery: *Lynmouth;
   the River Bank* (signed and dated 1844) and *Lynmouth;
   a Bend of the River*.
4. *Ibid.*, p.224. Letter to Benjamin Johnson, dated Lynmouth,
   August 16, 1844.
5. *Ibid.*, p.220. Solly (pp.220-1) also describes an upright oil
   (2'10" x 2'2") marked by the same qualities of transparency and
   purity of colouring. Exhibited at Wolverhampton in 1869, it was
   then in the collection of William Kenrick, Edgbaston, and was
   with Suzi Quadrat, Bristol, in December 1994.
6. Francis Greenacre and Sheena Stoddard *W.J. Müller 1812-1845*,
   Bristol, 1991, cat.no.172, p.165.
7. Solly, *op,cit.*, p.235
8. *Ibid.*, p.236.
9. *Ibid.*, p.238.

JOHN WILLIAM NORTH
1. *Wayside Posies: Original Poems of the Country Life*. Edited by Robert
   Buchanan, Routledge, 1867, p.18.
2. See Lindsay Stainton *British Landscape watercolours 1600-1860*,
   British Museum, 1985, no. 193, col. pl.133. The catalogue entry
   does not mention the connection with *Wayside Posies* but
   Pinwell's *King Pippin* is an illustration to a poem of the same name
   in which a small boy ('a pretty little man') receives apples from a
   young woman ('a beauteous maid'). North's watercolour may

conceivably be exploring the same text. Admittedly the child in
North's picture looks more like a girl, but the same is true of
Pinwell's illustration. Pinwell died in 1875 aged only thirty three.
In his posthumous sale at Christie's in March 1876 one lot was
Beer Church, South Devon (lot 77). It is tempting to think that he
may have been sketching in Devon with his friend North but no
supporting evidence can be found in G.C.Williamson's
G.J.Pinwell and his Works, 1900.

SAMUEL PALMER
1. Lister, *Letters*, vol. II, p.712. October 20, 1864.
2. *Ibid.*
3. A.H. Palmer, *Life*, pp. 55-6.
4. Lister, *Letters*, vol. II, p.715, November 1864. For Palmer's exhibited
   works see A. H. Palmer, *Life*, pp.405-21; R. Lister,
   Catalogue Raisonné of the Works of Samuel Palmer, Cambridge,
   1988. Devon subjects are cat.nos.195-201; 217-8; 476-85; 557;
   574. (Lister's cat.no.200 is also his cat.no.477 judging by the
   inscription).
5. Lister, *Letters*, vol. I, p.473. July 1849.
6. *Ibid.*, vol. II, p.692; p.721.

WILLIAM PAYNE
1. David Japes, *William Payne. A Plymouth Experience*, Royal Albert
   Memorial Museum, Exeter, 1992.
2. Japes, *op.cit.*, pp.38-40 for Payne's exhibited works.
3. *Ibid.*, p.41 gives a full list of the contents. The volumes are in the
   West Country Studies Library, Exeter.
4. For Payne at Okehampton see also Japes, *op.cit.*, cat.no.20. No.38
   in vol. II of the Payne album of watercolours (see note 3) is a
   view of *Oakhampton Castle and Town from the Park*.
5. T.H. Williams *Picturesque Excursions in Devonshire and Cornwall,
   Part I Devonshire*, 1804, p.92. Turner's views were made for the
   Picturesque Views in England and Wales, engraved in 1828, and the
   Rivers of England, engraved in 1825.

AARON PENLEY
1. Two watercolours inscribed 'Berry Pomeroy Lodge, Devon,
   July 1842' and 'Berry Pomeroy Castle, Devon, July 1842' are
   illustrated in John Steegman 'Aaron Penley - a forgotten
   water-colourist', *Apollo*, January 1958, pp.14-17. The Fitzwilliam
   Museum also owns a pencil drawing by Penley of 'Bickley Vale'
   which may be dated to 1842 for the same reasons.
2. *Plymouth, Devonport and Stonehouse Herald*, January 22, March 19
   and April 16, 1842. See also S.A.Smiles 'Plymouth and Exeter as
   Centres of Art, 1820-1865', unpublished PhD dissertation,
   University of Cambridge, 1982, p.106.
3. These exhibits were as follows. Plymouth, September 1842:
   (Unnamed landscape) (3) and a *View from Mount Edgcumbe* (4),
   Medora (59), *Peasant Girls at a Spring* (89); Exeter, October 1842:
   Part of Babbicombe Bay (46), *Medora* (82) and (unnamed) (47).
   See *Plymouth, Devonport and Stonehouse Herald*, September 3,
   1842; *Western Luminary* , October 25, 1842 and *Exeter Gazette*,
   November 5, 1842. *Study of A Turkish Merchant* and *A Sketch* were
   the Art Union prizes. See *Western Luminary* December 20, 1842.
4. See *Sketching from Nature* (above) note 15.

WILLIAM PITT
1. *Old Farm Yard at Beer, near Colyton, Devon* (1860) sold Christie's
   February 3, 1978, lot 203 (illustrated); *Near Tamerton, Devon*
   (1864) sold Sotheby's December 9, 1980, lot 101 (illustrated).
2. Charles Dickens and Wilkie Collins 'A Message from the Sea'
   in *All the Year Round*, 1860.

JOHN SKINNER PROUT
1. A lithograph vignette of *Clovelly* was published by Ackermann in
   the mid 1830s; a zincograph of *Fall of the West Lyn. Lynmouth
   Devon* was published by Trix of Lynmouth c.1840. The Victoria
   and Albert Museum has a painting of *Kynance Cove, Cornwall*,
   signed and dated 1838, which might also be derived from a sketch
   made on the same tour.

SAMUEL PROUT
1. Quoted in J.I. Roget *A History of the Old Water Colour Society*,

London 1891,vol. I, pp.348-9. *South Zeal, Devon* was presumably intended as a subject for Britton's *Beauties of England and Wales,* whose Devon volume was published in 1809, but it was not in fact included. Engravings after Prout's sketches constituted nine of the 21 Devon subjects engraved in Britton's publication.

2. A version is in the collection of the Royal Albert Memorial Museum, Exeter (57/1935).

3. Hendrik de Cort, who had worked as a drawing master at Ugbrooke in the 1790s had drawn picturesque cottages at Chudleigh in 1795, some of which were etched by G.Hollis and published by Colnaghi in 1817 as *Six Views in Chudleigh, Devonshire…made previously to the Fire in 1807.*

4. This was also issued as *Samuel Prout's New Drawing Book, in the Manner of Chalk: 12 Views in the West of England of Picturesque Cottages at Exeter, East Bourne, Tavistock, Lynmouth, Pennycross, etc.*, with the same plates bound in a different order.

JOHN INIGO RICHARDS

1. Two views of *Glastonbury* were shown at the Society of Artists in 1763; *Halswell House* (now in the National Museum of Wales, Cardiff) was shown there in 1764; *View of a Cascade at Hestercombe* was shown at the Royal Academy in 1769. There is a picture of two gentlemen contemplating a cascade at Stourhead with this title, although the waterfall looks very much like the one at Lydford in Devon instead. There are also watercolours by Richards of Hestercombe in the collection of the British Museum.

2. The British Museum collection includes a watercolour by Richards, 'Ruins of an Abbey, near Plymouth,' inserted in volume III (no.724) of the interleaved catalogues of the Society of Artists. The Witt Library has a photograph of a watercolour by Richards of Totnes in the Oppé collection.

3. A slightly larger picture by Richards, with a more extensive view, entitled *A View of Ivybridge* (1765) was at Sotheby's on November 10, 1982, lot 66 (illustrated). This 1765 version once belonged to William Jackson of Exeter.

4. *Ivy Bridge, near Plymouth* was engraved by F. Chesham and published in 1781. It is unclear when Sandby visited Devon, but there is a drawing entitled 'At Ilfracombe' in the collection of the British Museum.

5. Richard Warner *A Tour through Cornwall in the Autumn of 1808,* Bath, 1809, p.46.

THOMAS ROWLANDSON

1. See John Hayes, *Rowlandson. Watercolours and Drawings,* 1972 and J. Baskett and D. Snelgrove *The Drawings of Thomas Rowlandson in the Paul Mellon Collection,* 1977. Mitchell's name is also spelled Michell and the date of his death given as 1817 or 1819.

2. Baskett and Snelgrove, *op.cit.*, Nos.26, 27, 30, 34 for Devon subjects; also Leger galleries, *An Exhibition of watercolour Drawings by Thomas Rowlandson,* 1981, cat.nos.12, 18.

3. *A Guide to the Watering Places, on the Coast, Between the Exe and the Dart…,* 1817, p.28.

4. *The Tour of Doctor Syntax, In Search of the Picturesque,* 1812. There were nine editions in seven years. The illustrations by Rowlandson, with text by William Combe, had first appeared in the *Poetical Magazine* from 1809-1811. Rowlandson also etched two series of Cornish views in 1812 and 1822. Somers Cocks lists a View in Devonshire (no. 3480) of 1809, also published in 1818 (S.50).

5. Baskett and Snelgrove, *op.cit.*, No.27.

BRADFORD RUDGE

1. John Eagles, *The Sketcher,* 1856, p.194.

2. *Ibid.*, p.193.

3. Several wash drawings of Lynmouth and Linton are listed in Ronald Aquilla Clarke *Illustrating a City. Edward Rudge and Art in Coventry c.1760-1830,* Herbert Art Gallery, Coventry, 1992.

HENRY COURTNEY SELOUS

1. See Richard D. Altick *The Shows of London,* Harvard, 1978, pp.138, 181-2; Ralph Hyde *Panoramania! The Art and Entertainment of the 'All-Embracing' View,* Barbican Art Gallery, 1988, p.60.

2. *Exeter Flying Post,* July 14 and September 29, 1831. On this latter date the proprietors were exhibiting a new attraction, 'The Bombardment of Algiers.' Daguire opened again at the Freemasons' Hall, Cornwall Street, Plymouth, later in October. See *Plymouth, Devonport and Stonehouse Herald,* November 5, 1831. Daguire was one of a number of specialists in moving panoramas who toured their shows through the provinces. His advertisement states that the panorama of the French Revolution was painted by artists who had participated in the events. If this advertisement is to be believed it follows that these original artists would probably have remained in France and Daguire would have had need of an English artist to undertake any necessary repairs and refurbishments.

FRANCIS STEVENS

1. *Views of Cottages and Farm-Houses in England and Wales: Etched by Francis Stevens, from the Designs of the Most Celebrated Artists,* Ackermann, 1815.

2. *Western Luminary,* April 10, 1827.

3. Stevens had subscribed to Lewis's *Scenery of the River Dart,* 1821.

WILLIAM TOMKINS

1. His Devon exhibits at the Royal Academy were these. 1770: *View of Mount Edgcumbe, taken from the west end of the new rope-house, Plymouth Dock* (186); *View of Plymouth Sound, taken from the same* (187); 1772: two views of *Chudley Rock (sic) in Lord Clifford's Park* (256-7); *View of the Lary (sic) under Sultram (sic) wood…*(259); 1773: two views of *Mainhead (sic) in Devon the seat of Viscount Lisburne* (291-2); two views of *Tapley Devonshire (John Cleveland)* (293-4); 1780: *View of Maristow, on the Tavy* (8); *Ivy Bridge, Devon* (165); 1781: *View of Mount Edgcombe (sic) from Mutton Cove* (32); 1781: *Crab-tree slate quarry* (101); 1786: *View within three miles of Plymouth* (4). Work shown at the Society of Artists from Dorset (*Sherborne Castle,* 1765) and Somerset (*Pixton, near Dulverton,* 1768), together with two views of *Haswell Park* at the Royal Academy in 1771 suggest further success in securing west country patronage. He painted a panoramic view of Totnes (c.1765) which is illustrated in Arthur Ackermann and Son *The Pleasures of Observation,* May 1991, no.6. A number of his views can still be found in their original settings, especially at Dunster Castle and Saltram.

2. See Jonathan Coad 'The Development and Organisation of Plymouth Dockyard, 1689-1815.' in Michael Duffy et al. (eds) *The New Maritime History of Devon, Vol. 1: from Early Times to the Late Eighteenth Century,* Conway Maritime Press in association with Exeter University, 1992, pp.192-200. A painting by Nicholas Pocock (c.1800) in the National Maritime Museum, Greenwich, shows the full extent of Plymouth Dockyard following its late eighteenth century expansion. Some of this impressive complex still survives.

J.M.W. TURNER

1. Other series include the local drawing master T.H.Williams' *Picturesque Excursions in Devonshire and Cornwall* (1804), with 20 etchings of Devon landscapes; John Britton and Edward Brayley's *Devonshire and Dorsetshire* (vol. IV of *Beauties of England and Wales*) (1809) with 20 engravings of Devon buildings; Richard Ayton and William Daniell's *A Voyage round Great Britain* (1814-25) with 26 coloured aquatints of Devon subjects; and Daniel and Samuel Lysons' *Magna Britannia* (1822) with 17 engravings of Devon topography after Joseph Farington.

2. See Sam Smiles 'Turner in the West Country: From Topography to Idealisation' in J.C. Eade (ed) *Projecting the Landscape,* Humanities Research Centre, Australian National University, Canberra, 1987, pp.36-37.

3. A.J. Finberg *The Life of J.M.W. Turner R.A.,* Oxford, 1961, pp.182-3; W. Cosmo Monkhouse, *Turner,* London, 1879, p.84. Local writers were keen to make the most of this connection. *The Western Luminary* of September 30, 1845, talked of Devon as 'the county which has given a Sir Joshua, a Northcote, and a *Turner* to the world' and Cyrus Redding relates an anecdote in which Turner asks to be added to the roll-call of Devon painters. See C. Redding 'The Late Joseph Mallord William Turner,'

Fraser's Magazine, February 1852, p.151.

4. The 1811 tour to the West Country also produced nine images of Cornwall, eight of Dorset and two of Somerset for the *Southern Coast*. The Devon subjects were *Teignmouth, Devonshire* (Yale Center for British Art, New Haven); *The Mew Stone at the Entrance of Plymouth Sound* and *Clovelly Bay, Devonshire* (National Gallery of Ireland, Dublin); *Plymouth Dock, from near Mount Edgecumbe* (Private Collection); *Plymouth, with Mount Batten* (Victoria and Albert Museum); *Torbay, seen from Brixham, Devonshire* (Fitzwilliam Museum, Cambridge); *Combe Martin* (Ashmolean Museum, Oxford); *Ilfracombe, North Devon* (Private Collection); *Dartmouth, Devonshire* (Private Collection); *Mount Edgecomb, Devonshire* (present whereabouts unknown). Seven further images of Devon by Collins, Owen, Prout and Clennell were included by Cooke in the *Southern Coast*. The fullest account of Turner's topographical work in the west country is Eric Shanes *Turner's England, 1810-38*, Cassell, London, 1990. See also Howard J.M. Hanley *Turner in Dorset - Images from the Picturesque Views on the Southern Coast of England*, Weymouth, 1992.

5. *The Diary of Henry Woollcombe*, West Devon Record Office, 710/394. Entry for August 27, 1813.

6. One thinks, for example, of *Dido and Aeneas* (1814), the second version of *Lake Avernus* (1814-15), *Crossing the Brook* (1815), *Dido building Carthage* (1815) and *The Decline of the Carthaginian Empire* (1817). I have argued this interpretation at length in Smiles, 'Turner in the West Country,' 1987, pp.36-53.

7. Cyrus Redding 'The Late Joseph Mallord William Turner,' *Fraser's Magazine*, XLV, February 1852, p.154.

8. Cyrus Redding *Past Celebrities whom I have known*, London, 1856, p.53.

9. Smiles, 'Turner in the West Country,' 1987, pp.44-50.

10. For a full discussion see Sam Smiles 'The Devonshire Oil Sketches of 1813', *Turner Studies*, vol. 9, no.1, Summer 1989, pp.10-26.

11. Walter Thornbury *The Life of J.M.W. Turner, RA*, London, 1877, p.155.

12. See Sam Smiles 'Turner in Devon: some additional information concerning his visits in the 1810s', *Turner Studies*, vol. 7, no.1, Summer 1987, pp.11-14.

13. West Devon Record Office 710/520. This letter is undated but Woollcombe's *Diary* records a visit to Turner's studio on April 13, 1814. (West Devon Record Office, 710/394).

14. John Gage *Collected Correspondence of J.M.W. Turner*, Oxford, 1980, letter no. 52. I have argued elsewhere that the most likely sketchbook to record this trip is that known as *Devon Rivers No.2* (TB CXXXIII), which contains drawings of scenes on the Dart and Dartmouth itself. See Sam Smiles, 'Turner in Devon', 1987, pp.12-13.

15. Correspondence relating to this is collected in John Gage, *op.cit.*, nos.57, 58 and 59.

16. Private collection. Exhibited at Turner's gallery in 1812.

17. Petworth House. Exhibited at Turner's gallery in 1812.

18. Petworth House. Probably exhibited at Turner's gallery in 1812 as the seventh (unnamed) picture noted by the art critic of *The Sun* on June 9. *The River Plym* which that critic also records would then represent a further picture (now lost) derived from Devon. Hulks were not moored on the Plym and Turner is unlikely to have confused two such different rivers as the Plym and the Tamar.

19. Metropolitan Museum of Art, New York. Exhibited at Turner's gallery in 1812.

20. Tate Gallery. Exhibited at the Royal Academy in 1815.

21. See Sam Smiles 'Turner in the West Country,' 1987, pp.45-7.

22. Redding, *op.cit.*, 1852, p.156.

23. Tom Taylor (ed) *Autobiographical Recollections by Charles Robert Leslie, R.A.*, London 1860, p.70.

24. 'Ivy Bridge to Penzance' sketchbook (TB CXXV), p.47.

25. The engraving by J.C.Allen was eventually published on its own in 1821.

26. 'Devon Rivers No.2' sketchbook (TB CXXXIII), p.45. This sketchbook is the only one later than 1811 to include pencil drawings made on the river Dart which Turner visited in 1814. Shanes, *op.cit.*, p.283, has suggested that Turner may have also used the sketch on p.153 of the 1811 sketchbook 'Devonshire Coast No. 1' (TB CXXIII).

27. The 1811 sketches are in the 'Corfe to Dartmouth' sketchbook (TB CXXIV), pp.39, 40; the 1814 sketch is in the 'Devon Rivers No. 2' sketchbook (TB CXXXIII), p.48.

28. The relevant sketchbooks are 1811:'Devonshire Coast No.1' (TB CXXIII) and 'Corfe to Dartmouth' (TB CXXIV);1814: 'Devon Rivers No.2' (TBCXXXIII).

29. This form of transport was the chief means of moving goods when so many of Devon's roads were inadequate for wheeled traffic. Charles Vancouver describes them thus: 'The rapidity with which these animals descend the hills, when not loaded, and the utter impossibility of passing loaded ones, require that the utmost caution should be used in keeping out of the way of the one, and exertion in keeping a-head of the other. A cross-way fork in the road or gateway, is eagerly looked for as a retiring spot to the traveller, until the pursuing squadron, or heavily loaded brigade, may have passed by.' Charles Vancouver, *General View of the Agriculture of Devon*, 1808, p.371.

CORNELIUS VARLEY

1. Lt. Colonel Harding, *The History of Tiverton*, 2 vols, 1845, vol. I, pp.209-24. See also W. Gore Allen, *John Heathcoat and his Heritage*, 1958 and D.E. Varley, *John Heathcoat, 1783-1861. Founder of the Machine-made Lace Industry*, 1969 (first published in *Textile History*, vol. 1, No. 1, December 1968).

2. *The Route Book of Devon: A Guide for the Stranger and Tourist*, 2nd edition, n.d. (1840s), pp.102-3.

3. See M. Pidgley, 'Introduction' in *Exhibition of Drawings and Watercolours by Cornelius Varley*, Colnaghi, 1973, and M. Pidgley, 'Cornelius Varley, Cotman, and the Graphic Telescope', *Burlington Magazine*, November 1972, pp.781-6. A large drawing, *Vale of Exe from Tiverton*, dated June 7, 1824, is pl.xx in Colnaghi catalogue above. *Collefrere, Tiverton*, also dated June 7, is No. 50 (illus.) in Agnew's *English Watercolours and Drawings*, 1994.

WILLIAM FLEETWOOD VARLEY

1. Alfred T. Story *James Holmes and John Varley*, London, 1894, p.294.

2. C.M Kauffmann, *John Varley 1778-1842*, Batsford and Victoria and Albert Museum, 1984, pp.63-4.

3. Plate D explains Varley's aims. 'The general arrangement of subject in this composition is suggested by the view of Totness *(sic)* in Devonshire', but selected to suit the composition and effect.

4. Two works by Varley are signed and dated 1810: *Chudleigh Lime Rock* (also called *Palace Quay, Chudleigh*), and *Broadgate, Exeter* (also called *An Archway in Exeter*). Photographs of them are in the Witt Library. The picture collection at Ugbrooke is mentioned in *Devonshire Scenery; or, Directions for Visiting the Most Picturesque Spots on the Eastern and Southern Coast, from Sidmouth to Plymouth*, Exeter, 1826, pp.27-30. Co-incidentally on pp.43-4 of this guide the environs of Alphington are described: 'a sweet walk... through a path-field, overlooking the richly-wooded grounds, leads to a piece of water, around which are some noble trees; in the wood above, there is a walk, from whence the city is seen, and part of the Exe.'

JOHN RAWSON WALKER

1. Heather Williams 'The Lives and Works of Nottingham Artists from 1750 to 1914 with Special Consideration of their Association with the Lace Industry and Society at Large', unpublished PhD dissertation, University of Nottingham, 1981, pp.465-6.

2. He probably arrived in Exeter in the spring of 1845, for the local papers describe him as 'an artist of this city' and mention that his *Sun-rise off Teignmouth* was intended for the Royal Academy exhibition (where it was exhibited as (493) *Sunrise - Scene near Teignmouth, Devonshire*). See *Exeter Flying Post*, April 3, 1845 and *Western Times*, April 5, 1845. He exhibited at least seven pictures in the Exeter exhibition that autumn. Three of these were Devon landscapes: *Cottage Scene, near Kingskerswell* (43),

Scene near Teignmouth (184), *Scene on Heavitree Brook*
(watercolour)(217). See *Western Luminary*, 30 September 1845,
Exeter Flying Post, 23 October, 1845. In the Exeter exhibition of
1846 he exhibited *View of Anstey's Cove from the South West* (55)
and two other landscapes (102 and 160). See *Exeter Flying Post*,
September 24, 1846, *Western Luminary*, 29 September, 1846.
In local directories for 1848 and 1850 he is described as a resident
of Torquay.
3. See Williams, *op.cit.* pp.452-3.
4. They are memorably described in Sabine Baring-Gould *Devonshire
Characters and Strange Events*, 1908, vol. I, pp.16-20, who links
their arrival in Torquay to the later 1840s.

FRANCIS WHEATLEY
1. Mary Webster *Francis Wheatley*, Paul Mellon Foundation for
British Art, London, 1970, p.194. An undated view of
Stonehouse, Plymouth is illustrated on p.16. A watercolour of
The Mermaid Inn, near Mount Edgcumbe, Plymouth is in Bradford
Museum.

RICHARD WILSON
1. David Solkin, *Richard Wilson. The Landscape of Reaction*,
Tate Gallery, 1982, pp.239-40, and pp.105; 109-11. Solkin made
the identification of the subjects.
2. W. Daniell, vol. viii, 1825, p.12; *Devonshire and Cornwall Illustrated*,
1832, p.33.
3. *Beauties of England and Wales*, vol. IV, 1809, p.94.
4. Farington, *Diary*, November 3, 1810.
5. *The Route Book of Devon*, n.d. (1840s), p. 41.
6. *Devonshire and Cornwall Illustrated*, p.8.
7. Victoria and Albert Museum.

BIBLIOGRAPHY

(Anon) *Devonshire Scenery; or, Directions for Visiting the Most Picturesque Spots on the Eastern and Southern Coast, from Sidmouth to Plymouth*

(Anon) *The Route Book of Devon: A Guide for the Stranger and Tourist*, 2nd edition, n.d. (1840s).

(Anon) *A Guide to the Watering Places, on the Coast, Between the Exe and the Dart...*, 1817.

(Anon) *Guide in a Tour to the Watering Places, and their Environs on the South-East Coast of Devon*, (1802).

A Handbook for Travellers in Devon and Cornwall (third edition, revised), John Murray, London, 1856.

Acland, Arthur H.D. (ed) *Memoir and Letters of the Right Honourable Sir Thomas Dyke Acland*, 1902 (privately printed).

Adams, Eric *Francis Danby: Varieties of Poetic Landscape*, Paul Mellon Centre for Studies in British Art, Yale University Press, 1973.

Agnew's *English Watercolours and Drawings*, 1994.

Allen, David E. *The Naturalist in Britain - A Social History*, Harmondsworth, 1978.

Allen, W. Gore *John Heathcoat and his Heritage*, London, 1958.

Allom, Thomas and Bartlett, William *Devonshire and Cornwall Illustrated*, London, 1832.

Allthorpe-Guyton, Marjorie, *Henry Bright 1810-1873*, Norfolk Museums Service, 1986.

Art Journal.

Art Union.

Athenaeum.

Baker, Margaret *Discovering the Exeter Road*, Tring, 1968.

Baring-Gould, Sabine *Devonshire Characters and Strange Events*, London, 1908.

Baskett, Jane and Snelgrove, Dudley *The Drawings of Thomas Rowlandson in the Paul Mellon Collection*, 1977.

Beckett, R.B. *John Constable's Correspondence: VI - The Fishers*, Suffolk Records Society, vol. XII, 1968.

Bicknell, Peter and Munro, Jane *Gilpin to Ruskin. Drawing Masters and their Manuals, 1800-1860*, Fitzwilliam Musuem, Cambridge, 1988.

Brall, R. 'The Precocious Talent of John Middleton,' *Connoisseur*, November 1980.

Bray, Mrs. Anna *The Borders of the Tamar and Tavy*, London, 1836.

Britton, John and Brayley, Edward *Beauties of England and Wales*, vol. IV, *Devonshire and Dorsetshire*, London, 1809.

Browne, Hablot K. (Phiz) *Sketches of the Seaside and the Country*, London (1860s).

Buchanan, Robert (ed.) *Wayside Posies: Original Poems of the Country Life*, London, 1867.

Carrington, Henry *The Plymouth and Devonport Guide*, 1828.

Carrington, N.T. *Dartmoor- a Descriptive Poem*, London, 1826.

Carrington, N.T. et al. *The Teignmouth, Dawlish and Torquay Guide...*, Teignmouth, (1830).

Carrington, N.T. et al., *The Teignmouth, Dawlish and Torquay Guide; with an account of the surrounding Neighbourhood*, Teignmouth, n.d. (early 1840s).

Carus, C.G. *The King of Saxony's Journey through England and Scotland in the year 1844*, translated S.C. Davidsen, London, 1846.

Chanter, Charlotte *Ferny Combes. A Ramble after Ferns in the Glens and Valleys of Devonshire*, 1856.

Coad, Jonathan 'The Development and Organisation of Plymouth Dockyard, 1689-1815', in Michael Duffy et al. (eds) *The New Maritime History of Devon, Vol. 1: from Early Times to the Late Eighteenth Century*, Conway Maritime Press in association with Exeter University, 1992.

Collingwood, W. 'Reminiscences of J.D. Harding',

Magazine of Art, December 1897.

Collins, Wilkie *Memoirs of the Life of William Collins, R.A.*, London, 1848.

Copper Plate Magazine

Cox, David *A Treatise on Landscape Painting and Effect in Water Colours*, 1813, reprinted as a special number of *The Studio*, 1922.

Daniell, William and Ayton, Richard *A Voyage Round Great Britain*, London, 1814-1825.

Delamotte, P.H. *The Art of Sketching from Nature*, 1871, second edition, London, 1888.

(Dibdin, Charles) 'C. Dibdin's Account of Travelling in North Devon in 1801,' *Devon and Cornwall Notes and Queries*, vol. 22, 1942-46.

Dickens, Charles and Collins, Wilkie *A Message from the Sea* (published as the Christmas number of *All the Year Round*, 1860).

'E' 'Lines written in the West of England', *The Gentleman's Magazine*, May 1790.

Eagles, John *The Sketcher*, London, 1856.

Everitt, William *Devonshire scenery - its inspiration in the prose and song of various authors*, Exeter, 1884.

Exeter Flying Post

Exeter Gazette

Exwood, Maurice & Lehmann, H.L. (eds) *The Journal of William Schellinks' Travels in England, 1661-1663*, Camden Fifth Series, Offices of the Royal Historical Society, London, 1993.

Finberg, A.J. *The Life of J.M.W. Turner R.A.*, Oxford, 1961.

Francis, J.G. *Beach-Rambles in search of Sea-Side Pebbles and Crystals*, London, 1859.

Fraser, Robert *General View of the Agriculture of Devon with Observations on the Means of its Improvement*, London, 1794.

Gage, John *Collected Correspondence of J.M.W. Turner*, Oxford, 1980.

Garlick, K., Mcintyre, A. and Cave K., *The Diary of Joseph Farington*, New Haven and London, 1978-84.

Gilpin, William *Observations on the Western Parts of England*, London, 1798.

Girtin, Thomas and Loshak, David *The Art of Thomas Girtin*, London, 1954.

Gosse, Edmund *The Naturalist of the Sea Shore. The Life of Philip Henry Gosse*, London, 1896.

Gosse, P.H. *A Naturalist's Rambles on the Devonshire Coast*, London, 1853

Gosse, P.H. *Land and Sea*, London, 1865

Gosse, P.H. *Seaside Pleasures: Sketches in the Neighbourhood of Ilfracombe*, London, 1853.

Gosse, P.H. *The Aquarium: An Unveiling of the Wonders of the Deep Sea*, London, 1854.

Greenacre, Francis and Stoddard, Sheena *W.J. Müller 1812-1845*, City of Bristol Museum and Art Gallery, 1991.

Greenacre, Francis *Francis Danby*, Tate Gallery and City of Bristol Museum and Art Gallery, 1988.

Greenacre, Francis *The Bristol School of Artists - Francis Danby and Painting in Bristol 1810-1840*, City of Bristol Museum and Art Gallery, 1973.

Grigson, Geoffrey *Places of the Mind*, London, 1949.

Grigson, Geoffrey *The Harp of Aeolus and other Essays on Art, Literature and Nature*, London, 1948.

'H.J.', 'Sea-Side Life', *Once a Week*, August 2, 1862.

Hadfield, Charles *Atmospheric Railways. A Victorian Venture in Silent Speed*, Newton Abbot, 1967.

Hardie, Martin (ed.) *Edward Norgate Miniatura or the Art of Limning*,

(1648-50), Oxford, 1919.

Harding, Lt. Colonel *The History of Tiverton*, 2 vols, 1845.

Harris Museum and Art Gallery, Preston, *Anthony Devis (1729-1816) a 'picturesque traveller,'* 1993.

Hawcroft, F.W. *John Middleton. A Sketch of his Life and Work, The Saturday Book*, No.16, 1956.

Hawcroft, Francis *Watercolours by Thomas Girtin*, Whitworth Art Gallery and Victoria and Albert Museum, 1975.

Hayes, John *Rowlandson. Watercolours and Drawings*, Oxford, 1972.

Hayward Gallery, *Landscape in Britain 1850-1950*, London, 1983.

Heath, Francis *The Fern Paradise* , London, 1875.

Heath, Francis *The "Romance" of Peasant Life in the West of England*, London, 1872.

Holcomb, A., *John Sell Cotman*, London, 1978.

Hook, A.J. *Life of James Clarke Hook, R.A.* (3 vols., privately printed, 1929-32).

Houghton, Rev. W. *Sea-side Walks of a Naturalist with his Children*, London, 1860s.

Howard, Peter *Landscapes: The Artists' Vision*, London, 1991.

Howitt, William *The Rural Life of England*, London, 1838.

Illustrated London News.

James, Henry 'North Devon' from *English Hours* (1905), Oxford University Press, 1981.

Japes, David *William Payne. A Plymouth Experience*, Royal Albert Memorial Museum, Exeter, 1992.

Joppien, R. *Philippe Jacques de Loutherbourg, R.A., 1740-1812*, Kenwood House, London, 1973.

Kauffmann, C.M. *John Varley*, Batsford/Victoria and Albert Museum, 1984.

Kingsley, Charles *Glaucus: or the Wonders of the Shore* , London, 1855.

Kingsley, Charles *Westward Ho!* London, 1855.

Kingston, Jack 'The History of the Torpoint Ferry' *Old Cornwall*, vol. VII, no.5, 1969, pp.198-206.

Kitson, S.D. *The Life of John Sell Cotman*, 1937.

Laing Art Gallery, *John Frederick Lewis R.A.*, Newcastle upon Tyne, 1971, catalogue by Richard Green.

Laing Art Gallery, *Charles Napier Hemy R.A.*, Newcastle upon Tyne, 1984, catalogue by Andrew Greg.

Leger Galleries, *An Exhibition of watercolour Drawings by Thomas Rowlandson*, 1981.

Lewis, M., *John Frederick Lewis, R.A.*, 1978.

Lister, Raymond *The Letters of Samuel Palmer*, 2 vols., Oxford, 1974.

Lister, Raymond, *Catalogue Raisonné of the Works of Samuel Palmer*, Cambridge, 1988.

Liversidge, M.J.H. 'James Bourne - an assessment of his life and work,' *The Connoisseur*, vol. 163, Sept.-Dec. 1966.

Long, Basil *John Glover, Walker's Quarterly*, No. 15, April 1924.

Lysons, Daniel and Samuel *Magna Britannia*, vol. VI, 1822, *Devon*.

Marks, J.G. *Life and Letters of Frederick Walker, A.R.A.*, London, 1896.

Marshall, William *The Rural Economy of the West of England*, London, 1796.

Maton, W.G. *Observations relative chiefly to the Natural History, Picturesque Scenery, and Antiquities, of the Western Counties of England, Made in the Years 1794 and 1796*, Salisbury, 1797.

Monkhouse, W. *Cosmo Turner*, London, 1879.

Moore, Charles *A List of the Principal Castles and Monastries in Great Britain*, London, 1798.

Morris, Susan 'Two Girtin Discoveries' *Sotheby's Art at Auction*, 1989-90.

Morris, Susan *Thomas Girtin, 1775-1802*, Yale Center for British Art, New Haven, 1986.

Newall, Christopher and Egerton, Judy *George Price Boyce*, Tate Gallery, 1987.

Newall, Christopher *John William Inchbold, Pre-Raphaelite Landscape Artist*, Leeds City Art Galleries, 1993.

Once a Week

Palmer, A.H. 'The Story of an Imaginative Painter,' *The Portfolio*, 1884.

Palmer, A.H. *The Life and Letters of Samuel Palmer*, 1892; reprinted 1972.

Palmer, A.H. five essays on J.C. Hook, *The Portfolio*, 1888.

Parris, Leslie et al. *Landscape in Britain, c.1750-1850*, Tate Gallery, London, 1973.

Pavière, Sydney H. *The Devis Family of Painters*, Leigh-on-Sea, 1950.

Penley, A. 'On Landscape Painting in Water Colours,' *The Chromolithograph*, August 8, 1868.

Picturesque Views on the River Exe, Tiverton, 1819.

Pidgley, M. 'Cornelius Varley, Cotman, and the Graphic Telescope,' *Burlington Magazine*, November 1972.

Pidgley, M. 'Introduction' in *Exhibition of Drawings and Watercolours by Cornelius Varley*, Colnaghi, 1973.

Plymouth and Plymouth Dock Weekly Journal.

Plymouth, Devonport and Stonehouse Herald.

Pope, W.B. (ed) *The Diary of B.R. Haydon*, Cambridge, Mass., 1960-63.

Portfolio.

Potts, Alex *Sir Francis Chantrey*, National Portrait Gallery, 1980.

Prothero, R.W. *The Letters of Richard Ford, 1797-1858*, London, 1905.

Punch, June 26, 1852.

Redding, Cyrus 'The Late Joseph Mallord William Turner,' *Fraser's Magazine*, XLV, February 1852.

Redding, Cyrus *Past Celebrities whom I have known*, London, 1856.

Reynolds, Stephen *A Poor Man's House*, London, 1909.

Roget, J.I. *A History of the Old Water Colour Society*, London1891.

Rowe, Samuel *A Perambulation of the Antient and Royal Forest of Dartmoor*, Plymouth, 1848.

Royal Albert Memorial Museum, *John Gendall (1789-1865) 'Exeter's Forgotten Artist,'* 1979.

Rundle, Thomas *Letters of the late Thomas Rundle, L.L.D. to Mrs. Barbara Sandys*, Gloucester, 1749.

Saintsbury, G. (ed.) *The Paris Sketch Book and Art Criticisms by William Makepeace Thackeray*, vol. 2 of the Oxford Thackeray, n.d.

Scrase, David *Drawings and Watercolours by Peter De Wint*, Fitzwilliam Museum, Cambridge, 1979.

Shaw, Rev. S. *A Tour to the West of England in 1788*, London, 1789.

Sheldon, Gilbert 'Devonshire Scenery as depicted in English Prose Literature,' *Transactions of the Devonshire Association*, vol. LXIII, 1931.

Smiles, Sam 'Picture Notes: *St Mawes at the Pilchard Season; St Mawes Cornwall; Falmouth; St Mawes Cornwall,'* *Turner Studies*, vol. 8, no.1, Summer 1988.

Smiles, Sam 'Plymouth and Exeter as centres of Art, 1820-1865,' unpublished Ph.D dissertation, University Of Cambridge, 1982.

Smiles, Sam 'The Devonshire Oil Sketches of 1813', *Turner Studies*, vol. 9, no.1, Summer 1989.

Smiles, Sam. 'Turner in Devon: some additional information concerning his visits in the 1810s,' *Turner Studies*, vol. 7, no.1, Summer 1987.

Smiles, Sam 'Turner in the West Country: From Topography to Idealisation' in J.C. Eade (ed) *Projecting the Landscape*, Humanities Research Centre, Australian National University, Canberra, 1987.

Smith, Hammond *Peter De Wint*, London, 1982.

Solkin, David *Richard Wilson. The Landscape of Reaction*, Tate Gallery, 1982.

Solly, N. Neal *Memoir of the Life of David Cox*, London, 1873.

Solly, N. Neal *Memoir of the Life of William James Müller*, London, 1875.

Somers Cocks, J.V. *Devon Topographical Prints, 1660-1870 - A Catalogue and Guide*, Devon Library Services, Exeter, 1977.

(Southey, Robert) *Letters from England: by Don Manuel Alvarez Espriella. Translated from the Spanish*, London, 1807, reprinted Gloucester, 1984.

Stainton, Lindsay *British Landscape Watercolours, 1600-1860*, British Museum, 1985.

Staley, Allen *The Pre-Raphaelite Landscape*, Oxford, 1973.

Steegman, John 'Aaron Penley - a forgotten water-colourist,' *Apollo*, January 1958.

Stevens, F. *Views of Cottages and Farm-houses in England and Wales*, London, 1815.

Surtees, V. (ed.) *The Diaries of George Price Boyce*, Norwich, 1980.
Taylor, Isaac *Personal Recollections. VI - The Summer of the Comet
        of 1811. Devonshire and Dartmoor*, in *Good Words*, 1864.
Taylor, Tom (ed) *Autobiographical Recollections by
        Charles Robert Leslie, R.A.*, London, 1860,
        reprinted EP Publishing, East Ardsley, 1978.
Taylor, Tom *Birket Foster's Pictures of English Landscape*, London, 1863.
Thornbury, Walter *The Life of J.M.W. Turner, R.A.*, London, 1877.
Travis, John F. *The Rise of the Devon Seaside Resorts, 1750-1900*,
        University of Exeter Press, 1993
Tyler, Richard *Francis Place, 1647-1728*, York Art Gallery, 1971.
Vancouver, Charles *General View of the Agriculture of the County
        of Devon*, London, 1808.
Varley, D.E. *John Heathcoat, 1783-1861. Founder of the Machine-made
        Lace Industry*, 1969 (first published in *Textile History*,
        vol. 1, No.1, December 1968).
Walker, J. *The Itinerant: A Select Collection of interesting and Picturesque
        Views, in Great Britain and Ireland*, London,1799-1801.
Warner, Richard *A Tour through Cornwall in the Autumn of 1808*,
        Bath, 1809.
Warner, Richard *A Walk through some of the Western Counties
        of England*, Bath, 1800.
Warter, J.W. (ed) *Selections from the Letters of Robert Southey*,
        London, 1856.

Webster, Mary *Francis Wheatley*, The Paul Mellon Foundation
        for British Art, London, 1970.
Western Luminary.
Western Times.
White, Walter *A Londoner's Walk to the Land's End and a Trip to the
        Scilly Isles*, London, 1855.
White, William *History, Gazetteer, and Directory of Devonshire*,
        Sheffield, 1850.
Wildman, Stephen *The Birmingham School*, Birmingham City
        Museum and Art Gallery, 1990.
Williams, Heather 'The Lives and Works of Nottingham Artists from
        1750 to 1914 with Special Consideration of their
        Association with the Lace Industry and Society at Large,'
        unpublished Ph.D dissertation, University of Nottingham,
        1981.
Williams, Thomas Hewitt *Picturesque Excursions in Devonshire and
        Cornwall, Part I Devonshire*, 1804.
Wood, Rev. J.G. *The Common Objects of the Sea Shore*, 1861.
Woodall, Mary (ed.) *The Letters of Thomas Gainsborough*,
        London, 1963.
Woollcombe, Henry *The Diary of Henry Woollcombe*,
        West Devon Record Office 710/392-396.
Wragg, Arthur *Jesus Wept. A Commentary in black and white on
        ourselves and the world today*, London, n.d. (1930s).